WITHDRAWN
NDSU

THE HANDLING OF WORDS

THE HANDLING OF WORDS

and Other Studies in Literary Psychology

by VERNON LEE

Paget, Violet [handwritten], *pseud.* [handwritten]

Introduction by Royal A. Gettmann

UNIVERSITY OF NEBRASKA PRESS · LINCOLN

Introduction © 1968 by the University of Nebraska Press

All rights reserved

Library of Congress Catalog Card Number 68-13649

The Bison Book edition is reproduced from the 1927 edition published by John Lane, The Bodley Head Ltd., by arrangement with The Bodley Head Ltd.

CONTENTS

	Editor's Introduction	vii
	Vernon Lee: A Brief Chronology	xix
	A Note on the Text	xxiii
	Introduction	xxvii
I.	On Literary Construction	1
II.	On Style	34
III.	Æsthetics of the Novel	66
IV.	The Nature of the Writer	73
V.	Studies in Literary Psychology—	
	(A) The Syntax of De Quincey	136
	(B) The Rhetoric of Landor	157
	(C) Carlyle and the Present Tense	174
VI.	The Handling of Words	187
	(A) Meredith	192
	(B) Kipling	200
	(C) Stevenson	213
	(D) Hardy	222
	(E) Henry James	241
	(F) Maurice Hewlett	251
VII.	"Imagination Penetrative"	275
VIII.	Can Writing Be Taught?	287
IX.	What Writers Might Learn	302
X.	Conclusion	314

EDITOR'S INTRODUCTION

VERNON Lee's first book, *Studies of the Eighteenth Century in Italy* (1880), was at once recognized as historical art criticism marked not only by erudition but by originality and sensitivity. It, together with *Belcaro* (1881) and *Euphorion* (1884), opened up the Italian scene to Edith Wharton and her generation. Vernon Lee came to be acknowledged as the most subtle and thoughtful member of the æsthetic school, and when she proceeded to theorize about æsthetics, her work was respected by travellers and guides in that mazy domain, as it still is. (It is an irony of literary history that Oscar Wilde, who cheapened everything he borrowed from Walter Pater, should have been regarded by the public as the very definition of *æsthete*.) Even in her widely different kinds of writing Vernon Lee found favor with readers: her pacifistic polemic, *Satan the Waster* (1920), was warmly praised by G. B. Shaw; of her twenty volumes of fiction the Hoffmannesque tales have been admired; and *The Handling of Words* (1923) is pretty generally recognized as the first attempt to grasp firmly the elusive problem of prose style.

But the variety and volume of Vernon Lee's work presents this difficulty: her merits are not fully represented in any one work, and no single book has been taken by the general reader to his heart. It would be a mistake, however, to construe this variety of writing and this diffusion of energy as inconstancy of purpose or want of seriousness. On the contrary, the Vernon Lee who described the ugliness of the river Tyne at Newcastle and the sound of dropping chestnuts in Tuscany was very much the same writer who praised *The Marriage of Figaro* and analyzed the prose of Henry James. There is a drift—indeed, a current—running through and vitalizing all her work, and it is the purpose of the following paragraphs to indicate the direction and continuity of that current.

I

Vernon Lee has a firm place in that company of travel writers which includes Goethe, James, Gissing, and Douglas. Because she was born and reared on the Continent, she did not feel the expatriate's need to compare and appraise two different cultures; nor did she succumb to the tourist's too enthusiastic wonderment before romantic atmosphere.

To be sure, Vernon Lee was extraordinarily responsive to the genius of place, but her response was not an escape or a diversion: she never disowned her character and temperament or denied her store of past experiences. She also had a gift for translating colors, lusters, textures, shapes, and sounds into vivid words and ardent epithets. Some pages of her travel essays are indeed flecked with purple, but her characteristic practice was to place the acute observation and the

Introduction

deep-dyed sensuous particular in the context of her own memories and the historical experience of European man. The present moment is interpenetrated by knowledge, retrospection, and concern for the future.

Thus, leaning on a parapet fronting the Rhine, Vernon Lee sees the belfries of Cologne against the pale green sky and watches the dark swirls of water flowing away from a ferry boat. And she suddenly recalls Saint Geryon and Dante. This spontaneous recollection is not an ostentatious display of learning: it is related to her experience in a Cologne church earlier in the day. In other words, Vernon Lee is not quoting from Bædeker, nor is she simply remembering books she had passively read. She has taken possession of *The Divine Comedy*, or, to turn over the coin, she has permitted it to work upon her whole experience of life. In the churches of Cologne she has just seen relics of the distant past encased in silver filigree and jewelled gold, and she has inhaled the pungency of incense and dying flowers. She renders these sensations in forcible phrases, but she relates them to the meaning of devotion in the Middle Ages and to an abiding quality in man. In her travel essays Vernon Lee is never the detached, simply curious spectator in search of material for a versatile pen, nor does she indulge in private emotions generated by Beauty Spots or Ugly Places.

Vernon Lee wrote on both the silvery loveliness of the Cam back of King's College, reflecting the golden willows, and the polluted, leaden Tyne at Newcastle, flowing sluggishly through blackish cinders and chemical waste under a sky in which the sun was made invisible by smoke. As in all of her writing about places Vernon Lee is not content with the strongly felt momentary experience of these streams and the rendering of it in pungent phrases. Her evocations of the Cam and the Tyne are interwoven with her rich memories, her acceptance of her character and temperament, her awareness of her personal values, a knowledge of the art and aspirations of men in the past, and her anxious concern for the happiness and goodness of men in the present and in the future.

By way of a personal testimony to the quality of Vernon Lee's travel essays, I will recall a glorious eight days I spent in Ansbach a few years ago. The highlights included an awesome performance of *The Passion according to Saint John*, concluded just before the church bells tolled midnight; the poignant last four notes of *The Art of the Fugue* heard in the hushed big hall of the Residenz; a spirited performance of concerti in the Orangerie; and visits to such historic but still living villages as Wolframs-Eschenbach, Heilsbronn, Windsbach, and Markendorf. This span of time was splendid, but a later reading of Vernon Lee's essay on Ansbach—and it is not one of her best pieces—made me clearly aware of the inadequacy of my response to these places and to the ways in which they reflect the experience of mankind. Hence I was quite prepared to understand Bernard Berenson's entry in his diary of April 30, 1948: "After many years, I revisited Belcaro . . . . Vernon Lee's book, which I read while still at Harvard, invested the name

Introduction

with even more magic than other Italian place names."

Thus travel, in Vernon Lee's view, does not consist of exposure to scenes and the acquisition of tangential, isolated facts. It requires sensibility and sympathy, continuous intellectual activity, and the subtle ministry of the passage of time. It is an exchange between topography and personality, a fusion of external contours and inner landscape. Similarly the experience of paintings, marbles, buildings, and gardens is not a passive reaction to sensible images but a complex activity which permeates and alters memories and shapes expectations.

II

Vernon Lee, more than any other writer on æsthetics, was responsible for the widely-used—sometimes misused—term *empathy*. Though the concept had been broached as early as 1858 by Lotze in his *Mikrokosmus* and had been discussed fully by Lipps in *Raumæsthetik* (1893), *empathy* was put into common currency by Vernon Lee's influential *The Beautiful*, a Cambridge Manual published in 1913. But several years before that—and, it seems, prior to her reading of Lipps—Vernon Lee had put forward the concept of empathy in "Beauty and Ugliness," an essay published in *The Contemporary Review* (1897).

It is somewhat less than accurate to define *empathy*, in the words of a generally excellent dictionary of critical terms, as "the projection of one's feelings into a perceived object." This definition does not make sufficiently clear the kind of feeling and its cause. Moreover it suggests a Byronic egotism which is quite incompatible with Vernon Lee's view of empathy. Nor is it altogether accurate to think of it in terms of a translation of Lipps's statement about *einfühlung*, the process of "feeling . . . oneself into the æsthetic object." For Vernon Lee the crucial point is not projection, or feeling into, but a merging of the beholder and the object beheld. Empathy is neither egotistical absorption and projection nor a passive, empty surrender: it is a collaboration.

In a much-quoted passage in Chapter IX of *The Beautiful* Vernon Lee, starting from the expression "The mountain rises," defines *empathy* as "this complex mental process, by which we (all unsuspectingly) invest that inert mountain . . . with the stored up and averaged and essential modes of our activity . . . ." (The words that deserve italics are *complex, mental, stored up*, and *activity*.) In other passages Vernon Lee had called attention to such expressions as "the arches spring," "the towers point," "the lines balance," and "the verse moves"; and she declared that these statements imply that we are inside the picture, the arch, and the poem. Our response to a work of art is a twofold process: initially it arouses in us feelings of tactile pressure, tautness, balance, movement, and expectation, and then we project these feelings back into the art work or the object. Vernon Lee repeatedly insisted that her conception of empathy did not originate in abstract psychological speculation but from first-hand experience of individual works of art.

In 1897, Vernon Lee's view of the æsthetic experience was rather simple and physiological. This was in line with the then emphasis amongst psychologists and students of the fine arts upon the "organic sensibilities," kinæsthetic elements and incipient movements of muscle and eye. An example of that interest was William James's celebrated essay in *Mind* (1884) in which he advanced the hypothesis that we feel sorrow not because we have lost our fortune but because we have shed tears, that we experience anger not because we have been insulted by a rival but because we have struck him a blow. In brief our emotion depends, immediately, upon the bodily manifestation: the sequence is physiological. Another reflection of this trend may be seen in Bernard Berenson's *Florentine Painters* (1896) in which there are many such phrases as "muscular sensations of movement," tactile values," and "tactile imagination." Berenson declared that a painter's "first business . . . is to rouse the tactile sense" and that the response to a figure painting requires "the illusion of varying muscular sensations inside my palm and fingers . . . ."

Immediately after her first essay on the nature of the æsthetic experience Vernon Lee began to refine her conception of it. In doing so she was undoubtedly influenced by *Marius the Epicurean* (1878), Pater's grave romance, in which he scrupulously modulated and illustrated the advice he had given the young men of Britain in the concluding essay of *Studies in the History of the Renaissance* (1873)—namely, to burn with a hard gemlike flame and to love art for its own sake. Finally in 1924, in the long introductory essay to

Art and Man by C. Anstruther-Thomson, Vernon Lee retracted altogether her early emphasis on the "respiratory and muscular" aspects of the æsthetic experience. She now believed that they were a mere accompaniment—and only for a limited number of people—of the response to paintings, works of sculpture, and buildings: they were not an intrinsic part of the æsthetic experience.

One way in which Vernon Lee enriched and enlarged her view of æsthetic perception was to emphasize the function of memory. Early and late she had asserted that the æsthetic life is not accidental or sporadic, that the response to art is not transitory or inconsequential. In *The Beautiful* she repeatedly affirmed that the æsthetic experience extends beyond the particular moment; it deposits a "residue" which may be rehearsed and contemplated; it leaves a "potential condition" in the memory. Thus when I say "the mountain rises" I am drawing upon my general experience, and my response to a work by Leonardo involves my conception of a "Leonardo emotion," which is accumulated from my previous experiences of other works by Leonardo.

A second way in which Vernon Lee expanded her conception of the response to beauty was to stress its complexity. She more and more frequently declared that it is not a question of sensation, of response to a color, sound, taste, or, texture no matter how intense or agreeable. It is instead a question of contemplation. And contemplation is exercised upon *shape*—that is to say, spatial relations, movements, and reiterations of lines, curves, and sounds. In sum the æsthetic experience requires activity, attention, memory, and foresight; it involves the interweaving of past, present, and future.

Finally, Vernon Lee came to the faith that the æsthetic experience was somehow related to moral values. It called for orderliness, discipline, self-harmony, and selflessness. She did not, however, claim that the beneficent effect was immediate or direct or calculable, for she was skeptical of Ruskin's confident moralizing of buildings and pictures. Instead the effect of beauty was a process of irradiation, preparation, and gradual transfer.

III

Just as, in Vernon Lee's view, the response to a painting or a marble requires the active participation of the beholder, so reading is an active process. The reader is not a dry sponge or an empty nullity: he is of a given temperament; he has had particular experiences in which he was both agent and victim; he is in possession of a store of interwoven memories.

But there are limits to the activity of the responsive reader. He is not to be suspicious or disputatious or willful. He does not argue with his author from the first page or decide arbitrarily whether a particular statement is "true." Instead his activity is evoked and guided by the words on the page. Reading is a reciprocal process. In one sense the reader is possessed by the words of the author, and at the same time he takes possession of the meaning of the words on the page.

To paraphrase some of Vernon Lee's passages (pp. vii, 231, 235, 239) on this head: An effective prose style demands the active exercise of memory, foresight, and comparison. The mind of the reader is kept nimble by the tensions between ambiguity and certainty, past and present tenses, expectation and affirmation. Thinking, for the reader of imaginative writing, is not clear-cut abstract ratiocination: it is the realization of the concatenations of such elements as implied causal relationships, meaningful shifts in spatial and temporal planes, and connections between inner and outer landscapes. In this process of "ever giving, ever taking" the initial responsibility rests upon the author: hence lazy writing is the cause of lazy reading, and the merit of a prose style can be measured by the degree of energy it elicits from or imposes upon the reader.

There can be no doubt of Vernon Lee's enthusiasm for her strategy for analyzing and appraising prose style. The zest with which she keeps the score on De Quincey's verbs, and the energy, sweep, and urgency of her own sentences will be felt by every reader—indeed they may be questioned and even resisted by a few readers.

But in point of fact Vernon Lee is not dogmatic or doctrinaire. She is not urging upon us a complete system which is to yield the very last answer; she does not insist that the scrutiny of sentences will always carry us to our final destination. Thus in the two concluding paragraphs of her analysis of the passage from *Tess of the d'Urbervilles* Vernon Lee deliberately refrains from giving the screw the last turn. This softened conclusion has led David Lodge, whose *Language of Fiction* (1966) should be attentively read by all students of the novel, to suspect that Vernon Lee was here concealing a "failure of nerve" or "an inadequate method." But that charitable concluding paragraph, with its nod towards Hardy's "solitary and matchless grandeur of attitude," may be construed in another way—that is, as an acknowledgment that no single critical method is adequate to the whole task of criticism. To concede this is not to deny the usefulness of the given method or to undercut the seriousness of literary study in general: it is simply to recognize the great diversity of human utterance and the complexity of describing it and responding to it.

The same flexibility and tact may be found in the first chapter, "On Literary Construction," which deserves the praise it receives in Kenneth Graham's *English Criticism of the Novel 1865–1900* (1965). In this penetrating inquiry into the use of point of view in the novel Vernon Lee discerned and provocatively described the problems in the craft of fiction which Henry James was later to expound with copious subtlety. Although she declared in an effective passage (pp. 20 ff.) that point of view was "the supreme constructive question in the novel" and although she clearly preferred the Jamesian "showing" to the "telling" of the omniscient author, Vernon Lee unreservedly admired the novels of Tolstoy, whose greatness lay beyond James's view of the art of fiction.

If we think of literary criticism not as the articulation of a comprehensive system or as the handing down of final judgments on individual works but as an unceasing conversation amongst sensitive, responsible readers, then *The Handling of Words* can provide us with a very important topic in that conversation.

ROYAL A. GETTMANN

University of Illinois

VERNON LEE: A BRIEF CHRONOLOGY

1856 Violet Paget is born October 14 at Chateau Saint Leonard (Boulogne) to a Welsh mother and an English father. Her childhood years are spent in such places as Baden, Thun, Nice, and Rome.

1866 Violet Paget becomes intimately acquainted with the Sargents of Philadelphia. Mrs. Sargent, mother of the painter John Singer Sargent, awakens her interest in the art of Rome. From 1868 the Pagets spend their winters in Rome.

1870 Violet Paget's first published writing, reflections on a Roman coin, written in French, appears in a Lausanne paper.

1871 Violet Paget discovers near Rome the neglected villa where the Arcadian Academy had met during the eighteenth century.

1877 *Fraser's Magazine* publishes "Tuscan Peasant Plays," an essay by V. Paget. During the following year *Fraser's* publishes three more essays on the culture of Italy by "Vernon Lee."

1880 *Studies of the Eighteenth Century in Italy* is published in London and is warmly praised for its originality, learning, firm opinions, and vigorous prose style.

1881 *Belcaro: being Essays on Sundry Æsthetical Questions*, a volume of historical studies with signs of an increasing interest in æsthetic theory, is published and leads to Vernon Lee's acquaintance with such writers as Morris, Pater, Browning, and Stephen. Henceforward Vernon Lee pays an annual summer visit to London.

1884 *Euphorion: being Studies of the Antique and the Mediæval in the Renaissance* is published as well as *Miss Brown*, a three-volume novel satirizing the æsthetic-fleshly school.

1886 *Baldwin: being Dialogues on Views and Aspirations* reflects a concern about religious and social problems.

1892 *Vanitas: Polite Stories* is probably the best of Vernon Lee's several volumes of fiction.

1895 *Renaissance Fancies and Studies* is a farewell to art history in favor of the view that a work of art is an "active, positive, special factor of pleasure" in the life of the individual person.

1899 *Genius Loci: Notes on Places* is perhaps the best of Vernon Lee's seven books of essays on places.

1908 *Gospels of Anarchy, and Other Contemporary Studies* consists of essays on such "stirrers-up" of thought as Nietzsche, Tolstoy, William James, Ibsen, and Wells.

Chronology

1913 *The Beautiful: an Introduction to Psychological Æsthetics* is a summary of the theory of empathy which Vernon Lee had broached as early as 1897 in "Beauty and Ugliness" (*The Contemporary Review*).

1920 *Satan, the Waster. A Philosophic War Trilogy, with Notes and Introduction.* This polemic against war expresses attitudes which Vernon Lee, because of her long and varied experience of Europe, had begun to form during the troubled year 1911.

1923 *The Handling of Words, and Other Studies in Literary Psychology* is a selection from the essays on literature which Vernon Lee wrote from the mid-eighties onwards. It omits some early essays on the art of fiction which are well worth reading.

1929 *A Vernon Lee Anthology*, selected by Irene Cooper Willis, is published in The Week-End Library.

1932 *Music and its Lovers. An Empirical Study of Emotion and Imaginative Responses to Music* is a belated reflection of a lifelong interest in music.

1935 Vernon Lee dies in Florence on February 13.

A NOTE ON THE TEXT

THE present text of *The Handling of Words* is reproduced from the edition in The Week-End Library (1927). This was a reprinting, the fourth, of the first edition of the book (1923). In the Introduction Vernon Lee speaks of the essays which comprise *The Handling of Words* as being "so variously dated." This statement may be made more explicit: the first essay appeared in *The Contemporary Review* in September 1895. The third section of Chapter II was published in December 1894 in *The New Review*, then edited by W. E. Henley. Chapters IV and V appeared in *The Contemporary Review* during 1903–1904. The title essay was published in five issues of *The English Review* in 1910–1911. It had probably been accepted during the period of Ford Madox Ford's brilliant editorship. In sum, the several essays in this volume were published over a span of almost thirty years.

A scrutiny of sample pages in *The Handling of Words* indicates that the text is essentially the same as that of the essays as they appeared in periodicals. The alterations suggest that Vernon Lee polished the surface of her prose but did not rethink or rewrite. In making revisions she worked with a degree of care not always exercised by hard-pressed periodical writers. For example, a collation of four pages in the section on Thomas Hardy shows a total of forty-nine differences in punctuation and diction which resulted in a more idiomatic usage and a slight alteration in exactness and emphasis. Thus the phrase "movement of the day" was revised to "time of day," and "in that place" was changed to "in that neighborhood." In the discussion of Hardy's comparison of a green valley to a billiard table the criticism of Hardy's alleged slackness was slightly sharpened by altering "the flatness and greenness" to "the utterly dissimilar flatness and greenness." In the four pages one short sentence was omitted, and one was added. In none of these revisions is there any indication of a basic change in Vernon Lee's appraisal of Hardy's style.

TO

THE MANY WRITERS I HAVE READ

AND

THE FEW READERS WHO HAVE READ ME

LET ME GRATEFULLY DEDICATE

THESE STUDIES IN

WRITING AND READING

INTRODUCTION

IN the course of revising these so variously dated essays and notes, I have become aware, not only of changes of opinion which are sufficiently corrected by each other, but likewise of omissions on important points. Of these, according as space may allow, I shall try and make good one or two in a concluding chapter.

As regards the rest of the subjects discussed in this volume, and which range from the engineering of a whole narrative to the construction of single sentences, I shall leave the Student to discover their inner, though, as it seems to me, quite evident relationship.

Half a lifetime of additional reading and writing, and of ruminating over what I have read and have written, has brought some general conclusions clearer and clearer to my mind, the implicit growing explicit. And of course, and despite vehement self-reproach, I have fallen a victim to the lazy temptation of explaining too many effects by too few causes. Perhaps by one cause only! Namely: the fact that the efficacy of all writing depends not more on the Writer than on the Reader, without whose active response, whose output of experience, feeling and imagination, the living phenomenon, the only reality, of Literary Art cannot take place. This fundamental fact of literary psychology, indeed of all psychological æsthetics, appears to me both so all-important and so universally neglected that I am quite content that the make-up of this volume out of disconnected essays and lectures, should have resulted in the repetition thereof half a hundred times and in its exhibition from half a dozen angles. I may be stupider than some people, but surely not than all, and it is my experience that I have never really grasped any new or nearly new idea until I had been shown several different applications thereof. Which personal confession bears out my belief that so far as concerns the things of the spirit, there is no saying truer than Goethe's counsel :

> "Was du ererbt von deinen Vätern hast,
> Erwirb es, um es zu besitzen."

Or put in less epigrammatic form : that we must not expect to understand what others can tell us without extracting its significance for ourselves, and without making their ideas into our own.

So it is just as well for my alert student, besides being far more convenient for my rather weary self, that it be left to him to put such order as may be lacking into this bundle of random studies.

CHIPCHASE, NORTH TYNE,
26th August 1922.

THE HANDLING OF WORDS

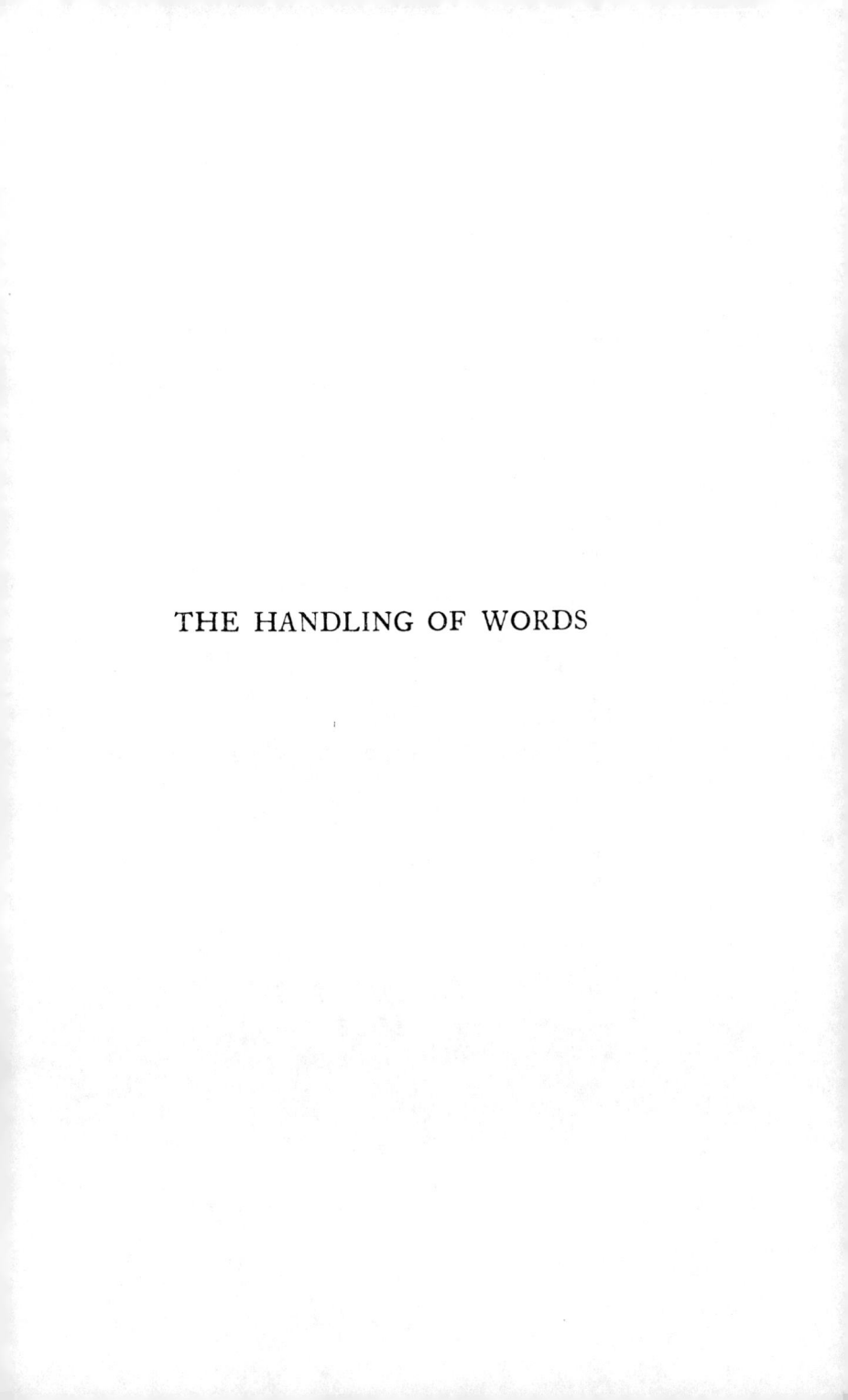

THE HANDLING OF WORDS

I

ON LITERARY CONSTRUCTION

THE craft of the Writer consists, I am convinced, in manipulating the contents of his Reader's mind, that is to say, taken from the technical side as distinguished from the psychologic, in construction. Construction is not only a matter of single words or sentences, but of whole large passages and divisions; and the material which the Writer manipulates is not only the single impressions, single ideas and emotions, stored up in the Reader's mind and deposited there by no act of the Writer's: the Writer deals likewise with those very moods and trains of thought into which he, by his skilful selection of words and sentences, has grouped the already existing single impressions, the very moods and trains of thought which have been determined by himself in the mind of the Reader.

I

We have all read Mr. Stevenson's *Catriona*. Early in that book there is a passage by which I can illustrate my meaning. It is David Balfour's walk to Pilrig:

"My way led over Mouter's Hill, and through an end of a clachan on the braeside among fields. There was a whir of looms in it went from house to house; bees hummed in the gardens; the neighbours that I saw at the doorsteps talked in a strange tongue; and I found out later that this was Picardy, a village where the French weavers wrought for the Linen Company. Here I got a fresh direction for Pilrig, my destination; and a little beyond, on the wayside, came by a gibbet and two men hanged in chains. They were dipped in tar, as the manner is; the wind span them, the chains clattered, and the birds hung about the uncanny jumping jacks and cried."

This half-page sounds as if it were an integral part of the story, one of the things which happened to the gallant but judicious David Balfour. But in my opinion it is not such a portion of the story, not an episode told for its own sake, it is qualifier of something else; in fact, nothing but an adjective on a large scale.

Let us see. The facts of the case are these: David Balfour, after the terrible adventures recorded in *Kidnapped*, having at last been saved from his enemies and come into his lawful property, with a comfortable life before him and no reason for disquietude, determines to volunteer as a witness in favour of certain Highlanders, whom it is the highest interest of the

Government to put to death, altogether irrespective of whether or not they happen to be guilty in the matter about which they are accused. In order to offer this testimony in what he imagines to be the most efficacious manner, David Balfour decides to seek an interview with the Lord Advocate of Scotland; and he is now on his way to his cousin of Pilrig to obtain a letter from him for that terrible head of the law. Now if David Balfour actually has to be sent to Pilrig for the letter of introduction to the Lord Advocate, then his walk to Pilrig is an intrinsic portion of the story, and what happened to him on his walk cannot be considered save as an intrinsic portion also. This would be true enough if we were considering what actually could or must happen to a real David Balfour in a real reality, not what Stevenson wants us to think did happen to an imaginary David Balfour. If a real David Balfour was destined, through the concatenation of circumstances, to walk from Edinburgh to Pilrig by that particular road on that particular day, why, he was destined also —and could not escape his destiny—to come to the gibbet where, on that particular day, along that particular road, those two malefactors were hanging in chains.

But even supposing that Stevenson had been bound, for some reason, to make David Balfour take that particular day the particular walk which must have brought him past that gibbet, Stevenson would still have been perfectly free to omit all mention of his seeing that gibbet, as he evidently omitted mentioning a thousand other things which David Balfour must have seen and done in the course of his adventures, because the sight of that gibbet in no way affected the course of the events which Stevenson had decided to relate, any more than the quality of the porridge which David had eaten that morning. And as it happens, moreover, the very fact of David Balfour having walked that day along that road, and of the gibbet having been there, is, as we know, nothing but a make-believe on Stevenson's part, and so there can have been nothing unavoidable about it. Therefore, I say that this episode, which leads to no other episode, is not an integral part of the story, but a qualifier, an adjective. It acts, not upon what happens to the hero, but on what is felt by the Reader. Again, let us look into the matter! This beginning of the story is, from the nature of the facts, rather empty of tragic events; yet tragic events are what Stevenson wishes us to live through. There is something humdrum in those first proceedings of David Balfour's, which are to lead to such hairbreadth escapes. There is something not heroic enough in a young man, however heroic his intentions, going to ask for a letter of introduction to a Lord Advocate. But what can be done? If adventures are invented to fill up these first chapters, these adventures will either actually lead to something further complicating a plot already quite as complicated as Stevenson requires; or—which is even worse—they will come to nothing, and leave the Reader disappointed, incredulous, less willing to attend after having wasted expectations and sympathies. Here comes in the admirable invention of the gibbet. The gibbet is, so to speak, the shadow of coming events cast over the smooth earlier chapters of the book. With its grotesque and ghastly vision, it puts the Reader in the state of mind desired: it means tragedy. "I was pleased," goes on David Balfour, " to be so far in the still countryside; but the shackles of the gibbet clattered in my head. . . . There might David Balfour hang, and other lads pass on their errands, and think light of him." Here the Reader is not only forcibly reminded that the seemingly trifling errand of this boy will lead to terrible dangers; but he is made to feel, by being told that David felt (which perhaps at that moment David, accustomed to the eighteenth-century habit of hanging petty thieves along the roadside, might not feel) the ghastliness of that encounter.

And then note how this qualifier, this adjectival episode, is itself qualified. It is embedded in impressions of peacefulness: the hillside, the whir of looms and hum of bees, and talk of neighbours on doorsteps; nay, Stevenson has added a note which increases the sense of peacefulness by adding an element of unconcern, of foreignness, such as we all find adds so much to the peaceful effect of travel, in the fact that the village was inhabited by strangers—Frenchmen—to whom David

6   The Handling of Words

Balfour and the Lord Advocate and the Appin murder would never mean anything. Had the gibbet been on the Edinburgh Grassmarket, and surrounded by people commenting on Highland disturbances, we should have expected some actual adventure for David Balfour; but the gibbet there, in the fields, by this peaceful foreign settlement, merely puts our mind in the right frame to be moved by the adventures which will come slowly in their due course.

This is a masterpiece of constructive craft: the desired effect is obtained without becoming involved in other effects not desired, without any debts being made with the Reader; even as is the case of the properly chosen single adjective, which defines the meaning of the noun in just the desired way, without suggesting any further definition in the wrong way.

Construction, that is to say, co-ordination. It means finding out what is important and unimportant, what you can afford and cannot afford to do. It means thinking out the results of every movement you set up in the Reader's mind, how that movement will work into, help, or mar the other movements which you have set up there already, or which you will require to set up there in the future. For, remark, such a movement does not die out at once. It continues and unites well or ill with its successors, as it has united well or ill with its predecessors. You must remember that in every kind of literary composition, from the smallest essay to

On Literary Construction

the largest novel, you are constantly introducing new *themes*, as in a piece of music, and working all the themes into one another. A theme may be a description, a line of argument, a whole personage; but it always represents, on the part of the Reader, a particular way of intellectual acting and existing, a particular kind of mood. Now, these moods, being concatenated in their progression, are thereby altered by the other moods they meet; they can never be quite the same the second time they appear as the first, nor the third as the second; they must have been modified, and they ought to have been strengthened or made more subtle, by the company they have kept, by the things they have elbowed, and been—however unconsciously—compared and contrasted with: they ought to have become more satisfactory to the Reader as a result of their stay in the Reader's own mind.

A few very simple rules might be made, so simple as to sound utterly childish; yet how many Writers observe them? For instance:

Do not, if you want Tom to seem a villain, put a bigger villain, Dick, by his side; but if, for instance, like Tolstoi, you want Anatole to be the trumpery wicked Don Juan, put a grand, brilliant, intrepid Don Juan—Dologhow—to reduce him to vulgar proportions. Do not, again, break off in the midst of some event, unless you wish that event to become important in the Reader's mind and to react on future events: if, for instance, you have had to introduce a mysterious stranger, but do not wish anything to come of his mysteriousness, be sure you strip off his mystery as prosaically as you can, before leaving him in the Reader's charge. And, of course, *vice versa*.

I have compared literary themes to musical ones. The novel may be considered as a tragic symphony, opera, or oratorio, with a whole orchestra. The essay is a little sonata, trio, sometimes a mere little song. But even in a song, how many melodic themes, harmonic arrangements, accents, and so forth! I could wish young Writers, if they have any ear, to unravel the parts of a fugue, the themes of a Beethoven sonata. By analogy, they would learn a great many things.

Leaving such learning by musical analogy alone, I have sometimes recommended to young Writers that they should draw diagrams, or rather *maps*, of their essays or stories. This is, I think, a very useful practice, not only for diminishing faults of construction in the individual story or essay, but, what is more important, for showing the young Writer what amount of progress he is making, and to what extent he is becoming a craftsman. Every one will probably find his own kind of map or diagram. The one I have made use of to explain the meaning to some of my friends is as follows: Make a stroke with your pen which represents the first train of thought or mood, or the first group of facts you deal with. Then make another pen-stroke to represent the second, which shall be proportionately long or short according to the number of words or pages occupied, and which, connected with the first pen-stroke, as one articulation of a reed is with another, will deflect to the right or the left according as it contains more or less new matter; so that, if it grow insensibly from stroke number one, it will have to be almost straight, and if it contain something utterly disconnected, will be at right angles. Go on adding pen-strokes for every new train of thought, or mood, or group of facts, writing the name along each, and be careful to indicate not merely the angle of divergence, but the comparative length of lines. And then look at the whole map. If the Reader's mind is to run easily along the whole story or essay, and to perceive all through the necessary connection between the parts, the pattern you will have traced will approximate most likely to a circle or ellipse, the conclusion reuniting with the beginning as in a perfect logical exposition; and the various pen-strokes, taking you gradually round this circle or ellipse, will correspond in length very exactly to the comparative importance or complexity of the matter to dispose of. But in proportion as the things have been made a mess of, the pattern will tend to the shapeless; the lines, after infinite tortuosities, deflections to the right and to the left, immense bends, sharp angles and bags of all sorts, will probably end in a pen-stroke at the other end of the paper, as far off as possible from the beginning. All this will mean that you have lacked general conception of the subject; that the connection between what you began and what you ended with is arbitrary or accidental, instead of being logical and organic. It will mean that your mind has been rambling, and that you have been making the Reader's mind ramble hopelessly, in all sorts of places you never intended; that you have wasted his time and attention, like a person pretending to know his way in an intricate maze of streets, but not really knowing which turning to take. Every one of those sharp angles has meant a lack of connection, every stroke returning back upon itself a useless digression, every loop an unnecessary reiteration; and the entire shapelessness of your diagram has represented the atrocious fact that the Reader, while knowing what you have been talking about, has not known why you have been talking about it, and is, but for a number of random pieces of information which he must himself rearrange, no wiser than when you began.

What will this lead to? What will it make the Reader expect? What will it actually bring the Reader's mind to? This is the meaning of the diagrams. For, remember, in literature all depends on what you can set the Reader to do; if you confuse his ideas or waste his energy, you can no longer do anything with him.

II

I mentioned just now that in a case of bad construction the single items might be valuable, but that the Reader was obliged to rearrange them. Such rearrangement is equivalent to rewriting the book; and, if any one is to do that, it had better not be the Reader, surely, but rather a more competent Writer. When the badly arranged items are themselves good, one sometimes feels a mad desire to hand them over thus to some one else. It is like good food badly cooked. I think I have scarcely ever been so tormented with the wish to get a story rewritten by some competent person, or even to rewrite it myself, as in the case of one of the little volumes of the Pseudonym Series, a story called *A Mystery of the Campagna*. I should like every young Writer to read it, as a perfect model of splendid material, imaginative and emotional, of notions and descriptions worthy of Mérimée (who would have worked them into a companion piece to the wonderful *Vénus d'Ille*), presented in such a way as to give the minimum of interest with the maximum of fatigue. It is a thing to make one cry merely to think of: such splendid invention, such deep contagious feeling for the uncanny solemnity, the deathly fascination of the country about Rome, worked up in a way which leaves no clear impression at all, or, if any, an impression of trivial student life in restaurants.

One of the chief defects of this unlucky little book of genius is that a story of about a hundred pages is narrated by four or five different persons, none of whom has any particular individuality, or any particular reason to be telling the story at all. The result is much as if you were to be made to hear a song in fragments, fragments helter-skelter, the middle first and beginning last, played on different instruments. A similar fault of construction, you will remember, makes the beginning of one of our greatest masterpieces of passion and romance, *Wuthering Heights*, exceedingly difficult to read. As if the step-relations and adopted-relations in the story were not sufficiently puzzling, Emily Brontë gave the narrative to several different people, at several different periods, people alternating what they had been told with what they had actually witnessed. This kind of construction was a fault, if not of Emily Brontë's own time, at least of the time in which many of the books by which she had been most impressed were written, notably Hoffman's, from whose *Majorat* (Rolandsitten) she borrowed much for *Wuthering Heights*. It is historically an old fault for the same reason which makes it a fault with beginners, namely, that it is undoubtedly easier to narrate in the first person, or as an eye-witness; and that it is easier to co-ordinate three or four sides of an event by boxing them mechanically as so many stories one in the other, than to arrange the various groups of persons and acts as in real life, and to change the point of view of the Reader from one to the other. These mechanical divisions also seem to give the Writer courage, like the series of ropes which take away the fear of swimming: one thinks one might always catch hold of one of them, but, meanwhile, one usually goes under water all the same. I have no doubt that most of the stories, of the older generation at least,[1] we have all written between the ages of fifteen and twenty were either in the autobiographical or the epistolary form; that they had introduction set in introduction like those of Scott, that they shifted narrator as in *Wuthering Heights*, and altogether reproduced, in their immaturity, the forms of an immature period of novel-writing, just as Darwinians tell us that the prehensile feet of babies reproduce the feet of monkeys. For, odd as it is to realize, the apparently simplest form of construction is by far the most difficult; and the straightforward narrative of men and women's feelings and passions, of anything save their merest outward acts, the narrative which makes the thing pass naturally before the Reader's mind, is by far the most difficult, as it is the most perfect. You will remember that *Julie* and *Clarissa* are written in letters, *Werther* and *Adolphe* as confessions with postscripts; nay, that even the *Odyssey* and the *Arabian Nights* cannot get along save on a system of narrative within narrative; so long does it take to get to the straightforward narrative of *Vanity Fair*

[1] This lecture was delivered about 1895.

(since even Thackeray is not always absolutely direct in the *Newcomes*), let alone that of Tolstoi.

But a narrative may be in the third person, and may leave out all mention of eye-witness narration, and yet be far from what I call straightforward. Take, for instance, the form of novel adopted by George Eliot in *Adam Bede, Middlemarch, Deronda*—in all save her masterpiece, which has the directness of an autobiography—*The Mill on the Floss*. This form I should characterize as that of *the novel built up in scenes*, and it is well worth your notice because it is more or less the typical form of the former English three-volume novel. It represents a compromise with that difficult thing, straightforward narrative ; and the autobiographical, the epistolary, the narration-within-narration dodges have merely been replaced by another dodge for making things easier for the Writer and less efficacious for the Reader, the dodge of arranging the matter as much as possible as in a play, with narrative or analytic connecting links. By this means a portion of the story is given with considerable efficacy ; the dialogue and gesture, so to speak, are made as striking as possible ; in fact, we get all the apparent lifelikeness of a play. I say the *apparent* lifelikeness, because a play is in reality excessively unlifelike, owing to the necessity of things which could not have happened together being united in time and place, to quantities of things being said which never could have been said nor even thought ;

the necessity of scenes being protracted, rendered explicit and decisive far beyond possibility, merely because of other scenes (if we may call them scenes), the hundred other fragments of speech and fragments of action which really made the particular thing happen, having to be left out. This is a necessity on the stage because the scene cannot be changed sufficiently often, and because you cannot let people remain for an instant without talking either to some one else or to themselves. But this necessity, when applied to a novel, actually mars the action; and, what is worse, alters the conception of the action, for the form in which any story is told inevitably reacts on the subject.

Take *Adam Bede*. The hero is supposed to be exceedingly reserved, more than reserved, one of these strenuous natures who cannot express their feelings even to themselves, and run away and hide in a hole whenever they do know themselves to be feeling. But, owing to the division of the book into scenes, and connecting links between the scenes, one has the impression of Adam Bede perpetually *en scène*, with appropriate background of carpenter's shop, and a chorus of village rustics; Adam Bede always saying something or doing something, talking to his dog, shouldering his tools, eating his breakfast, in such a way that the dullest spectators may recognize what he is feeling and thinking. Now to make an inexplicit personage always explain himself is only equalled by making an unanalytical person perpetually analyse himself; and, by the system of scenes, by having to represent the personage walking immersed in thoughts, hurrying along full of conflicting feelings, this is the very impression which we get, on the contrary, about Arthur and Hetty, whose misfortunes were certainly not due to overmuch introspection.

Now you will mark that this division into scenes and connecting links occurs very much less in modern French novels: in them, indeed, when a scene is given, it is because a scene actually took place, not because a scene was a convenient way of showing what was going on; and I think you will all remember that in Tolstoi's great novels one scarcely has the sense of there being any scenes at all, not more so than in real life. Pierre's fate is not sealed in a given number of interviews with Hélène; nor is the rupture between Anna and Wronsky —although its catastrophe is brought about, as it must be, by a special incident—the result of anything save imperceptible disagreements every now and then, varied with an outbreak of jealousy. Similarly, in Tolstoi you never know how many times Levine went to the house of Kitty's parents, nor whether Pierre had twenty or two thousand interviews with Natacha; you only know that it all happens as it inevitably must, and happens, as most things in this world do, by the force of accumulated action.

There are some other questions of construction in

novels connected with this main question of the really narrative or partially dramatic form of construction, of the directness or complication of arrangement. One of these is the question of what I would call the *passive* description, by which I mean the setting up, as it were, of an elaborate landscape, or other background, before the characters are brought on the stage. The expression I have just used, " brought on the stage," shows you that I connect this particular mode of proceeding with the novel in scenes. And it is easy to understand that, once the Writer allows himself to think of any event happening as it would on the stage, he will also wish to prepare a suitable background, and, moreover, most often a chorus and set of supernumeraries ; a background which, in the reality, the principal characters would perhaps not be conscious of, and a chorus which, also in the reality, would very probably not contribute in the least to the action. Another drawback, by the way, of the construction in scenes and connecting links is, that persons have to be invented to elicit the manifestation of the principal personage's qualities : you have to invent episodes to show the good heart of the heroine, the valour of the hero, the pedantry of the guardian, etc., and meanwhile the real action stops ; or, what is much worse, the real action is most unnaturally complicated by such side business, which is merely intended to give the Reader information that he either need not have at all, or ought to get in some more direct way.

18   The Handling of Words

Note that there is all the difference in the world between an episode like that of the gallows on the road to Pilrig, which is intended to qualify the whole story by inducing a particular frame of mind in the Reader, and an episode like that of Dorothea (in *Middlemarch*) sharing her jewels with her sister on the very afternoon of Mr. Casaubon's first appearance, and which is merely intended to give the Reader necessary information about Dorothea; information which might have been quite simply conveyed by saying, whenever it was necessary, " Now Dorothea happened to be a very ascetic person, with a childishly deliberate aversion to the vanities." This second plan would have connected Dorothea's asceticism with whatever feelings and acts really sprang from it; while the first plan merely gives you a feeling of too many things happening in one day, and of Mr. Casaubon appearing, not simply as a mere new visitor, but as the destined husband of Dorothea. For, remember that the Reader tends to attribute to the personages of a book whatever feelings you set up in him, so that, if you make the Reader feel that Casaubon is going to be the bridegroom, you also, in a degree, make Dorothea feel that she is to be the bride. And that, even for Dorothea, is rather precipitate.

Another question of construction is the one I should call the question of *retrospects*. The retrospect is a frequent device for dashing into the action at once, and putting off the evil day of explaining why people are doing and feeling in the particular way in which we find them, on the rising of the curtain. This, again, is a dramatic device, being indeed nothing but the narrative to or by the confidants which inevitably takes place in the third or fourth scene of the first act of a French tragedy, with the author in his own costume taking the place of the nurse, bosom friend, captain of the guard, etc. The use of this retrospect, of this sort of folding back of the narrative, and the use of a number of smaller artifices for foreshortening the narrative, seems to me not at all disagreeable in the case of the short story. The short story is necessarily much more artificial than the big novel, owing to its very shortness, owing to the initial unnaturalness of having isolated one single action or episode from the hundred others influencing it, and to the unnaturalness of having, so to speak, reduced everybody to be an orphan, or a childless widow or widower, for the sake of greater brevity. And the short story, being most often thus artificially pruned and isolated, being in a measure the artificially selected expression of a given situation, something more like a poem or little play, may even actually gain by the discreet display of well-carried-out artifices. While, so far as I can see, the big novel never does.

There is yet another constructive question about the novel—the most important question of all—whose existence the lay mind probably does not even suspect, but which, I am sure, exercises more than any other the mind of any one who has attempted to write a novel; even as the layman, contemplating a picture, is apt never to guess how much thought has been given to determining the place where the spectator is supposed to see from, whether from above, below, from the right or the left, and in what perspective, consequently, the various painted figures are to appear. This supreme constructive question in the novel is exactly analogous to that question in painting; and in describing the choice by the painter of the point of view, I have described also that most subtle choice of the literary craftsman: choice of the point of view whence the personages and action of a novel are to be seen. For you can see a person, or an act, in one of several ways, and connected with several other persons or acts. You can see the person from no particular body's point of view, or from the point of view of one of the other persons, or from the point of view of the analytical, judicious author. Thus, Casaubon may be seen from Dorothea's point of view, from his own point of view, from Ladislaw's point of view, or from the point of view of George Eliot; or he may be merely made to talk and act without any explanation of why he is so talking and acting; and that is what I call nobody's point of view. Stories of adventure, in which the mere incident is what interests, without reference to the psychological changes producing or produced by that incident, are usually written from nobody's point of view. Most sensational books and books for children; much of Wilkie Collins, even when there is a sequence of narrative as in the *Moonstone*, is virtually written from nobody's point of view; and so are the whole of the old Norse sagas, the greater part of Homer and the *Decameron*, and the whole of *Cinderella* and *Jack the Giant Killer*. We moderns, who are weary of psychology —for poor psychology is indeed a weariness—often find the lack of point of view as refreshing as plain water compared with wine, or tea, or syrup. But once you get a psychological interest, once you want to know, not merely *what* the people did or said, but what they *thought* or *felt*, the point of view becomes inevitable, for acts and words then come to exist only with reference to thoughts and feelings, and the question arises, Whose thoughts or feelings?

This is a case of construction, of craft. But it is a case where construction is most often determined by intuition, and where craft comes to be merged in feeling. For, after having tried to separate the teachable part of writing from the unteachable, we have come at last to one of the thousand places—for there are similar places in every question, whether of choice of single words or of construction of whole books—where the teachable and the unteachable unite, where craft itself becomes but the expression of genius. So, instead of trying to settle what points of view are best, and how they can best be alternated or united, I will now state a few thoughts of mine about that which settles all questions of points of view, and alone can settle them satisfactorily—the different kinds of genius of the novelist.

III

I incline to believe that the characters in a novel which seem to us particularly vital are those which to all appearance have never been previously analysed or rationally understood by the author, but, on the contrary, those which, connected always by a similar emotional atmosphere, have come to him as realities ; realities emotionally borne in upon his innermost sense.

Some day mental science may perhaps explain by the operation of stored-up impressions, of obscure hereditary potentialities, and all the mysteries of the subconsciousness, the extraordinary phenomenon of a creature being apparently invaded from within by the personality of another creature, of another creature to all intents and purposes imaginary. The mystery is evidently connected, if not identical, with the mysterious conception—not reasoned out, but merely felt, by a great actor of another man's movements, tones of voice, states of feeling. In this case, as in all other matters of artistic activity, we have all of us, if we are susceptible in that particular branch of art (otherwise we should not be thus susceptible) a rudiment of the faculty whose exceptional development constitutes the artist.

And thus, from our own very trifling experience, we can, perhaps not explain what happens to the great novelist in the act of creation of his great characters, but guess, without any explanation, at what is happening in him. For, in the same way that we all of us, however rudimentally, possess a scrap in ourselves of the faculty which makes the actor; so also we mostly possess in ourselves, I think, a scrap of what makes the novelist; if we did not, neither the actor nor the novelist would find any response in us. Let me pursue this. We all possess, to a certain small degree, the very mysterious faculty of imitating, without any act of conscious analysis, the gestures, facial expression, and tone of voice of other people; nay, more, of other people in situations in which we have never seen them. We feel that they move, look, sound like that; we feel that, under given conditions, they would necessarily move, look, and sound like that. Why they should do so, or why we should feel that they do so, we have no notion whatever. Apparently because for that moment and to that extent we *are* those people: they have impressed us so forcibly, at some time or other, they or those like them, that a piece of them, a pattern of them, a word (one might think) of this particular vital spell, the spell which sums up their mode of being, has remained sticking in us, and is there become operative. I have to talk in allegories, in formulæ which savour of cabalistic mysticism; for

I am not trying to explain, but merely to recall your own experiences; and I am sure you will recognize that these very mysterious things do happen constantly to all of us.

Now, in the same way that we all feel, every now and then, that the gestures and expressions and tones of voice which we assume are those of other people and of other people in other circumstances; so likewise do we all of us occasionally feel that certain ways of facing life, certain reactions to life's various contingencies—certain acts, answers, feelings, passions—are the acts, answers, feelings, passions, the reactions to life's contingencies, of persons not ourselves. We say, under the circumstances, *I* should do or say so and so, but Tom, or Dick, or Harry will do or say such another thing. The matter would be quite simple if we had seen Tom, Dick, or Harry in exactly similar circumstances; we should be merely repeating what had already happened, and our forecast would be no real forecast, but a recollection. Now the point is, that we have *not* seen Tom, Dick, or Harry doing or saying in the past any of what we thus attribute to him in the future. The matter would also be very simple if we attained to this certainty about Tom, Dick, or Harry's sayings and doings by a process of conscious reasoning. But we have not gone through any conscious reasoning; indeed, if some incredulous person challenges us to account by analysis for our conviction, we are most often unable to answer; we are occasionally even absolutely worsted in argument. We have to admit that we do not know why we think so, nay, that there is every reason to think the contrary; and yet there, down in our heart of hearts, remains a very strong conviction, a conviction like that of our own existence, that Tom, Dick, or Harry would, or rather *will*, or rather—for it comes to that—*does* say or do that particular thing. If subsequently Tom, Dick, or Harry is so perverse as not to say or do it, that, oddly enough, does not always obliterate the impression of our having experienced that he *did* say or do it, an impression intimate, warm, unanalytical, like our impressions of having done or said certain things ourselves. The discrepancy between what we felt sure must happen and what actually did happen is, I think, due to the fact that there are two persons existing under the same name, but both existing equally—Tom, Dick, or Harry as felt by himself, and Tom, Dick, or Harry as felt by us; and although the conduct of these two persons may not have happened to coincide, the conduct of each has been perfectly organic, inevitable with reference to his nature. I suppose it is because we add to our experience, fragmentary as it needs must be, of other folk, the vitality, the unity of life, which is in ourselves. I suppose that, every now and then, whenever this particular thing I am speaking of happens, we have been tremendously impressed by something in another person—emotionally impressed. not intellectually, mind; and that the emotion, whether of delight or annoyance or amusement, which the person has caused in us, in some way grafts a portion of that person into our own life, into the emotions which constitute our life; and that thus our experience of the person, and our own increasing experience of ourselves, are united, and the person who is not ourselves comes to live, somehow, for our consciousness, with the same reality, the same intimate warmth, that we do.

I hazard this explanation, at best an altogether superficial one, not because I want it accepted as a necessary premiss to an argument of mine, but because it may bring home what I require to make very clear—namely, the absolutely sympathetic, unanalytic, subjective creation of characters by some novelists as opposed to the rational, analytic, objective creation of characters by other novelists; because I require to distinguish between the personage who has been borne in upon the novelist's intimate sense, and the personage who has been built up out of fragments of fact by the novelist's intelligent calculation. Vasari, talking of the Farnesina Palace, said that it was not "built, but really born,"—*non murato ma veramente nato.* Well, some personages in novels are built up, and very well built up; and some—some personages, but how few!—are really *born.*

Such personages as are thus not built up, but *born,*

seem always to have been born (and my theory of their coming into existence is founded on this) of some strong feeling on the part of their author. Sometimes it is a violent repulsion—the strongest kind of repulsion, the organic repulsion of incompatible temperaments, which makes it impossible, for all his virtues, to like our particular Dr. Fell, the reason why, we cannot tell. Our whole nature tingles with the discomfort which the creature causes in us. Such characters—I take them at random—are (for myself at least) Tolstoi's Monsieur Karénine and Henry James's Olive Chancellor. But the greater number, as we might expect, of these really *born* creatures of unreality are born of love—of the deep, unreasoning, permeating satisfaction, the unceasing, ramifying delight in strength and audacity; the unceasing, ramifying comfort in kindliness; the unceasing, ramifying pity towards weakness; born of the emotion which distinguishes the presence of all such as are, by the necessity of our individual nature and theirs, inevitably, deeply, undyingly beloved. These personages may not happen to be lovable, or even tolerable, to the individual Reader—the Reader may thoroughly detest them. But he cannot be indifferent to them; for, born of the Writer's real feeling, of the strongest of real feelings, the love of suitable temperaments, they are real, and awaken only real feeling. Such personages—we all know them!—such personages are, for instance, Colonel Newcome, Ethel Newcome;

Tolstoi's Natacha, Levine, Anna, Pierre; Stendhal's immortal Duchess and Mme de Rênal; and those two imperfect creatures, pardoned because so greatly beloved, Tom Jones and Manon Lescaut. Their power—the power of these creatures born of emotion, of affinity, or repulsion—is marvellous and transcendent. It is such that even a lapse into impossibility—though that rarely comes, of course—is overlooked. The life in the creatures is such that when we are told of their doing perfectly incredible things—things we cannot believe that, being what they were, they could have done—they yet remain alive, even as real people remain alive for our feelings when we are assured that they have done things which utterly upset our conception of them. Look, for instance, at Mr. James's Olive Chancellor. It is inconceivable that she should have ever done the very thing on which the whole book rests—taken up with such a being as Verena. Yet she lives. Why? Because the author has realized in her the kind of temperament, the mode of feeling and being most organically detestable to him in all womankind. Look again at Meredith's adorable Diana. She could not have sold the secret, being what she was. Well, does she fall to the ground? Not a bit. She remains and triumphs, because she triumphed over the heart of her author. There is the other class of personage—among whom are most of the personages of every novel, most of the companions of those not built up, but born;

and among whom, I think, are all the characters of some of those novelists whom the world accounts as the greatest philosophers of the human heart—all the characters, save Maggie and Tom, of George Eliot; most, I suspect, of the characters of Balzac.

Such are the two great categories into which all novelists may, I think, be divided, the synthetic and the analytic, those who feel and those who reason. According as he belongs to one category or the other, the novelist will make that difficult choice about points of view. The synthetic novelist, the one who does not study his personages, but *lives* them, is able to shift the point of view with incredible frequency and rapidity, like Tolstoi, who in his two great novels really *is* each of the principal persons turn about; so much so, that at first one might almost think there was no point of view at all. The analytic novelist, on the contrary, the novelist who does not *live* his personages, but studies them, will be able to see his personages only from his own point of view, telling one what they are (or what he imagines they are), not what they feel inside themselves; and, at most, putting himself at the point of view of one personage or two, all the rest being given from the novelist's point of view; as in the case of George Eliot, Balzac, Flaubert, and Zola, whose characters are not so much living and suffering and changing creatures, as illustrations of theories of life in general, or of the life of certain classes and temperaments.

It is often said that there are many more wrong ways of doing a thing than right ones. I do not think this applies to the novel, or perhaps to any work of art. There are a great number of possible sorts of excellent novels, all very different from one another, and appealing to different classes of minds. There is the purely human novel of Thackeray, and particularly of Tolstoi—human and absolutely living; and the analytic and autobiographical novel of George Eliot, born, as regards its construction, of the memoir. There is the analytic, sociological novel of Balzac, studying the modes of life of whole classes of people. There is the novel of Zola, apparently aiming at the same thing as that of Balzac, but in reality, and for all its realistic programme, using the human crowd, the great social and commercial mechanisms invented by mankind—the shop, the mine, the bourgeois house, the Stock Exchange—as so much matter for passionate lyrism, just as Victor Hugo had used the sea and the cathedral. There is the decorative novel—the fantastic idyl of rural life or of distant lands—of Hardy and Loti; and many more sorts. There is an immense variety in good work; it appeals to so many sides of the many-sided human creature, since it always, inasmuch as it is good, appeals successfully. In bad work there is no such variety. In fact, the more one looks at it, the more one is struck at its family resemblance, and the small number of headings under which it can be catalogued. In examining it, one finds, however superficially veiled, everlastingly the same old, old failings: inefficacious use of words, scattered, illogical composition, lack of adaptation of form or thought; in other words, bad construction, waste, wear and tear of the Reader's attention; incapacity of manipulating his mind; the craft of writing absent or insufficient. But that is not all. In this exceedingly monotonous thing, poor work (as monotonous as good work is rich and many-sided), we find another fatal element of sameness: lack of the particular emotional sensitiveness which, just as visual sensitiveness makes the painter, makes the Writer.

IV

For writing—I return to my original theory, one-sided, perhaps, but certainly also true in great part—is the art which gives us the emotional essence of the world and of life; which gives us the moods awakened by all that is and can happen, material and spiritual, human and natural, distilled to the highest and most exquisite potency in the peculiar organism called the Writer. As the painter says: "Look, here is all that is most interesting and delightful and vital, all that concerns you most in the visible aspect of things, whence I have extracted it for your benefit"; so the Writer on his side says: "Read; here is all that is most interesting and delightful and vital in the moods and thoughts awakened by all things; here is the quintessence of experience and emotion; I have extracted it from the world and can transfer it to your mind." Hence the teachable portion of the art of writing is totally useless without that which can neither be taught nor learned—the possession of something valuable, something vital, something essential, to say.

We all of us possess, as I have remarked before, a tiny sample of the quality whose abundance constitutes the special artist; we have some of the quality of the philosopher, the painter, the musician, as we have some of the quality of the hero; otherwise, philosophy, painting, music, and heroism would never appeal to us. Similarly, and by the same proof, we have all in us a little of the sensitiveness of the Writer. There is no one so dull or so inarticulate as never in his or her life—say, under the stress of some terrible calamity—to have said or written some word which was memorable not to be forgotten by him who read or heard it: in such moments we have all had the power of saying, because apparently we have had something to say; in that tremendous momentary heightening of all our perceptions we have attained to the Writer's faculty of feeling and expressing the essence of things. But such moments are rare; and the small fragments of literary or artistic faculty which we all are born with, or those are born with to whom literature and art are not mere dust and ashes, can be increased and made more efficient only to a limited degree. What we really have in our

On Literary Construction

power is either to waste them in cumbering the world with work which will give no one any pleasure; or to put them to the utmost profit in giving us the highest degree of delight from the work of those who are specially endowed. Let us learn what good writing is in order to become the best possible Readers.

II

ON STYLE

I

I MUST begin by saying that what I am about to attempt will be, at best, a very partial account of the great thing we mean by Writing. I shall have to omit a good many sides of the subject; and a good many other sides, which certainly must exist, I do not probably even suspect of existing. In intellectual vision, as in physical, the possible points of view are several; and according to which of these points of view we make our own, we shall see the subject in one of a variety of possible arrangements of perspective: the central point, whence all radiates or whither all converges, will shift, even as the apparent centre of a scene seen now from one hill, now from another; lines will connect or not connect, and certain tracts will occupy a greater or smaller portion of the visual field, quite irrespective of their absolute proportions. Hence, according to the point of view, all relative importance varies, and items are omitted, telescoped, enlarged, or made conspicuous. As regards the present case, I had better say at once that the point of view from which, as a matter of individual preference perhaps, I look upon the subject of Writing, is the one which would be roughly defined as psychological. What interests me, what I have thought about, are the relations of the Writer and the Reader. All literary problems, all questions of form, logic, syntax, prosody, even of habit and tradition, appear to me to depend upon the question of Expression and Impression; and Expression and Impression mean merely the Writer and the Reader. I conceive that literature, whenever it is a free art and not merely a useful process, is the art of evoking in the Reader images and feelings similar to those which outer circumstances have evoked, and inner peculiarities have brought forward, in the Writer. I conceive the actual book or poem or essay to be but a portion of the complete work of literary art, whose completion depends upon the response of the Reader to the suggestions of the Writer; I conceive therefore—but I had better not forestall the conclusions which are beginning to force themselves upon me about the finality of the written thing. Just now I will merely sum up, for the easier following of what must necessarily be disjointed remarks, that I conceive Writing to be, spiritually: the art of high and delightful perception of life by the Writer; and technically: the craft of manipulating the contents of the Reader's mind. Hence I consider Writing as, in very special sense, an emotional art.

In a totally different sense from the visual arts, and even music, Writing is an art of emotion, because whereas every art aims at awakening its own specific emotion of pleasure, and even occasionally subordinates everything to the awakening of some other kind of emotion besides that, Writing (inasmuch as a free art, and not a mere mechanism for transferring facts or theories) also employs emotion as the actual material for producing more emotion. The Writer, in so far as an artist, does not aim at producing either a complete picture or a convincing syllogism; he does not try to reproduce things either in their relations in space, or their relation in time, or, save when he now ceases to be an artist and becomes a scientific worker, in their relations of cause and effect. The relations between things which he feels impelled to register, the relations which he desires to transfer from his own consciousness to his Readers, are the relations which we call a *frame of mind*, a *mood*, an *emotion*. This frame of mind is produced in himself by a great many items—sights, sounds, words, gestures, and his own vague conditions of being. But—and here we come to an important distinction between Writing and the visual arts, it is not produced by the *whole of anything*. These items come in contact with the Writer only at limited points; their whole import is not needed, or at all events is not felt to be operative. His consciousness carries, so to speak, only fragments on its surface, instead of the comp'ete visions of the painter or sculptor; and fragments, moreover, quite heterogeneous, called up by all the senses we know of, and often by more senses than we can account for. But these fragments contain the active essence, the taste, perfume, *timbre*, the something provocative of the mood. And it is among these fragments that he selects when he wishes to pass on his mood to others, or to preserve it for himself. Therefore, while Hegel said that all art tends to the condition of music, we might say, more truly, that all Writing, in the highest artistic sense, tends to the condition of the Lyric.

II

This great emotional art of Writing, emotional in its aims and in its means, can be divided, like every other art, into two parts, one which cannot be taught, and one which can. You cannot teach the Writer to *feel life* in such a manner as to make it desirable that his feelings be communicated to others; but you can teach the Writer to communicate such feelings as he may already have, worthy or not of communication, by manipulating the contents of the Reader's mind. In order to make this distinction as clear as possible, let us consider the two totally different meanings in which we are accustomed to use the word *Style*.

The first sense in which this word is used, for instance in the famous saying, "*Le style, c'est l'homme*," relates to the unteachable portion of the art of Writing. Style in this sense means, not a method of presenting the Writer's ideas to the Reader, but the quality of the Writer's ideas, and the manner in which they present themselves to the Writer; a quality and a manner which can be mimicked as we mimic a man's gait, disposition, and temper, but cannot be taught any more than we can teach a man to have such or such relations of arms and legs, liver, heart, and brain. It is, in fact, so much of the man's individual relation with the universe at large as can by any possibility be conveyed in words, for there remain the other portions of those relations which require for their conveying colours and shapes and sounds; moreover, others which no human being can convey to another, and which remain pleasurable, painful, or of subdued, vague, mixed quality, locked up, like his vitality, within himself.

It is, perhaps, only in attempting to analyse style according to its first meaning, that we learn the extraordinary differences which exist in man's power and manner of perceiving, of feeling, one might almost say, of living. These differences sometimes group individuals, however unlike, into men of the same race or men of the same time, like the tendency to see all things as abstractions, which tempts one to think that the men of the eighteenth century really wrote about words picked out of Johnson's Dictionary, not about the shining, coloured, sounding, hot, cold, bitter, sweet things which must have touched and smitten their senses; or again, that orderly vision of detail, dab of colour next to dab of colour, nothing unseen or misty, which distinguishes the French from the English, and connects men so different as Hugo, Flaubert, Zola, and Gautier, and which, judged by the Anglo-Saxon, sometimes almost amounts to visual hyperæsthesia.

The difference between individuals is more subtle : they may construct their sentences much in the same way : but their nature is playing each a different sort of game with the world without. Some men, like Pater, seem to pass as in trance through the steps of an argument and awake only at its conclusions ; others, like Herbert Spencer, are incapable of raising their feet so as to clear a single step. Pater seems to perceive Nature in definite moments and pictures only at rare intervals ; out of a mist there arises a vision, exquisite, but reduced to the bare essentials, all else blotted away. Pater stands half-way to Stevenson in the tendency to note rather the emotion caused by an object in himself than to reproduce the object and trust to its reproducing its impression. Stevenson tells you what he feels, and his feeling awakens a vision in you. Another writer, Mary Robinson, in her wonderful little poem " Stars," for instance, would give you the starry heaven, the depth of the night, the outline of the trees, the sound of the insects and breeze, where Stevenson, in an immortal passage (in the *Cévennes*), sums up the emotions, the suggestions which that night had awakened.

Some men see objects by their movement or the movement they produce in us; others merely by their visible qualities. There are men who, with the utmost psychology and the subtlest connections of moods, are yet, like Browning, far more objective than subjective. Others, like Wordsworth, tell us little of the Nature they are for ever contemplating, save the supreme quality of this contemplation. Such differences ramify in the minutest distinctions: the kind of emotion, the combination of colour, the effects of light which the man perceives first, those which he perceives second; how his eye or his soul glances heedlessly over a foreground, or leaves in vagueness a distant object; what among the many things he sees and feels, among the very few with which he must strain his Reader's unwilling attention and sympathy, he rejects and what he retains. All these differences, if the man has command over words, his words will reveal; and that revelation of a peculiar manner of being, through a peculiar manner of writing, is the heaven-born, unteachable portion of the art of writing: *Poeta nascitur*.

The second sense in which we ordinarily speak of style refers to the portion of the art of Writing which *can*, to some small extent, be taught; it is not the quality of the Writer's ideas, but the method of presenting those ideas to the Reader. It means such a manner of dividing and arranging a subject, of selecting words, as will convey the meaning of the Writer to the Reader with the least possible difference between the effect produced and that intended, and also with the least possible wear and tear of the Reader's capacity and goodwill.

To this great craft (for it is a craft, that is to say, a teachable practice explicable by rational, scientific reasons), belongs infinitely more subtlety than one might guess: it is the triumph of practical good sense, and self-criticism. It is based upon the psychological fact that, to a greater extent than in other arts, the literary work of art is dependent on two persons, the one who speaks and the one who listens, the one who explains and the one who understands, the Writer and the Reader. And this resolves itself into the still more fundamental one, that the words which are the Writer's materials for expression are but the symbol of the ideas already existing in the mind of the Reader; and that, in reality, the Reader's mind is the Writer's palette.[1] The Writer wishes the Reader to realize so far as possible the same thoughts, emotions, and impressions as himself. To do this he must, as it were, drive the Reader to a certain goal along a certain road of his choice; and the Reader is perpetually on the point of stopping, of turning round, or of going off at a wrong turning, let alone his yawing from side to side with intolerable loss of time and effort; therefore, like a horse, he has to be

---

[1] This and other similes occur over and over again in these essays and lectures. I let them stand because I want these useful formulæ learned by heart.

always kept awake, and kept extra awake whenever any new turn is coming, so that much of the craft of writing consists in preventing the Reader from anticipating wrongly on the sense of the Writer, going off on details in wrong directions, lagging behind or getting lost in a maze of streets. Few persons realize that the Writer has not only to make his Reader think or feel the right thing, but also to prevent his perpetually thinking or feeling the wrong one; for stupidity manifests itself most frequently in laying hold of the wrong portion of a page or a sentence, just as inattention shows itself worst in perceiving only one word isolated and in straggling off after the unimportant, so that the important can never be overtaken. Nor is it necessary even to suppose either stupidity or inattention. People catch naturally at what is most familiar to them, as a horse turns naturally down the streets he knows; and considerable attention on the part of the literary coachman is required to forestall such effects of habit. So the Reader must be perpetually forestalled, perpetually kept in the right path, perpetually kept awake. This is the teachable portion of the art of writing; this is style as *a craft*; and about this it is, mainly, that I wish at this moment to talk.

III

I believe that all such portion of the literary art, prose or verse, as does not depend upon the special mode of seeing and living and being of the individual Writer, but is, on the contrary, susceptible of becoming the common property of all gifted persons, a thing which can be taught by explanation and example, improved by practice, and stored up by tradition—that all *literary craft* can be summed up under the heading *Construction*. Now this intellectual construction, which constitutes the teachable portion of literature, even like the physical construction of the builder in stone and brick, and whether the object be a single row of bricks, or an arch or a whole cathedral, will be satisfactory just in proportion as the craftsman realizes the how and why of carrying and pushing and pulling in general, and the specific nature of the materials he is employing in particular. It is a question of mere common sense ; of that common sense which when it acts rapidly and almost unconsciously we call intuition; and, when it deals unexpectedly with new, unthought-of combinations, we sometimes call genius.

The material with which the Writer constructs, out of which he builds the image of his own feelings and thoughts, must be regarded in two ways — a more external and practical way, and a more intimate and essential one. The Writer's materials are *words*, and those groupings, larger and smaller, of words which we all call sentences, paragraphs, chapters, and also other groupings such as parenthetical passages, explanations, retrospects, and so forth. The Writer's materials are words, and it is by arranging these that he copies, so to speak, his own feelings and ideas. But these words, you must remember, are merely *signals* which call up the various items—visual, audible, tactile, emotional, and of a hundred different other sorts—which have been deposited by chance in the mind of the Reader. The words are what the Writer manipulates in the first instance, as the pianist manipulates in the first instance the keys of his instrument. But behind the keyboard of the piano is an arrangement of hammers and strings; and behind the words are the contents of the Reader's memory; and what makes the melody, the harmony, is the vibration of the strings, the awakening of the impressions in the consciousness. The Writer is really playing upon the contents of the Reader's mind, as the pianist, although his fingers touch only the keyboard, is really playing on the strings. And the response to the manipulation is due, in both cases, to the quality of what is at first not visible: the Reader's potential images and emotions, the string which can be made to vibrate.

The efficacy of any word or class of words depends upon the particular nature and experience of the individual reader or class of Reader. It is evident, for instance, that a man born blind will not respond to words intended to awaken visual images; and that a man in possession of his sight, but employing it only so far as indispensable for his convenience, will perceive

On Style

the efficacy of visual nouns and adjectives only in a negative way. Moreover, the experiences of each individual Reader will have given some kinds of stored-up impressions a greater tendency to reappear in his mind than others; we all know how different people will single out different passages of the same book. A soldier, for instance, will be more impressed by those words and sentences in a story by Mr. Kipling which evoke, or can evoke, images and feelings connected with barrack life; while a painter, no doubt, will scarcely notice those words and sentences, but will feel very keenly the passages, the adjectives and metaphors evoking aspects of sky and water and moving outlines of figures. Words will be efficacious for various reasons: chiefly their familiarity on the one hand, and their unfamiliarity on the other. A word which is very frequently employed and in a very great variety of circumstances, will tend to become very wide in meaning and very *massive*, as psychologists express it, in the kind of feeling it awakens; each successive use of the word, implying, as it does, a state of mind, a way of thinking or feeling, leaves clinging to that word something of that state of mind, of that way of thinking and feeling. In this way the word becomes something like a composite photograph: through the accumulation of different meanings which have been connected it will enlarge its general meaning, and enlarge also, to the extent of sometimes obliterating all special quality, the feeling attached to it. Think of such a word as *Sea*. It awakens in our mind an incredible number of possible visual, audible, sensible, and emotional impressions: wide, deep, wet, green, blue, briny, stormy, serene, a thing to swim or drown in, connecting or severing countries; moreover, a word which may awaken in our mind, because it has been accompanied with so many different ones, feelings of gladness or terror or sorrow. Thus, the word *Sea* is one of those which suggest most, but also most confusedly; and it is a word, also, which we probably none of us hear without a degree of emotion, more emotion than, say, a word like *Bay* or *Gulf*, but an emotion so compounded of different emotions as to be quite unclassifiable, and perceptible only as a very vague, general excitement. These images and states of mind, which a word brings up because they have accompanied it, are what I should wish every Writer to analyse as a deliberate exercise, unless he is already extremely aware of their peculiarities; and those are what I mean by the *connotations of words*.

I have now come to the point where I want to direct your attention to the most important question in all literary craft, the question, if I may call it so for greater briefness, of the Adjective. I believe that you will find in dictionaries and grammars that the Adjective *is the word which serves to qualify a noun*. I am taking it in a much wider sense, and as including, besides the kind of word grammatically licensed to qualify nouns, and the other kind of word, namely, the adverb, grammatically licensed to qualify verbs, every kind of word of whatsoever category which serves to qualify another word; and also, every form of speech comparison, metaphor, or even descriptive or narrative fragment, which does duty to qualify other parts of speech or statements. For all writing consists in two processes, very distinctly separate : a process of awakening ideas which are already existing, ready for combination in the mind of the Reader; and a process of qualifying those ideas by the suggestion of others, in order that the principal ideas or sets of ideas be not only matched as closely as possible with the ideas or sets of ideas occupying the mind of the Writer, but that these principal ideas or sets of ideas should lead more irresistibly or easily to the other ideas or sets of ideas which are to follow. For we must remember always that the business of writing is not with effects coexistent like the effects of painting, but rather successive, existing essentially in time, like the effects of music. I have been pointing out to you that a word taken separately, for instance any noun, awakens an image in the mind which is apt to be complex and vague, susceptible to self-contradiction, or at least to alternatives, because every time that the word has been used it has been used in slightly varying circumstances, a deposit of each of which has been left, more, or, as already remarked, less faintly, in the mind. Nearly every word has meant, turn about, so many different main calls on our attention; the word *Sea* has meant, turn about or simultaneously, an impression of sight, colour, sound, smell, breath, and so forth, and what is more, a different kind of emotion, so that in order to awaken the particular impression we want, we have to cut off the possibility of some or all the others being revived. We have to shut the doors to impressions we do not want and to canalize, in a particular direction, those which we do want.

That which thus acts as a door to exclude irrelevancies, as an embankment to concentrate impressions, and again, as a signpost (forgive this sequence of metaphors) to indicate the direction of future impression, nay, as a window through which to catch glimpses of the impressions we are heading for,—this qualifier, adjective, adverb, or adjectively or adverbially employed metaphor, simile, or bare fact,—is the chief instrument by which the Writer can rearrange the thoughts and feelings of the Reader in such a way as to mirror his own.

Hence one might take it as one of the first precepts of writing *that no adjective, by which I mean no qualifier, is ever without a result.* You may, perhaps, waste principal items, facts, nouns, and verbs which are not acting as qualifiers; but you cannot merely waste an adjective or qualifier: an adjective, if it does not help you, goes against you.

Adjectives are usually imagined to *add something* to nouns. What they really do is to cut off something, some of the possible meanings of a noun. A noun is almost always the representative of reiterated experiences of a similar kind, and it is inevitably the representative of a simultaneous combination of many kinds of impression: it recalls different modes of perception or emotion, even if it does not recall different occasions on which these different modes of perception or emotion have been united. Now, it is most improbable that the Writer will ever want to recall at once *all* the impressions grouped simultaneously under the heading of this noun; and I think I may boldly say that it is *impossible* he can ever want to recall at once all the impressions which, on successive occasions, have become stored up as part and parcel of it. Consequently, one principal use of the adjective will be to direct the Reader's attention to the particular portions of that noun which *are* to be recalled; the adjective will *limit* the noun; so, for instance, when we speak of the stormy sea, or the blue sea, we are not *adding* to the impressions conveyed by the word *sea*, but, on the contrary, diminishing them. It is probably the increasing richness of connotation of nouns, a richness due to the constant addition made by every human being's experience, which accounts for the increasing use of adjectives. The Ancients, the Northern writers of the Middle Ages, did not require to use adjectives as much as we do, because their nouns were poor in significance, had, so to speak, few aspects, and they had no need therefore to limit the significance, to select the aspect. Much the same applies, as regards all visual impressions, to the Writers of the eighteenth century: they cared little for the visible aspects of things, and words therefore suggested to them but very few visible aspects among which to select: a hill was a hill, not a rounded hill or a peaky hill, etc. etc., so it was quite enough to say *hill*, or at most to say that it was a *horrid hill*; since to those comfortable sedentary people there existed only two kinds of hill: the hill easy to climb and with a meditative seat at the top, and the hill without a seat, and, owing to its difficulty of climbing, practically without a top.

The other way in which an adjective qualifies a noun is by connecting it with another noun, by extracting, so to speak, from among the impressions to be evoked by a word that particular impression which belongs also to some other set of impressions, to be evoked presently by another word. This is what I have called the canalizing power of adjectives. Let us suppose, for instance, that you are speaking of the sky, that the impression which you wish to evoke is that of the sky at night: if you wish to speak afterwards of the stars, you will do well to limit, to canalize, your impressions of the night by using the adjective *clear*, *bright*, or so forth, because, by so doing, you cut off and

On Style

throw away at once the other impressions possibly connected by the word *night*, for instance, the impression of blackness, or of diffused moonmist; and, when you come to speak of your stars, you will find them ready, unimpeded by other things, to quiver into existence in the Reader's mind. This connective power of adjectives, this power of qualifying what is coming next, is one of the facts which give most trouble to inexperienced Writers, and which show the finest intuition on the part of the heaven-born genius. Short of being such a heaven-born genius, one has to be for ever trying in one's mind the action of adjectives, calculating their operation, what they will lead to, what new roads they may force you to diverge into, what vantage grounds, highly desirable later, they may be cutting you off from. Let us suppose that we wish to describe a rocket. The better to evoke this rocket, we will evoke that which is its background, and press our finger down on the note *sky*. We have now *rocket* and *sky*. But *sky* is very general: there are all sorts of skies; the one we want is a *blue* sky for the *gold* of the rocket does turn the sky peculiarly blue. But the word *blue*, connected with *sky*, usually evokes the notion of the sky by day, because most people do not have occasion to remark that, alongside of lamps, rockets, or even stars, the night sky is often an intense though different blue. Therefore we should have to say the night-blue sky. But we want something even more definite in evocation. Shall we say the starry sky? That gives us the night sky, presumably its colour also, and the fact of its being a vault, for the impression of stars brings the impression of a vault, and a vault is exactly what we want for the parabola of our rocket. Also the stars, thus evoked, are solidly fastened in heaven; they bring out, by their stability and eternity, all that is moving, leaping up, falling down, utterly ephemeral in the poor rocket. So far, *starry* seems immensely to improve the sky for our rocket. But . . . but the stars are very luminous, and, moreover, innumerable, and the vision of their splendour utterly dims the wretched rocket. So we strike out *starry*, having found that, although we gained much by its use, we also lost what was more essential. Thus, half the qualifying words, and similes, and sentences which arise in our mind or are written down on our paper have to be rejected; delightful things which enhanced the present but jeopardized the future; interesting lines and colours which spoilt the pattern of the picture or building, delightful arrangements of orchestration which hampered the rhythm or modulation of our music. I take it that the heaven-born Writer actually, at the moment of writing, perceives in his mind only the impressions, the qualities which aid a given general effect. His very act of feeling is selective, according to literary necessities. He is a specialized organism.

On Style

The strings of the piano, whose vibrations the pianist selects and groups into patterns, have been arranged to suit the necessities of piano playing. They represent the convenience of generations of pianists. Moreover, the strings of the piano stay quiet when they are not struck by the hammer which the pianist's finger brings down on them by touching the keys; and a note does not suddenly ring out, and then another note, quite unexpectedly, because some third note has been struck with which they had some affinity unknown to the player. But the instrument played upon by the Writer, namely, the mind of his Reader, has not been arranged for the purpose of thus being played upon, and its strings do not wait to vibrate in obedience to the Writer's touch, but are always on the point of sounding and jangling uninvited.

The impressions, the ideas and emotions stored up in the mind of the Reader, and which it is the business of the Writer to awaken in such combinations and successions as answer to his own thoughts and moods —these, which you must allow me to call, in psychologist's jargon, *Units of Consciousness*, have been deposited where they are by the random hand of circumstance, by the accident of temperament and vicissitudes, and in heaps or layers, which represent merely the caprice or necessity of individual experience. From the Writer's point of view, they are a chaos; and, what is worse for him who wishes to rearrange them to suit his thought or mood, they are chaos of living, moving things.

For the contents of our mind, the deposit of our life, have a way of their own, obey a law on which depends all the success and all the failure of writing: the law of the Association of Ideas; that is to say, the necessity, whose cause is one of the great problems of mental science, of starting into activity in the relation in which they were originally stored up, so that the various items united in our real experience tend to awaken one another in our memory. We all know this phenomenon: for instance, a certain impression, say, the shape of a particular house, when recalled to our memory, will bring with it, not merely in succession but in actual coexistence sometimes, a particular tone of voice, a certain philosophical opinion, a vague sense of warmth, a dull consciousness of sorrow, and perhaps the smell of wet earth or of warm fir trees; and this because these items of consciousness did really once come at the same time or in rapid succession, all together into our life. But, besides this storage of the Reader's thoughts and feelings (or their rudiments) in layers answering to the accident of life, there is another typical kind of such storage which will give the Writer, in his attempts to rearrange the Reader's mind, an equal amount of trouble, I mean the storage by the process of rough-and-ready practical classification, which comes as the result of life also. Let me say it once more:

a certain shape of house, a certain tone of voice, a certain philosophical view, a certain sensation of warmth, a smell of wet earth or warm fir trees have been stored up together accidentally ; but the operation of constantly comparing and sorting one's own impressions which the very fact of living, of ordering our conduct, is constantly forcing on us, and which goes on for ever in the individual and the race, may have rearranged these impressions in special abstract pigeon holes ; *that* particular shape of house will have been thrust unconsciously into the same heap with other shapes of houses ; the tone of voice, the contralto notes, say, will have been bundled together with other tones of voice, other contraltos, and probably with tenors and basses and trebles ; the philosophical opinion will have been thrown on to the other philosophical opinions, and the sensations of warmth, the smell of wet earth or warm fir trees, will be somewhere in the same box as other sensations of temperature and other smells. Hence, there is as much possibility of any of these items of consciousness, if touched by the Writer, if made to vibrate under the pressure of the signalling word—there is as much probability of any of these items of consciousness evoking its neighbours in the dull, abstract order of workaday classification, as in the vivid emotional order of actual individual experience.

And out of this accidental chaos, out of this rough-and-ready classification, out of twenty different possibilities of storage and neighbourhood, the Writer must summon up such items of the Reader's consciousness as he wants for his particular purposes. The Writer must select, for the formation of *his* particular pattern of thought or fact or mood, such as he requires among these living molecules of memory, such and such only as he wants—not one other, on pain of spoiling that pattern. And for this he has to make use of that very fact of Association of Ideas which seems so much against him, finding the secret of wakening ideas by other ideas and the secret of putting ideas to sleep no less.

Here is an illustration : You are writing about a man who, like most of the heroes of Balzac, is torn between the desire to take a cab and the knowledge that he cannot afford it. Speaking of this cab, bringing it forward, making it roll into the Reader's awareness, you may insist upon various aspects of the cab : you may speak of cabs from the sentimental point of view, as things which carry people to the places they delight in, or away from the persons they love ; cabs as factors of mere change of place. Or you may speak of cabs from the side of colour and form, the yellow wheels of the cab on the lilacky shiny asphalt, etc. ; or of cabs as constructed on such a system, by such a man, with such wheels, tyres, such or such a system of harnessing, capable of rolling so-and-so. But you do not happen to want to open up the vista of sentimental change, for in your story no one is arriving suddenly, or going to meet anyone, or going to part for ever. On the other hand, in your story you have no reason to open up the vista, in the Reader's mind, of the possible picturesqueness of London streets : you do not wish him to think next of the blue mist closing the view, the vague towers looming far off, or the network of telegraph wires and advertisements in the sky. Still less do you want the Reader to compare cabs with broughams, omnibuses, drays, locomotives, bicycles,[1] and to speculate on the laws of the movement of wheels and the effect of easy locomotion on civilization in general. You want the Reader to think of the cab in relation to the hero's desires and his poverty. To do this, you will insist, if you must insist on something, upon the cab being expensive on the one hand, and convenient or socially desirable on the other.

I have no time to speak of the power of words as mere sounds ; and, although even in prose such sound-power is undoubtedly operative, it is only in verse that any large and active effects can be obtained by the arrangement of words with reference to their sound. What I wish to insist upon is the choice and arrangement of words considered with reference to their meaning merely, by the selection of their connotative values, and the action and reaction of these connotative values

[1] Written in the later nineties. How fast have the motor-car and taxi dashed into being as the years rolled by !

determined by the combinations in which we place them. It is by this selection, by this continual modification of what each word evokes by the thing evoked by another word, that we obtain in writing the equivalent to texture and weight and perspective, to what are called *values* in painting; and to what is equivalent to phrasing and orchestration in music : the right presentation of the idea.

It is by this selection and arrangement of the *essential virtues* (if I may use the expression) of words that we communicate not merely the facts of life, but, so to say, the *quality* of those facts ; that we make the Reader feel that these are facts, not merely of life in general but of the life of one particular kind of temperament and not of another.

There are words which, owing to their extreme precision—a precision demanding time for thorough realization, or to their excessive philosophical generality, forcing the mind to lose time in long divagations— there are words which make the Reader think and feel, in a way make him *live*, slowly ; and there are other words which make the Reader think, feel, and live quickly ; and quickly and smoothly, or quickly and jerkily, as the case may be. Above all, there are arrangements of words—combinations of action and reaction of word upon word, which, by opening up vistas or closing them, make the Reader's mind dawdle, hurry, or bustle busily along. Now, by one of the most important laws of our mental constitution, whatever kind of movement a picture, a piece of music, or a page of writing sets up in us, that particular kind of movement do we attribute to the objects represented or suggested by the picture, the music, or the writing; it is from no idle affectation, no mere conventional desire to make things match, that we resent the lengthy telling of a brief moment, the jerky description of a solemn fact. We dislike it because two contrary kinds of action are being set up in our mind; because the fact related is forcing us to one sort of pace, indeed to what is even more important, one sort of rhythm, while the words relating that fact are forcing us to another pace, to another rhythm. Conversely, some of the most notable mishaps in literature are due to the accidental, unconscious meeting of a subject and a selection of words which reinforce one another too much : neither the fact nor the wording is in itself overwhelming, but the joint action of the two becomes intolerable. Somewhat similarly, Flaubert, by his enormous abundance of precise visual adjectives, by his obvious elaboration and finish, turns passing effects into unchanging attributes. On the other hand, lack of concordance between subject and wording defeats the Writer's intention : thus there is probably twice as much adventure, hairbreadth escape, intrigue, and so forth, in *Salambô* as in the *Master of Ballantrae*, yet while the personages in Stevenson's story affect us as in perpetual agitation, the people in Flaubert's great novel seem never to be doing anything but posing in *tableaux vivants*, or, at the utmost, moving rhythmically for the display of costumes and attributes, like figures in a grand ballet. Another curious instance is afforded by d'Annunzio's prose, magnificent though it is. His long, latinized sentences, where adjectives are rare and verbs vague, leave the impression of everything happening far slower than it possibly could in reality; his people take as long to put on their hat and walk to the door as real mortals to change all their clothes and walk to the other end of the town; hence a feeling of watching colossal ghosts or huge, unfinished, barely animated statues; an impression of something empty, featureless, gaping, but irresistibly emphatic, eerie and tragic, which allows one to read the most revolting or preposterous stories without, as one otherwise would, disbelieving in their possibility outside a madhouse.

On the other hand, George Eliot, with her passion for abstract scientific terms and scientifically logical exposition, often sacrifices entirely that evanescent, nay sometimes futile, quality without a degree of which life would wear us out in six months. And for this reason she conveys a wrong impression of characters whom, considered analytically, she understood thoroughly. Thus, Hetty Sorrel, whom we ought to think of as a poor little piece of cheap millinery, remains for our feelings, for our nerves, a solid piece of carpentering (please note by the way how the everlasting reference to carpentering weighs down, ruler-marks, and compass-measures the whole novel)—a Hetty dove-tailed and glued, nailed and screwed, and warranted never to give way! Moreover, George Eliot's scientific dreariness of vocabulary and manner of exposition explains very largely why her professed *charmeurs* and *charmeuses*, Tito, Rosamond Vincy, Stephen Guest, are so utterly the reverse of charming. They are correctly thought out as mere analyses, and never do anything psychologically false or irrelevant; but they are wrongly expressed; although, as I am more and more convinced, and as I hope some day to prove to you, such wrong expression is due, in the last resort, to imperfect or wrong emotional conception, as distinguished from intellectual, analytical comprehension. George Eliot has another mannerism which alternates with this to create an impression different from the one she is aiming at; for she has also a little dry, neat, ironical essay-style (imitated from Fielding and the Essayists) which creates an impression of the excessive trumperiness of human struggles and woes which, Heaven knows, she never felt to be trumpery; while at the same time she is making the limited feelings of obscure individuals into matters of state of the Cosmos by the use of terminology usually devoted to the eternal phenomena of the universe.

These peculiarities in the selection of words and their

arrangement, like the even more important peculiarities in modes of exposition of the whole subject, are, I think, largely matters of inborn tendency; they express the Writer's way of seeing, feeling, living, much more than we are apt to think. So that the art of the Writer consists less in adapting his style to the subject, than his subject to his style. George Eliot—although not one of her books is, from the artistic standpoint, a great book, had, nevertheless, a side on which she was a great Writer: the happy passages in her books, for instance the analytic autobiographical chapters (not unlike Rousseau's) in the *Mill on the Floss* seem to indicate what her real field of artistic supremacy might have been. As it is, the bulk of her work leaves a sense of wearisome conflict, conflict between what she has determined to say and the manner in which she is able to say it, and this because she ignored her inherent peculiarities of style when choosing a subject. Stevenson and Pater, on the contrary, seem to me to show, in two totally different kinds of work, the most perfect fusion of style and subject. In Mr. Pater's *School of Giorgione*, for instance, and in the Bass Rock episodes of *Catriona*, it is quite impossible to say where style begins and subject ends. One forgets utterly the existence of either, one is merely impressed, moved, as by the perfectly welded influences of outer nature, as by the fusion of a hundred things which constitute a fine day or a stormy night.

Instead of summing up these remarks on the selection of words, on the action and reaction which their connotations provoke, I will merely add that one does not want to *open up side vistas* in a narrative which is intended to speed through time; and that one does not want adjectives which narrow down, nor definite and highly active verbs, in the description of a mood: it must float, wave, and give the notion of impalpable transitoriness.

You will have noticed that, in what I have just been saying, I have gradually, almost unconsciously, slid into speaking of something much more considerable than the choice of words. I believe have even used the expression "exposition of the subject." These two merge; while still speaking of construction in the narrower sense, I am obliged to forestall the treatment of construction in the wider. For it is all construction, whether we be manipulating what I called single units of consciousness, and the words which bid them start forward; or whether we deal with the whole trains of thought, the whole states of feeling into which these units of consciousness have been united, and which are themselves ordered about in groups of sentences, paragraphs, or chapters. Whatever we may be doing, so long as we are writing, we are manipulating the consciousness of the Reader.

But why, one asks oneself, why should this rearrangement of the ideas and feelings of the Reader be such a difficult matter, since all we are aiming at is, after all, to awaken the trains of thought and the moods which already exist in the Reader? Why all this manipulation and manœuvring? Why not photograph, so to speak, the contents of the mind of the Writer on to the mind of the Reader? Simply because the mind of the Reader is not a blank, inert plate, but a living crowd of thoughts and feelings, which are existing on their own account and in a manner wholly different from that other living crowd of thoughts and feelings, the mind of the Writer. We are obliged to transmit our thoughts and feelings to others in an order different from the one in which they have come to ourselves, for one very important reason: that they are *our* thoughts. Being *our* thoughts means that they are connected with our life, habits, circumstances, born of them; it means that they are so familiar that we recognize them whether they come out head foremost or tail foremost, and into however many and various splinters they may be broken. To the Reader, on the contrary, they are unfamiliar, since they are not his; and the habits and circumstances of the Reader, so far from helping him to grasp them, distract him by sending up other thoughts and feelings which are his own. Add to this that the mere activity of original feeling and thinking, of literary creation in ourselves, puts weight on in a manner which no amount of merely receptive attention can replace. All writing, therefore, is a struggle between the thinking and feeling of the Writer and the thinking and feeling of the Reader. The heaven-born Writer is he whose thoughts, by some accident of his constitution, tend spontaneously to arise in his *own* mind in the order and values most resembling the order and values in which these thoughts are most easily communicated to other minds. While the thoroughly schooled Writer is he who is able most quickly and thoroughly to exchange the order and values in which his thoughts have come to himself, for the order and values in which experience and analysis have taught him that these thoughts can best be transmitted to others.

These are a few of the facts of literary construction of the craft of manipulating the stored-up contents of other folks' minds, in the very elementary domain of arrangement of words and sentences, of exposition of the subject in paragraphs and passages. But all the rest is construction also, however far we go, although the construction of a whole book stands to the construction of a single sentence as the greatest complexities of counterpoint and orchestration stand to the relations of the vibrations constituting a single just note. It is always, in small matters and in large, the old question of what movements we can produce in the Reader's mind; and of what other movements we must prevent or neutralize in order that those we desire should have free play.

III

ÆSTHETICS OF THE NOVEL

THERE seems a general notion that wherever literature is cultivated for its own sake it must become a fine art like painting and music; and that the novel, more especially, since it gives pleasure, must give the special pleasure due to beauty; and, as a result, we call many things in a book beautiful, and imagine them to be analogous to a fine picture or a lovely song, which, honestly considered, are simply and utterly ugly.

It has taken me years to get rid of this prejudice; and cost me several pangs to admit to myself that it is otherwise. Yet it ought merely to prove the richness of human nature thus to find that the novel, for instance, has ample resources for fascinating our attention without the help of the very special quality called beauty. In the first place, *we like words*, and, above all, *we like a statement*; the forms made by logical thought are full of the special attractions of logic, and the material in which all that concerns our ego is expressed, is steeped, it would seem, in a sort of interesting egotistic solution. Certain it is that there must be a real pleasure in such things, since it is sufficient to overcome the effort of gathering up thoughts and interpreting words. Think of the quite unnecessary statement and argument in which mankind indulges, and the eager, often delighted manner in which people will talk and listen about anything, particularly about nothing at all. The attraction of all kinds of literature is primarily based upon this double pleasure : the pleasure of using words and the pleasure of realizing a statement or demonstration ; neither of which pleasures are more æsthetic than are those of moving our limbs or of indiscriminately using our eyes. For this reason we often take up a book or newspaper, absolutely irrespective of its contents ; and if a book, why not a novel ? After this elementary attractiveness of the spoken or written word come the satisfactions (rather than definite pleasures) of expectation and fulfilment, of watching movement and of sympathetic participation therein ; of emotional excitement (there is an undoubted pleasure, for instance, even in being annoyed and certainly in being angry) ; the immense and altogether superior satisfaction of leaving one's own concerns behind and freeing oneself from the routine of life by identification with other folk ; a kind of play, masquerade, eminently a holiday satisfaction, to which is closely allied the agreeable sense of irresponsibility which seems to grow with the perception of the responsibility of the characters we are watching, a feeling, by the way, in no way connected with fiction as such, since we have it equally in reading the newspaper, histories, and memoirs; are we not always ready to treat other folks' affairs as mere inventions, being delighted to rid ourselves of the perpetual consequences and complications which prevent our life from being the mere amusing play of perception and volition which it might be? Add to this, in greater or lesser degree, the perception, which is pleasant, of skill and tact on the part of the author; sometimes (what to some critical natures is equally pleasing) the lack of skill and tact of the author. When we have summed up these various items of literary satisfaction, we can pass on to a new kind of factor of pleasure, which is immensely attractive to certain minds, and which is especially present in the novel—I mean the gaining (or thinking we gain) a knowledge of mankind and of life. For when we are young, particularly, we are troubled by a delusive longing for such knowledge, and hoodwinked by a false sense of capability whenever we think we have got it.

These are what I should call the non-æsthetic attractions of the novel, attractions frequently sufficient to compensate for the most rough-and-ready disregard for all our instincts of beauty and harmony. The æsthetic attractions are wholly different. The novelist can show us beautiful places, make us live in company with delightful personalities—from Stendhal's Duchess to Tolstoi's Natacha, from Robinson Crusoe to Diana

Warwick. I do not mean merely *ethically laudable* persons (no one, I am sure, would care to live with Romola or Daniel Deronda), but creatures whose vigorous, harmonious personalities, sometimes mainly physical, the author has felt as he would feel a melody or a sunset, and, in consequence, conveyed to us not by mere reproduction of their characteristics, but by the far more efficacious means of direct emotional contagion: his admiration, love, delight, inevitably kindling ours. Besides this, there is the specific æsthetic quality of literature. What it is, I do not, and I suppose nobody nowadays does, know: a charm due to the complex patterns into which (quite apart from sound) the parts of speech, verbs and nouns and adjectives, actives and passives, variously combined tenses, can be woven even like lines and colours, producing patterns of action and reaction in our mind, our nerve tracks—who knows? in our muscles and heartbeats and breathing, more mysterious, even, than those which we can dimly discern, darkly guess, as effects of visible and audible form. In so far as any of these effects are produced by the novel, the novel participates in the nature of other æsthetic productions; I do not say of other works of art, for we are continually reverting to the old use of *art* as mere craft, and confusing with beauty what is mere logic, dexterity, technical knowledge, or tact.

But the novel can get along perfectly without any

such æsthetic qualities, as I hope to have shown by my enumerations of the many other factors of pleasure, or, at least, of interest, which the novelist has at disposal. And such non-æsthetic interest is sufficient, not merely for the Readers who are more scientific, or more dramatic, or more practical, or more technically ingenious, than æsthetic; but sufficient even for æsthetic Readers in their scientific, or dramatic, or practical, or technical moments and capacities; for even the most æsthetically sensitive persons must have other sides to their characters, else they would be dunces, criminals, paupers, bores, and general incapables. The difference between the people who are æsthetically sensitive and those who are not (and here we have the key to the varying power of reading novels like, let us say, Zola's *Pot-Bouille*), is not merely that the æsthetic people ask for beauty as the scientific do for knowledge and the dramatic for human emotion, but that the æsthetic people suffer very acutely whenever the novel contains downright ugliness; suffer in a much more positive manner than the scientific or dramatic Reader suffers from glaring absurdity or hopeless tameness of situation; for in the one case there is irritation or boredom, in the other something verging on physical disgust. So that, regarding the novel, the question becomes simply: which, in the individual case, happens to be the stronger, the satisfaction of the many non-æsthetic capacities for pleasure; or the displeasure inflicted on the æsthetic instinct by subject or treatment which do not in the least offend any other craving of human nature? It is a question, in fact, between the individual Writer and the individual Reader; and I doubt whether it can ever be made a question of right and wrong. Some persons *can* read *A Vau l'Eau* [1] without any misery and with much satisfaction, even getting up from their reading decidedly the richer in knowledge and sympathy. Others are so harrowed that any possibilities of pleasure or profit are absolutely paralysed, and there is no sort of use in going on with the book. A third class can get through the novel in a middle condition of balanced, neutralized satisfaction and dissatisfaction, occasionally varied by a momentary predominance of pleasure or loathing.

I have ventured to say that in such questions there is no absolute right or wrong, and that a book like this (I have purposely chosen the most excessive instance) may increase the spiritual health of some Readers and momentarily jeopardize that of others, all equally estimable persons. But what, I hear a class of Readers (and that class is represented, as well as the others, in my own person), what is the use of being utterly depressed and sickened by a hundred and fifty pages of trivial hideousness? The sickening and the depression do no good, quite the contrary; and, as I said, where there is nothing else, the book had best be thrown into the fire. But the stimulation which the book can give

[1] I *think*, by Huysmans.

to sympathetic understanding is a good, a very good thing, since we can never have enough of it in life. A novel like *A Vau l'Eau* can give the right kind of Reader an increased insight into the commonest, but also the most powerful, needs and passions of mankind, and in so far it can tend to make his attitude and action in life more useful, or at least less mischievous. It can teach, moreover, pity for people who may, perhaps, be helped; teach also resolute idealism in our own persons by disclosing the very unideal sloughs above which our common human nature has so insecurely and so partially raised itself. But in the question of novels, as in all others, the most useful thing, perhaps, is to be at the same time very æsthetic and very capable of momentarily shelving our æstheticism, or rather of being able to see and understand dispassionately, while keeping the most passionate aversions and preferences.

IV

THE NATURE OF THE WRITER

I

RUSHING through villages, along ridges, with the kingdoms of the earth on either side, all yesterday in the motor-car; sitting in the heather, hearing the wind in the pines, the distant hurtle of trains; all this, and the millions of other things of sight, sound and feeling, are transformed in the Writer's mind into words; words, if so be, transmissive, evocative. And in the mind of the Reader?

For the things which we write in our books, the Reader has to read into them.

Of course all art depends as much upon memory as upon actuality; it lives as much, so to speak, in our past as in our present. Because, in however unconscious and hidden a manner, all art deals with habits of perception and association, which are but the tracks of the endlessly repeated deeds of our life. Because it is in memory that our impressions are stored; and (what is more important) that our preferences and repulsions have become most strongly organized. Or, if you prefer, because it is in our whole Past that we really think and feel, when we seem, superficially, to be thinking and feeling only on this unclutchable point, without parts or magnitude, the Present. All art is due to our being creatures of experience, of recollection; but literature, the mere written or spoken word, art or not, to a much more visible and greater extent. For, if, as the new science of æsthetics is beginning to teach, the preference for a picture, a building or a song, indeed, the feeling and realizing of its presence, depends upon stored up and organized experience of our own activities, how far more exclusively does the phantom-reality called literature exist only in the realm of our recollections! It is not composed of objective, separately perceptible lines, masses, colours, note-sequences and note-consonances; it has no existence, no real equivalent, outside the mind; and the spoken sound, the written characters, have no power unless translated into images and feelings which are already within us. *What's Hecuba to me?* We are not much impressed by writings which deal with people and circumstances outside our own experience; and not impressed at all by writings, however eloquent, in a language which we do not understand.

Now *understanding a language* means simply that certain symbolical sounds or marks awaken in us echoes, images, feelings, which were already latent within us. The Writer makes his book not merely out of his own mind's contents, but out of ours; and in the similarity, the greater or lesser equivalence, of these contents, lies all the possible efficacy of literature. The newborn infant, could he see and spell, spell the very longest words and, from an innate gift, comprehend at once the hang of sentences, would yet be blind and deaf to literature. Why? because he was newborn, had no life behind him, nothing for literature to evoke, to rearrange, to subdue him with.

II

The Writer frames the patterns with which, like every other artist, he encloses, subdues and satisfies the soul, out of material given entirely and solely by the memory. This fact, to which I shall revert over and over again, accounts for the chief characteristics of literature, and for its particular relation to life. Let us, therefore, look at this stuff given by memory to the Writer.

We are apt to speak of recollected things and actions as if they were copies, a trifle faded and fragmentary, of the things and actions of reality; and as if what applied to the one must therefore be true of the other. This is not the case. The mere fact of being faded and fragmentary means more than it seems, for it is due to a circumstance we are apt to overlook, namely, that recollections do not exist (save in dreams and visions) in space and time, reserved, so to speak, for themselves;

but that they exist in minds perpetually traversed in all directions by a close and moving web of impressions from the present. We should think of recollections as something similar to ghosts, whom we can tell from living realities because they lack the corroboration of surroundings, the bulk, vividness and warmth which come of various modes of perception acting together. Like ghosts, recollections can enter by closed doors, occupy seats already filled, flit about in inappropriate places, baffle our attempts to clutch or scare them; but like ghosts they can only be seen and not touched, only heard and not seen; moreover, reality walks right through them. The presentment of the inner eye or ear, however vivid (and otherwise we should be mad and lured to destruction), cannot compete with the testimony of the senses; and if recollections are faint and vacillating, it is because they are blurred and interrupted by present reality.

I have been speaking of those recollections which are most like realities, and which imitate, to a certain degree, the multifold existence of all real things in space and time. But this is only the least part of what memory furnishes; and even it, as we shall see, is liable to singular processes of compression and expansion, of intensifying and fading, under the varying pressure of life and thought.

I have alluded to the competition of recollections with present impressions. There is, also, the competition between recollections and recollections. In the ceaseless crowding of impressions, a hundred, a thousand times exceeding our powers of storage, only those are accepted in memory which are connected with our habits and interests, which bear, so to speak, a kinship to other impressions already become recollections. These they sometimes replace, the fresher detail hiding the older one; and, in most cases, they coalesce with them, new and old being crushed down together into composite images, abstractions and diagrams, bulkless *ideas*, mere definitions "without space or magnitude"; while, every now and then, some individual feature, some forgotten peculiarity, will start into unexpected vividness.

Nor is this all. Even if the storage of memory were unlimited, the hurry of life, its lack of spare time and energy, the necessity for rapid, unhesitating and almost automatic action, would reduce the recollections we habitually use to the barely necessary. Thus the name of a thing or deed awakens, nine times out of ten, the notion of only one or two qualities or uses, becomes a counter to reckon by, or a label of most varying suggestion, serving to direct our momentary choice. If, as is the case, we see only so much of reality as individually concerns us in a given circumstance, how much less do we see of that more docile, more easily compressed, cut down, pushed aside, momentarily abolished, world of the past which is carried in ourselves! And here I revert and must enlarge upon this possibility not merely of appearing and vanishing, but of shrinking and dilating, of fading and intensifying, of shedding parts and integrating them afresh, a possibility which is the most singular, the most essential and the most pregnant characteristic of memory, although it seems, oddly enough, the one least taken into account by those who make such subjects their study. Recollections behave very much like congregated soap bubbles, which the breath through the straw makes bigger or smaller; now one, now another takes body or loses it, expands and swallows up its neighbours, shrinks into one of a minute subsidiary cluster; detaches itself to float in solitary iridescence, or to burst unnoticed into nothingness.

This adaptability of all recollections, so utterly different from the irreducible relations in space and time of present impressions, is what makes literature, because it has previously made unwritten, unspoken thought, into a construction entirely unlike anything in real experience; a construction answering not to the necessities of outward things, but to the needs of the inner nature, the microcosm, the soul.

To sum up: memory deals with the potential and tends to the essential rather than the actual; it is conditioned by our interests as much as by the qualities of things; it has to do with the resultant mood as much as with the object which produces it.

The Nature of the Writer

On these characteristics of memory depend, as I shall continue to repeat, the imperfections of literature, but also its compensations, so often surpassing all it lacks. For literature is vaguer, more superficial, less massively efficient than the other arts, and infinitely less æsthetic.[1] But, for that very reason, it is more closely connected with life, more universal and more permeating, and answers better to the preferences and repugnances of each individual case. It is more docile to our manifold wants because it deals with what our feelings have already sifted and manipulated: with recollections, and nothing but recollections.

Consider this. Each Reader, while receiving from the Writer, is in reality reabsorbing into his life, where it refreshes or poisons him, a residue of his own living; but melted into absorbable subtleness, combined and stirred into a new kind of efficacy by the choice of the Writer. Again: round every suggestion given by a book there gathers a halo of vague *something else*; and besides the succession of images determined by the words of the Writer, there arises in the Reader another succession, or more properly, a simultaneous *continuum* in which it all takes place. Thus the Reader's own experience, moving beneath the pressure of the word, brings into consciousness how many sights, how many

---

[1] By *æsthetic* I do not mean *artistic*. I mean, as in my Cambridge Manual, *The Beautiful*, that which relates to the contemplation of such aspects as we call " beautiful " whether in art or in nature.

feelings of which the author of that word can have no notion :—*Galeotto fu il libro, e chi lo scrisse.* It is on this stirring of half-conscious and, at best, confused recollections, upon this halo surrounding all clear literary suggestion, that depends very largely the fittingness or the reverse of certain Writers to certain Readers.

And the supremacy of literary genius is due, most probably, to its onward stride, its unwavering course; the great Writer ploughing through these vague crowding things of the Reader's memory, and with such strength and directness that all irrelevancies fall aside, or become compacted, lost, in his own masterful thoughts.

But one of the chief characteristics of literature is a comparative vagueness; and even the greatest Writer probably lacks the definite vision of his own work which is possessed by the painter or the composer. Even in his own mind the magical structure, the Solomon's and Abt Vogler's palace of thoughts, is but a fitful and varying mirage. And he is doomed never to know what it will become in its real destination, in that unexplored country, the soul of the Reader.

In the Reader's soul the thoughts evoked (if they *are* evoked) at the Writer's command are bound, as we have seen, to compete with the thoughts suggested by reality; the Writer's intention, even if not actually cast forth, is limited by the temper and experience of the Reader;

it is, at the best, transformed by unforeseen mixture till it becomes, sometimes, as enigmatic as a sphinx, half goddess and half beast, and often quite as monstrous. What have not commentators seen in Dante or Shakespeare? What did not theology read into the epithalamium of the Shulamite?

Letting alone such extreme cases, think of the quite normal addition which we make, most unintentionally, to all we read! Say we are low-spirited, have recently returned from a journey or parted with one beloved, our irrelevant sadness will steep the Writer's thought in melting mists; and the outlines of those recently seen hills and buildings, the vibration of that recent presence, will overlay the Writer's suggestion, or combine with it like the harmonies of some disquieting instrument.

The Writer must break himself of any curiosity, and never hope to know what he has really created. For his work, when complete, is just that various, fluctuating, inscrutable form which owes its being to the Reader as much as to himself, and which is hidden from him by the impenetrable wall of flesh separating one soul from the other.

III

In the foregoing pages I have paraphrased a remark once made to me by the one among all my friends who has always struck me as most sensitive to literature, living (though no Writer) essentially in and by means of the art of words. It is that the really great Writer seems to move along irresistibly and unflaggingly among ideas, driving them on, transposing them, bringing up more and still more from an unguessed rear, from unfathomed hidden depths in himself and in his Reader. Ever since hearing it I have found myself thinking in the terms of this remark, which is one of those wellings up from deeply organized modes of feeling, such as rise to the lips of genius or of passion. For it points to one of the main facts of the psychology of all art as well as of literature : the great Writer or artist is a creature who lives in a way more intense and more unified than the rest of us, in those fields, at all events, which specially concern him. And hence he can lay hold of our perception and emotion, make it move at a pace surpassing our own, and compel our labouring thoughts, our wandering attention, our intermittent feelings, into patterns consistent, self-sufficing, vigorous, harmonious, unified ; in the presence of which all else dwindles and is forgotten.

These patterns, in which the artist's vitality spontaneously works itself out, and in which our own vitality is made, however briefly and imperfectly, to move also—these patterns are, in all arts save literature, the visible and audible forms which the artist composes. The soul of the artist lives, and our soul is made to live also, in the shafts, architraves and vaultings of the

The Nature of the Writer

building; in the outlines and masses of the statue or picture; in the onward moving, backward falling melodies, the embracing harmonies, the balancing, striving, checking and interweaving counterpoint of the symphony.

But in the case of literature, the pattern is made, even more completely, of *us*; not merely of our soul's motions, but of our memory's contents. And of this dust of impressions, this stuff of our shapeless and aimless daydreams, the man who thinks and feels in the concentrated modes of the word elaborates a logical, coherent, organic representation, more satisfying than any experience of our own; and, in its vigour, balance and self-containedness, surviving in our mind among the moving chaos of our own thoughts and feelings; nay, persisting long after every word through which this miracle is wrought has been totally forgotten.

What were the words in which Meredith told me of that sunrise on the Adriatic, or Stevenson of the starry night in the Cévennes? Not one of those words has remained in my mind. But there is the shape into which they have moulded my thoughts and emotions, unchangeable, enduring.

IV

I have remarked on the fact that, having the Reader's memories for material, literature lacks the definiteness, the massive certainty of the other arts.

But while memory fails to preserve separate experiences in all their vividness, it distils, in this very crushing together of the single facts of life, an essence such as no other art (no, not even music) has at disposal: an essence of which one drop, one whiff, can change, by its subtle directness, the whole of our being of the moment. It is to this *essential* quality of memory that is due, more than to anything else, the unrivalled wonder of literature. A whole apparatus of shown things, of harmoniously combined forms, of convergent associations, is needed before a picture can inspire a mood undoubted and irresistible like that of Giorgione's Pastorals or Perugino's Adorations; in the case of architecture, the very body of the spectator needs to be transported inside a building, to be impinged upon not merely by its shape, but by its lighting and its real magnitude. Even the musician is comparatively slow; he needs a phrase or two with which to grip your vitals; and even then, the impression is of a definite kind, excluding all others. But the Writer—and here let me call him by his real name, the Poet, can, with one little word—that word *palmy*, for instance, applied to Rome, create a whole state of consciousness; and with a half-dozen words, make shadows and iridescences of feeling shiver one through the other; give the same vision in alternate flame of passion or in frost. And thus we have not merely the page which goes to our head with its especial fumes of feeling, all else forgotten; but what is far more wonderful, the page, the half-dozen stanzas (like some of Browning's lyrics) epitomizing all the human moods, making us feel that in the world's composition there is sadness, triumph, irony, the taking of all things in earnest, and the fine lightness of the individual recognizing his unimportance in the face of it all. Thus, what architecture compasses with interchange of uplifting and down-pressing forces, by vaulting-shafts seen between colonnades and chancels rising in answer to crypts descending; what music brings about with the combination of parts which take us in front, rear, flank, wheeling us along in various phrases of similar motion—this, the greatest of art's achievements, is accomplished by literature in dealing with such poor things as mere blurred recollections. But those recollections are steeped in feeling; and the counterpoint of the poet is composed, directly, of the essence of emotion.

V

On this connection with memory it depends also that literature can—how shall I put it?—risk giving us more pain than the other arts. This singularity, and the appearance that, in the drama and novel especially, we even extract some satisfaction from being hurt, has exercised the ingenuity of philosophers. The explanation thereof is, perhaps, *that literature does not hurt us so much as we think.* For we are apt to think in names and definitions rather than in the terms of intricate and obscure fact; and the fact, the " what is really happening" in literature, is most uncommonly obscure and intricate. What we find first of all is the label, the official subject of discourse, defined by what we deem (from its greater clearness) the essential part of the sentences, the big nouns and verbs, as, for instance: A man and woman who have loved unlawfully and been murdered by an injured husband, are now expiating in the whirlwinds of Hell the guilt, the fate, which one of them explains to the Poet Dante. This is the subject of the episode of Francesca da Rimini as it might be given in the doggerel argument prefixed in old-fashioned editions of the *Divine Comedy*. There seems little to rejoice at here; nor should we rejoice at all were we transported into this situation; sinful love, murderous death, eternal damnation and all. But we are not. Not even in the sternest reality, under the stress of closest fellow-feeling, is the most sympathizing of human beings transported into the true situation of a suffering neighbour. Not so much because imagination, and its short-cut sympathy, are weak, for they are, on the contrary, amazingly strong: strong, since they can countervail the fact that all of us, besides the realities which we mirror in our soul, are dealing with realities far more direct and cogent. It is our own life, trifling as it may seem, but imperious by being *ours*, which must for ever check, deflect and alter whatever of the life of others attempts to mingle with it. Our own life. Yes, even when, compared with what we understand and imagine, we seem to have none. Opposite to the life of Cordelia, Othello, Werther, in their vivid, definite fragmentariness (and we may write the names of our dearest friends in lieu of these heroes and heroines), there is our own life, so commonplace that we scarcely notice it, but such a solid, inextricable, living web of little habits, feelings, interests, sensations, references, hopes and fears, which, taken singly, are trumpery, invisible; but which just happen to be continuous, organized, *to be ourselves*. To each of us there has come, at least once, the sense of impotence and isolation because we could not enter into the depths of joy or sorrow of our best beloved; we know the humiliation at the petty irrelevancies which recall our faltering sympathy from out of the twilight of anxiety, the gloom of utter woe into which we have peered along the footsteps of that other soul: some worthless pleasure, or undignified habit, food, sleep, the appeal of a mere sensation, a hundred trifles we are ashamed to mention, make us turn our head, call us back after a minute, a second, of—oh, such partial absorption in that alien feeling! Like Persephone, but contrariwise, we have eaten of the magic pomegranate; only the fruit was grown in reality, its savour is our life, and even as she could not remain on earth, so we, indifferent mortals, cannot, until our own hour comes, tarry in realms of death.

It is thus when reality is pitted against reality, and when love and shame help our effort. If we reflect that in the poem, play or novel, the struggle in our consciousness is between our reality, familiar, direct, continuous, manifold, in a word *ourself*, and *another* merely imagined, and that by someone else, expressed in a few large strokes, or shown upon an actor's rouged and whitened surface; when we reflect on these odds the wonder is not that we should endure such make-believe painfulness, but rather that we should feel it at all. That we do feel it, against the whole testimony of our personal life, proves that mixed in this unreal pain there must be elements of pleasure to bribe our attention: the satisfaction of watching and understanding, the tickle of curiosity, and even the famous self-congratulation of the mariner looking at the storm from safe shores. Highly intellectual natures experience such things in real life, and derive some satisfaction, I will not repeat cynically with La Rochefoucauld, from the misfortunes of friends, but from their own pains and distresses; they suffer, but they think; and thinking, to a thinker, is a form of fighting, of building, of triumphantly using one's enemy, and so far pleasant. So it is in real life. How far more in the case of mere written things! false, or, if what we call true, remote in origin, artificial in shape and substance like the mummies of a museum; and then transmitted, of all things, through the medium of words! And here we return to words and their peculiar nature and virtues. I have alluded to the episode of Francesca da Rimini. The *argument*, the label thereof, we found to contain nothing that was not painful; though even into it there comes a fact of strange fascination: Love. That word we all love most, that bare verbal fact, *Love*, is a good starting-point for our analysis. In these few verses the mere word *Amore* recurs nine times, the episode irradiated with its charm from various points of that storm-coloured gloom; and, of a sudden, it is repeated in three consecutive and symmetrical phrases: "Amor ch'a cor gentil ratto s'apprende"; "Amor, ch'a null'amato amar perdona"; "Amor condusse noi ad una morte"; forming a sort of triple fountain of mystic light, in which float wondrous suggestions of beauty and bliss: the "gentle heart"—"the lovely person"—"the pleasure of loving"—and those tragic facts, all solemnly enounced, to wit: that love forces the beloved to love; and that, loving in such wise, there is no parting possible even in hell. There is something in this episode besides murder, sin and eternal punishment; and of different quality! The veritable subject is, therefore, found to be oddly altered from the argument at the head of the canto. Moreover, this, which turns out to be a kind of hymn to Love, is presented in a series of pictures which, to say the least, have nothing very painful. I take them at random. The allusion to the place of Francesca's birth, with the gravity of the sea, the sweetness of the great river and its followers seeking peace therein; the pathetic and solemn reference to the "King of the Universe," and to the prayers for Dante's peace (peace again!) with which the lovers, "if He were their friend" (note this suggestion again) would reward the poet's compassion. Then the vague crowds of antique knights and queens, their very names symbols of valour and beauty, out of which the two lovers of Rimini come forth; crowds glorious like those of Tintoretto's Paradise: with, clear in front, Paris and Tristram, Cleopatra, Helen, even the "great Achilles who fought at last for love." What a triumphal galaxy! And then the world of romances corresponding to this, into which, with the story of that first kiss, those lovers disappear, the book of Launcelot and Guinevere. Then notice the attitude of Dante imploring and listening to the tale; his *loving cry*, "O, suffering souls, speak unto us," which, for very strength, carries through that tempest; Dante in whom they recognize at once a creature "gracious and benign"; who listens with reverent, bowed head, faints from sheer sympathy; and, more significant than all, makes to Virgil that most marvellous answer: "Alack, how many sweet thoughts, and how much longing was needed to bring these to this grievous pass"; an answer gathering up, with the poet's sweeping glance, all the love, joy and sadness the world has known. Another point, but important: this Dante, whose passionate fellow-feeling sighs at the thrill of Francesca's narrative, is always, for our fancy, the *Poet*, and his companion also ; so that through this thunder-purple whirlwind of hell the two are visible with the solemn serenity of their laurel crowns. One might instance much more without exhausting this canto : thus, it is significant that three times a flight of birds breaks through and renders breathable that atmosphere of hell : the cranes, with their association of happier climes ; the starlings, suggestive of clear autumn frosts, and finally those doves, " called by desire, flying to their sweet nest on wide and steady wing " ; with whom, by the most direct symbol, we return, as usual, to the triumphant theme of Love.

All the foregoing is, however, an analysis of actual subject-matter which, in the process of exposition, Dante has worked into the argument in hand. To follow the literary transmutation of the subject, one must take the statistics, so to speak, of the very words employed, showing the constant recurrence of suggestions of gentleness, sweetness, dignity and supreme value and longing. And only after some such analysis would it be possible to see why this account, as the argument crassly puts it, " of the sinners through lust perpetually driven by most cruel winds symbolical of their unbridled passions "—has never been held, by lovers and poets, as a very serious warning against Love. Also, what concerns us philosophic creatures more closely, why all this painful business results, baffling the critical eye, in giving an enormous dose of pleasure which the pricks, the scars of trifling pain, only help to sink quicker and deeper into the Reader's soul.

VI

But, you may object, all the painful things in literature are not made by any means so—well, so *pleasant* as this particular piece of penetrating pathos. Philoctetes and Ophelia, and even the death of Gretchen, *do* give pain, and no mistake about it. Of course. Pain of so real a kind that, for my part, I confess my frequent inability to face it. I can remember in my childhood the positive dread, bodily almost, with which I looked forward to the harrowing details of certain books my mother read out loud, trying even to miss hearing them by some ingenious stratagem; and the relief of the thought that the autobiographical form guaranteed the survival of at least the principal personage, a minimum of woe. And even now, if I must tell the truth, I am as likely as not to skip the story of Le Fevre and such like; only the other day did I not catch myself putting off a slight sensation of inconvenience which accompanied in my throat, the selling of Stevenson's donkey, *Modestine*, at the end of the Cévennes journey?

Now, if you ask me why we occasionally not only endure, but court, pain, *real pain really felt as such*, there seems a reason for this apart from all survival of early brutality or all weak-nerved hankering after stimulants;

apart even from a very singular and mysterious exception, which I shall advert to, respectfully, later on. This reason is simple enough and not without solemnity. Even in real life we sometimes court the full savour of pain from an obscure instinct bidding us temper our soul to the inevitable, cauterize evil by thorough realization, master by our magnanimous forestalling the buffets of fortune. Nay, more, because, feeling ourselves the living and thinking fragments of a whole, we need to watch and listen to all that whole's mysterious ways; and have the irresistible impulse to mingle in the forces which are making, and which are destroying also, our little evanescent persons.

VII

This is the place for a parenthesis in our praise of literature, which has taken for granted (as our praise of institutions, laws and habits also does) that the thing is always of the very best; that there exists no literature which is not noble, or at least no Readers who are not pining to have it noble. Now the multiplying power of print gives the direct lie to such a notion. In this one branch of human affairs it is easy to be guided by that kindly Princess's advice, and eat *brioche*—shilling classics—when enough bread is not baked from day to day. And this being the case, the supply of other literature must answer to a demand, a real need, for intellectual food which, even if harmless, is not very spiritually nourishing.

The plain truth is that the bulk of mankind as at present existing, educated mankind quite as much as uneducated, has no use for the finer kind of literature. We have seen—if we have seen anything in the foregoing pages—that literature, for its perfect existence, requires the co-operation of the Reader with the Writer: the Reader must bring all his experience to the business, all his imagination and sympathy; he must enter deep into the Writer's work, help to make it live, and thus receive a strengthened and purified life in exchange. Now, in our very imperfect civilization, most people, even among the well-endowed and energetic, are too fagged, and even among the idle are too busy, for any such process. They invest their energies in necessary or unnecessary work and virtue, and rarely have a penn'orth to spare. They are, in the most literal sense, the Poor in Spirit; I use these words respectfully and in view of certain items of blessedness and future glory attendant on that state. For are they not the reserve material of mankind's to-morrow? and even if they do not toil in mines and mills and offices, have they not fostered those virtues and those inventions which every now and then were thrust upon them by the riotously living spirits of the past?

Such as they are—and they are everybody, including, turn about, our precious superfine selves—the Poor in Spirit require intellectual food in proportion almost to their inability to pay its proper price. It is because of their fatal tendency to bore themselves, to stagnate, that they require to be amused, tickled, shaken up; because they do not naturally see or feel beyond their cramped and cabined personal or class experience that they need violent enlarging of their life's horizon. But all this, owing to their poverty of spirit, in the cheapest, shoddiest and, alas! least efficacious manner. What they are like, even the proudest of us superior creatures has some notion of when ill, worried, tired, or merely in a fit of such demoralization as all creatures may suffer from; *then*, by something which is almost like a providential arrangement against a kind of sacrilege, we instinctively turn from every poem, play, novel, essay which we normally care for as we turn from our wholesome food and refuse our habitual exercise when we are sick.

Of course, as the world progresses and less energy is spent in exhausting labour, unintelligent learning, useless duty and dull relaxation, the number of the Poor in Spirit, as of the poor in health, money or virtue, may gradually diminish; and inferior or even unwholesome literature, like bad eating and worse drinking, will tend to disappear. But meanwhile, there the need is: the need to increase the soul's activity and improve its temperature with as little outlay of energy as possible, and therefore with the help of stimulants of various degrees of badness. Thus it is patent that thousands of Latins will patiently labour through a masterpiece of Zola or d'Annunzio, allured by the obscenities mingled in its humane observation or its stately far-fetched beauty. Whereas a hankering after brutal adventure and creepy detail enabled the majority of Anglo-Saxons to accept even Stevenson after his strange moral lapse in *Dr. Jekyll and Mr. Hyde*. But without going to such unusual lengths, one can safely say that a good proportion of books and papers are read because they appeal to covetousness, to social vanity, to the delight in degrading others and similar not very amiable human peculiarities. Such appeals exist, let us remember, not merely in the writings which are forgotten to-morrow, but in those handed down for their merits, and, alas! also for their vices, from centuries back: it is not merely for their immortal beauty and wit that people still read the *Iliad*, the *Inferno*, Rabelais or Swift.

All this is rather disconcerting; and, as a natural consequence, we nobler minds are apt to blink it. Even apart from stimulation of man's baser parts, we do not like to think that so much great literature finds Readers, and so much poor literature finds many more, for the sake of the plot interest, the details of kings and queens, the satisfaction given to calf-love or tearful sentimentality even if nothing worse; nay, to the most universal of all human needs, the need of company, of someone else and someone else's business, no matter who and what.

Very disconcerting all this, no doubt, to our contemplations of the double-peaked Parnassus, with Apollo and the Muses on the top, fiddling and singing quite irrespective of an audience. But there is nothing to be really distressed or in the least scornful about. No art, as I have already repeated to satiety, ever came into being or remained there for the sake of its mere artistic perfections; and beauty, harmony, nobility, are qualities which we cherish and seek for, but only in things and occupations answering to some more special need, bodily or spiritual: there would be no beautiful patterns unless there had first been stuffs and vessels, no architecture or sculpture unless people had wanted idols to propitiate and temples to keep them in; no music unless people had shouted and danced about for various reasons or no reason at all. And there would have been no literature if talking and writing, besides being practically useful, had not met the thousand different wants, whims, nay vices, of the soul of man.

What goes on, to our admiration, in those high valleys of Parnassus, where we imagine we live between Apollo and his sisters, with clear rills of poetry and wisdom for ever bubbling under the hoof of a well-broken, well-groomed Pegasus—what goes on up there (which is what we are talking about in these pages) is an exception, though, like all fortunate ones, an exception tending to increase. Everywhere below there is and ever has been an unceasing, incalculable output of written matter, serving or not its purpose in random fashion, and with the varying amount of waste and litter and nuisance incident to the satisfaction of all human wants; going, nine hundred and ninety-nine thousandths of it, to swell the dust heaps and kitchen middens where anthropology seeks for the traces of extinct manners and customs. But as a result of all this toiling and moiling and messing and muddling, there has emerged occasionally a written thing so noble, so significant or lovely, that, handy or useless, futile or instructive, we recognize in it an inexplicable higher utility, a certain immortality, on account of which we put it among our treasures, and bequeath it to our heirs.

VIII

We are mistaken, therefore, in looking on literature as an art exactly like the others; and still more so in allowing the other arts to inflict pain or leave dissatisfaction, because pain is an inevitable result of human sympathy, and dissatisfaction a result of all pursuit of truth. For only the art of words can thus enlarge our moral and intellectual life, and only it, therefore, has a right to the price of such expansion of experience and understanding.

Every art, until art falls into decay, is based upon some need quite independent of the pursuit of pleasure; although pleasure, ninety-nine times out of a hundred, stamps the need's satisfaction as useful to the race and

The Nature of the Writer

individual. It is my intention to review the various spiritual needs, or, if you will, cravings, to which literature ministers blindly and without inquiring after their goodness or badness. Before so doing I would point out, in connection with the end of my last chapter, that we often subject ourselves to pain at the Writer's hands on the deliberate understanding that the pain is but insufficiently redeemed by any pleasure, submitting to it for the health or the safety it may bring us. I have already confessed that, speaking for myself, a good deal of literature, whatever its other qualities, is so predominantly painful that I would rather not read it again, that I am tempted to skip, turn the page. But there is more than that. Reading, for instance, the second part of *Werther*, I am almost terrified by its picture of the downfall of a nature in which I find kinship to myself and some of my friends. Despite the mitigations of beautiful writing and charming episode, the mitigations of impersonality and distance belonging to all art; despite the amusement of noting the admirable fidelity to life, the skill employed, etc.; despite the pleasurableness of my own intellectual activity and consciously enlarged experience, the total effect is painful, and *ought to be painful*: I intend to be warned and chastened through that very pain. We have all of us a racial instinct—or, at least, a cultivated habit—of this kind of asceticism; we know that the spirit, more than the flesh, is weak, and recognize the cruel bracings, the harsh disciplines, required to strengthen it.

Symmetrically to this there has come to be in all decent creatures an instinctive turning away from other kinds of literature because racial experience tells us their pleasantness is bad. What we call *dirty* or *disgusting* (often neither in the literal sense) literature is such mainly from the experience that it soils or saps our souls, and from the immediate foretaste of degradation which that experience causes. A certain humourousness will, in some cases, allow endurance; the lightness of mood and general topsyturviness of laughter doubtless preventing the thing in question from staining deep into our nature; the comic being, essentially, superficial and transient. Such lightness—the lightness of Aristophanes, Rabelais, Voltaire—means the possibility of shaking certain degradations off our mind's surface; while the shame and ill-will aroused by similar subjects treated without laughter, safeguard those sanctuaries of memory and expectation on which depend so much of life's bodily and mental health. Our spiritual organization is full of such safety valves and compensations, due to incalculably repeated survival of useful variations. And this explains once more the differences between literature and the other arts. Painting, for instance, possesses the direct suggestiveness of represented scenes and objects; music makes for our nerves in even more violent or insidious manner. Whereas the written word must always, as I have so often insisted, fight its way against the thoughts and feelings already occupying our consciousness; and cannot do it without employing forms created by reasoning and therefore calling reason into play; literature is, two-thirds, intellectual, and thereby loses half its dangers of over-stimulating or blunting or perverting our sensibilities. Of course, however, literature is chaste (and under chastity we should surely include cleanness from cruelty quite as much as from lust) just in proportion as the Reader is literary. The child, the savage or the diseased person, goes straight for the gratification of his one desire; his energies cannot be drafted off by reason, nor his feelings be purified and disciplined by the hierarchic, nay, hieratic, influence of form. The lewdest and most brutal literature is always the least excellent; and the Reader for whom the higher qualities of literature do not exist will naturally magnify all traces of the lower. Hence, we should not lose patience even with prudishness; and, on the whole, sin rather in making literature too much of a church than in letting it become a free space for processes best performed in private and for proceedings best not permitted at all.

The creature for whom literature really exists goes to it very much as to science or to religion, from a desire, however unformulated, to learn what is, and also what ought, or ought not, to be. And the powers common to all art, the powers of soothing, vitalizing and harmonizing, enable us to endure and court such enlightenment and edification.

But besides these definite and utilitarian aims of literature, or rather below them, and in confused and less obvious regions of the soul, the written word ministers to a number of instincts and cravings, mostly unknown to other arts, and further differentiates literature from all and any of them. It is of these underlying reasons for writing and reading that I next wish to treat.

IX

That literature, so far from being a mere fine art, is in reality the fare which caters for the least artistic of human wants, is illustrated by one's own preferences in early life. I do not mean the books which children care for, though the remark applies, of course, also to them. I am alluding to the extraordinary things which passed for poetry before the age when one begins to care for . . . well, for what one calls *poetry* in later years. Thus, I can remember wild pleasure at the aphoristic and witty sayings scattered throughout the works of Pope and Young. "And wretches hang that jurymen may dine," seemed positively sublime; and how could my elders be insensible to the poetic quality of "for she's before her Maker and Mankind"? A perversely prosaic child? Perhaps I was. But I have heard grave and reverend signiors speak as if the "greatness" of Shakespeare lay in his "philosophy," that is to say, certain statements as obvious, as partial (and as flatly contradicted by similar statements) as those of the Book of Proverbs, or rather of *a* book of proverbs.

But apart from the knowledge of human nature extracted from poetry, my childish mind was also sensitive to the mere charms of expression. "The inverted silk," meaning a drawn-off stocking, has remained in my memory as one of the chief beauties of Thomson's *Seasons* and of the British Classics. And from the fact that he wrote it, and was printed and read for his pains, I presume that a good many persons of maturer years but less recent date must have had exactly the same taste as mine was as a child. The thing—I mean "the inverted silk" and my liking for it—becomes less astounding when we note the part played in the greatest classic poetry by the veiling of ordinary concerns under learned allusion and inappropriate expression. Our ancestors must have taken pleasure not merely in showing off, however irrelevantly, their various kinds of learning, but, what is to the credit of their good heart, in witnessing such display on the part of others. Such flowers of rhetoric gave the satisfaction of riddles, whether answered or "given up"; and of the various pedantic games on bits of paper ("Who said Divide and Govern?" "What cost us our Colonies?") or the sad Bible games of certain nurseries. Our ancestors revelled, no doubt, in all that talk of Numbers, Essences, Planets, Gods, Hebrew Kings, that emptying out of obsolete encyclopædias which constitutes half the obscurity of Dante, maddening some of us to fury. They were children, those solemn mediæval worthies. And we can all remember our own lively childish satisfaction in saying to others, nay, in being said to: "Do *you* know who Cyrus was? How puppies are born? What's French for shoe string?" Nay, if my own experience can be trusted, some children will play with dictionaries and encyclopædias as a kind of finer riddle guessing.

All such "pleasure in power," as Nietzsche and Dr. Adler would say, attached to the acquisition and display of irrelevant learning, is probably a feature of the growing mind, in the race as in the individual; perhaps, moreover, of the mind which has ceased to grow, or never grown at all! To us there is something funny in people having extracted pleasure from "the learned and ingenious devices" in which past ages hid and sought platitude and bathos. Yet it is perhaps to the taste for such ingenuity that we owe perspective, counterpoint, theology, metaphysics; that we owe more recently the metrical and linguistic complications of Parnassians and Symbolists. Anyhow, this is one instinct which literature has appealed to.

We can now proceed to more general considerations.

Exorbitantly on the Writer's part, and in only less degree on the part of the Reader, the need for literature is explained by one of the primary impulses of the human being: the impulse to revive impressions when they are important, to revisit, or failing that, to talk about all places, persons and things which have a power over our feelings. Oddly enough the theorizers on Art, and on the Play Instinct supposed to underlie art, have done scant justice to this impulse; yet instances of it crowd at every step, and the utility of it to the individual and to the race is manifest. Thus it is evident that the pleasure in make-believe at the core of all childish games is the pleasure in the thought of the horse, the lion, the wild Indian, and with small girls, of the baby, the wardrobe and the kitchen; these items can put the child into a pleasant frame of mind, an agreeable excitement; and the child, by that process of make-believe, sets about reviving that pleasure. The instinct continues throughout life. We all quote the classic lover who cuts his beloved's name in the bark of trees and sings it to the echoes; he intensifies in so doing his recollection, and procures a feeling of real presence. Indeed, the gloating over the fair one's portrait has much less of æsthetic contemplation than of such stimulation to feeling: a lock of hair, a withered flower, will do as well and better (and the relics of all kinds of piety have the same function); nay, the expectant mother is knitting at the tiny sock less because the baby will want it soon than because she wishes, already, to forestall the emotion of the little one's being there. For when all is said and done, what the poor human being requires is not things, but the effect of things upon himself; not food, but to be satisfied and nourished. And such beneficent emotions not only still the soul's hunger and thirst, but remake the soul's tissues. A shallow utilitarian explanation of the world has overlooked these fundamental facts, limiting usefulness to such objects and actions as directly further man's material life, and leaving out of account those which increase the life of the instincts and the emotions. And, in view of this, it is a useful provision that a sight, a feeling, may last, or serve twice over; as useful, at least, as the precautions to secure the germinating of a seed or the supply of a commodity. Indeed, it is not merely of sentimental conditions that we thus seek the reviviscence through speech or symbol. And by this hangs the unflagging boringness of specialists of all kinds : like Uncle Toby, they can give themselves all the emotions of a campaign (and without risk of another musket wound) over these few yards of entrenched lawn and their jackboot cannons; nay, without any apparatus, and by the help only of a stick drawing in the sand, and a lot of long words, as we all know to our cost and to their satisfaction. Even I, though proud of my intellect, can "talk weather" quite happily with any polite person at an afternoon call. "The peasants foretell heavy snow this winter"—for I see the blue lowering clouds and rolls of mist like wadding, and the mountains pale or glittering under next day's sun; nay, the heavy berried ivy, and hedges full of hips and haws.

Hence it comes that we are, all of us, more or less playactors, or, at all events, playing children, imitating those we love and admire the better to taste our secret emotions; or talking about the places and persons we care about in order to renew our enjoyment: they are so important, our neighbours and posterity really have a right to hear all about them! And of this sort is the impulse of Dante, solemn in the conviction that he must write of Beatrice "such things as have been said of no other lady."

But the miracle of literature is this: that the love for that one woman, Beatrice, ceases to be the private concern of that one man Dante; and becomes, for each of the readers of the *Vita Nuova*, his own love;—the love he feels, has felt, will feel; or which is destined, peradventure, to lie dormant and stir once only in his life, at that touch of the poet.

X

Literature is the universal confidant, the spiritual director of mankind. It revives, relieves and purifies the Reader's feelings by telling him of similar but nobler ones. It makes the Reader give, and thereby possess, his own soul through the illusion of having for a moment possessed that of the Writer.

I repeat : through the illusion. For we must guard against being misled by the private life of Writers having become the *corpus vile* of gossiping analysis ; a mere accident due to the preservation of famous people's letters and to the autobiographical matter contained, like every other sort of observed item, in their works. Being misled, I mean, into thinking that the Writer is revealing, giving away, cheapening, his innermost feelings. He may, indeed, feel poignantly that he is thus exposing his own self, and take pleasure or pain or a bitter-sweet mixture, in making himself a motley to the view. But, taking the act of literary communication for what it really is, it becomes clear that the Writer is exposing, evoking, only the Reader's own experience ; though widened, generalized by the universal experience stored up in the very language he makes use of. The Reader, meanwhile, persuaded, no doubt, that what he feels is the Writer's experience, is in reality feeling his own : his own experience, but *sub specie humanitatis*, so to speak. This is inevitable in the artistic phenomenon, since all artistic form is three-quarters of it an heirloom, handled by mankind and fashioned by its repeated handlings. There is no real unveiling of Dante in the *Vita Nuova*, nor of Goethe in *Werther* ; but an unveiling of the Reader to himself under the pressure of a greater personality than his own, and by the spell of processes which generations have elaborated. And under the name of Beatrice or Charlotte he falls into contemplation of his own mistress, or of the mistress of his dreams. If it were different it would be a case of What's Hecuba to me?

XI

The real revelation of the Writer (as of the artist) comes in a far subtler way than by such autobiography; and comes despite all effort to elude it; indeed, such effort and its methods are merely one of the means of revelation. For what the Writer does communicate is his temperament, his organic personality, with its preferences and aversions, its pace and rhythm and impact and balance, its swiftness or languor, aloofness or clinging or brooding attitude; and this he does equally whether he be rehearsing veraciously his own concerns or inventing someone else's. For the revelation is not so much in the facts, as in the choice and arrangement thereof; and in the manner, words, mode of seeing, explaining, condensing, eliding, expanding; weighing down here and springing off there, in fact in the conception of the subject, in the style. And by this projecting of himself in style and conception the Writer subdues his Reader into living for the moment, his own, the Reader's, experiences in modes of life which are the Writer's. Modes of life not as a person, a man with an address and a biography, but as a

Writer; that is to say, an individual spontaneous organism, itself subjected to those modalities of art which have been fashioned by the needs of all foregoing mankind.

Once we have grasped these facts and their dependence on the great process of give and take of all perception and interpretation, and so far grasped likewise the part played in works of genius by the universal and the eternal—once these things understood, there comes to be something contemptible and excusable, futile and harmless, in all such controversies as have raged round, let us say, *Elle et Lui*, or the Carlyle Letters. We have been talking not merely about things we do not know, but about things which scarcely exist, save in the knowing, in the minds of the talkers. How much more so when, instead of attempting to interpret *bona fide* documents and records, we try to reconstruct fact out of real works of art, like Shakespeare's *Sonnets*! We may guess at incidents underlying them, we can gossip about what may have happened. But the emotional drama is of our own making, and constructed out of our own experience. More than in any other art there is illusion in all literature, nay, rather *delusion*, the delusion of mistaking what the Writer has evoked in us for that which the Writer has felt, seen, been, himself. To the highest extent we receive from the Writer in proportion to what we can give.

XII

But literature is beneficent not merely by the personality it stirs within us. It helps us even more by being, sometimes, impersonal.

Every religion, of course, has ministered to this occasional need for shuffling off our ego, and, like Dante's Piccarda, seeking peace in a will transcending our own. And here I would remark that literature seems destined to replace many of religion's functions; and has even now already become, what religion was in its palmy days (when man's activities were but little specialized), the universal caterer for all such needs as are neither directly practical nor purely intellectual; needs ambiguous and shamefaced, as well as clear-eyed and majestic. Nor is the parallel made less precise when we remember, what sentimental unbelievers tend nowadays to forget, that the religion of the past had not merely its true saints, but its Archigalli, Corybantian cymbal-clashers, Flagellants or merely practically minded pietists, retiring, like the excellent Jung Stilling, to pray for funds towards housekeeping and conviviality. . . .

Be this as it may, the healing virtues of impersonal contemplation are, fortunately, to be met on many sides. For some of us of the laity they issue from whitewashed laboratories with their furnaces and odd-shaped glassware, as Besnard has expressed it in his wonderful decorative panels, where arise visions of worlds and times empty of mankind's fretting and fuming; also in the tower whence storms are made to write themselves down in purple and queer zigzags, and the flight is watched of migratory birds, themselves carrying our purified thoughts into distant climes of serenity. *The Cherub Contemplation*; Milton was right to seek him in high places.

To other sorts of minds, or at other moments, the same impersonal passion may be given by archæology; and I have heard of a man, sorely tried in all human matters, digging up peace, so to speak, with buried cities; superposed layers of rubbish, say, of the seven times burnt towers of Ilium. Nay, the extraordinary power which Rome has ever had over wounded or tragically restless natures is but a case in point. An hour's ramble among the great arches and the little belfries, plucking the tufts of fennel, or scraping, with idle fingers, that odd, lilac friable earth which looks like burnt-down cities and human ashes; an hour of contemplation in that mild, yellow, Roman sunshine; and the soul, so long galled by personal fears and sorrows, arises, feels itself new and whole. And, its eyes washed clean, like Dante's with the dew of Purgatory, it goes its way in peace; or ascends, in humility and greatness, to the seats *ad dexteram domini*, there to participate in the inevitable and universal.

XIII

In dealing with the question of inferior literature I have spoken of the usefulness of certain of its lowest forms as a mere excitant, or the least harmful among mere excitants, to minds fagged or numbed by the monotony and narrowness of life.

Except as such, a less offensive substitute for drink, betting, bull-fighting or nautch-dancing, Western as well as Eastern, I find it difficult to understand that excessive or painful emotion should ever be a desirable result of any kind of art. But experience has taught me to be more diffident before the mysteries of the human soul, its various sorts and varying needs. And although my temperament and my whole philosophy (such as it is) bid me look with suspicion and aversion on the kind of art which Nietzsche named, for all times, *Dionysiac*, I recognize that its fumes and agonies may be required for a small number who are the very opposite of that multitude I have dealt with as the Poor in Spirit. As the world, in its deep imperfection, goes, there seems room for certain exceptions, dangerous but salutary: creatures, perhaps, less sound than we, but gifted with powers transcending ours, with intensity of energy and passion out of keeping with life's even tenor, but requisite to correct life's everyday poverty; the mysterious brotherhood, known to us by our instinctive awe, of voluntary and destined martyrs, however uncanonized, nay, however untried. For such creatures as these, shadowed for us in the sublime first page of De Quincey's *Levana*, creatures so made for suffering that they accept it (for the world's good) as their element, thirst can be slaked only if hyssop, not honey, tip the rod held to their lips. For these tense and sombre souls, acquainted from childhood with bitterness and agony, the intolerable masterpieces from which some of us shrink, Œdipus, Lear, Wagner's death of Iseult, are not a *more* which almost breaks the spirit, but a *less* : the very stuff of their life, made solemn and gentle by kinship with the happier, less tragic soul of others. I cannot assert these things as certain, but only suspect them ; and I pass alongside of that Dionysiac art, in lack of understanding, but in awe and humility.

XIV

In the foregoing pages I have often spoken as if literature were an art just like the others ; but this, as I have hinted, is the reverse of my opinion. For while art encloses us completely in a world of its own, literature is in great measure an intensification, but also a prolongation, of real life. Our spirit has high needs besides the need for beauty and dignity : desire for sympathy, for self-expression, craving for intelligibility and permanence ; and these other requirements, like our meaner instincts, seek satisfaction in literature

But above all else Experience—the completion of what life teaches us by snatches—is what we seek for in the written word. Life puzzles, frightens us, yet we want more of it. Life is for ever propounding problems, showing us samples and diagrams which are snatched from our sight, effaced or inextricably overlaid, just as we seem to seize them. Have we ever the map of a square foot of existence, the sufficient formula of any character, even our own, nay, least of our own? Do we ever understand the real *why* of any action, or rather its real *how*? Yet it seems urgent to know, and we hunger and thirst after such knowledge. We are intellectual creatures as well as practical and æsthetic ones; and we want life's intellectual essences, we ask its meaning. Hence the great Writer is always the man of experience, the thinker, the philosopher. Having seen more, he should be able to tell us. . . . But he must have really seen more; not perhaps as actual objective fact, but as inner feeling and interpretation; and if we suspect that what he tells us is second-hand or for the nonce, adieu to his prestige! This is why we are so disturbed by everything savouring of rhetoric or formula: the pedant, the bookworm, the superfine attitudinizer, the most talented phrase-and-image monger is cheating us when we ask for the knowledge, felt or thought, of life.

This is a large order; but by no means all. There is, besides, the fact that human beings thirst for the human being; while in reality that human being appears but fitfully in our neighbours and in ourselves. We follow the glance of certain eyes, the smile or the bitter twist of a mouth; we follow a gesture, an outline. But the human being, most often, is not revealed to us pursuing it; indeed, we may lose all sight of it, masked, absorbed into conventionality. There are few things we want so much (and this methinks is, perhaps, why there is a certain compensation about all suffering) and get so little, as human contact; by which I mean the realizing of other people's feelings. Even with our nearest and dearest we rarely have it; indeed, least, perhaps, with them; so that the passing stranger is sometimes, for his brief second, closer to us, sinking deeper in. This passing stranger with the eyes promising the secrets after which we strain, and with the hands whose clasp our nerves have been longing for; this satisfying stranger can be given us by the spell of the Writer. Literature can evoke for us creatures entirely human, intelligible, whom we can love, clasp, perhaps also fight with, our fill! Creatures existing merely as human forces, as brothers, lovers, children, enemies, with none of reality's wrappings and trimmings; from Helen, mere power of beauty, to Iago, mere power of baseness. The innumerable hosts, more potent than the heavenly ones, created by poet and novelist are, in great measure, the consolers of our inevitable secret loneliness: they are those to whom, by the deed of fancy, we can give ourselves utterly, as we give only to that which we have chosen and, may be, to that we have created. Among these, less clear, but how much more potent for his illusive reality, is the Writer himself! Every Writer is, to our fancy, an essential man, because he shows us only his essence, keeping the casual and deciduous for actual life. Hence, we expect in the Writer a man of deeper life, higher power, than ourselves or our neighbours. And in the very great Writer, the typical poet, we really find him. Not as he sits at meat, or goes to his office, or converses (even with his Boswell or Eckermann), but *as he writes*. Nay, in the very greatest, we expect, we get, and *we make*, this typical man (such as Emerson taught of) even in the ordinary concerns of life. Hence the commanding quality of figures like Goethe, or Johnson, or Shelley; the fascination of Stevenson.

The very great Writer *must* be, potentially at least, a great personality, else how can he know more than we, feel more than we, see more than we? He cannot, like the artist, be a specialized genius tacked on to a mediocrity. And for yet another reason. Perhaps the most æsthetic demand we make of literature (though at first sight it may not seem so) is for a definite philosophy of life; since philosophy of life means the essentials of æsthetic contemplation: a standpoint, a unified vision, a definite mood or temperament. And note that all the greatest poets, those whom we put in the first line, Dante, Shakespeare, Goethe, Browning, are all philosophers of life.

It is the ignorance of this which makes the foolish failures of *art for art's sake*, the jejuneness of all the Gautier, Leconte de Lisle, Heredia kind of poetry; of men even like Baudelaire and Swinburne, the wearisome hollowness of magnificent artists in words like d'Annunzio or Barrès. However well they speak, there seems no call for their speaking. Let them paint pictures in words, build temples and grottoes, score symphonies of metaphors and allusions. But what can they tell of other life or do with their own? They are of the stuff no reasonable creature cares to know about; certainly not of the stuff that dreams are made of. We are apt to judge them with undue harshness, because they disappoint a need of ours: *poseurs*, hypocrites, *histriones*. For at the bottom of much of our desire for great poetry is our desire for the greater life, the deeper temperament, the more powerful mind, for the great man.

XV

A question arises at this point, frivolous and indiscreet, as it is usually put; but taken seriously, important and most instructive in many ways. Must the great Writer be a great Man?

The greatest Writer quite inevitably, and in the most everyday acceptance of the term. The less great, in

The Nature of the Writer 119

no such sense of human greatness; but merely, I would add, because his fragmentary and special superiority, his literary genius, has, to a greater or lesser extent, benefited by the greatness of character which his betters, Readers as well as Writers, have worked into the art of words.

For words, such as they come to hand, are steeped in association; syntax is but the cast left by long repeated acts of thought; all eloquence has originally welled up under high pressure of feeling. And the same quality of intellectual and moral greatness which transports the Reader into a world finer than his usual one, will make the literary artist, the creature specially sensitive to such verbal suggestion, think and feel, as long as he writes, in a way quite foreign to his individual habits; because, to whatsoever extent, he is doing so in words imposed on him by others. Of course, however, the smaller Writers (and among them many whom we call classics) are liable to lapses from this high state of being. I believe, if we watched (and even without watching!), we should always find them out. They hesitate and swerve, or exceed, exaggerate; however elaborate their skill, they are unequal, and, although most often piquing themselves on taste, on judgment, they offend against it.[1] For nothing can replace the unflagging directness, the unhesitating intention of greatness; that energy which, hastening

[1] See my further chapter on De Quincey and Landor.

steadily along, gives all things their just weight, fills out or neglects obedient to a central necessity, concentrates everything from sheer unity of purpose, and sweeps all irrelevant matter away in the irresistibleness of habitual and organized power.

And by a well-known psychological law, such superior vitality is necessarily self-forgetful, in a way altruistic ; the great Writer never dreams of making a point, doing a fine thing, showing off to advantage ; his outgoing energy flows into the matter in hand, however trifling ; he is impressed, moved (little guessing by his own genius) as it seems by the necessities of the case. In humble terms, he has the faculty of unceasing, complete interest, which means gift of oneself, superabundance of life ; and there is in his proceedings the concentration on the desired object which gives an air of being rapt, and is indeed a kind of higher automatism.

Judicious and faithful artists of *art for art's sake*, disdainers of *subjectivity* and of *self-exhibition*, classics and Parnassians of all times and countries, has the suspicion never crossed your ingenious brains that you are able to give your graceful or ostentatious performances, to play about seriously and to no purpose, simply because other men have thought, have felt, have lived, with inevitable, self-unconscious entireness ?

Here I must gather up a dropped thread of this intricate subject ; and explain exactly what I mean, speaking of literary genius, by the words *self-unconscious*

The Nature of the Writer

and *entire*; and, if I can, also by that expression *living*, when applied to a Writer. For quite a number of great Writers, *e.g.* Henry James, as compared with other persons, seem scarcely to live at all, the storms in their existence, when no longer magnified by our admiration, being often of teacup proportion. Let alone that writing means a special activity, and very often a steady drudgery, that is to say, a derivative, in the French medical sense, from living as most men mean life. I am not, therefore, prying into the private concerns of Writers, which do not differ, except by being often less interesting, from those of other folk. The actual biography of human beings is determined by their character, but also, quite two-thirds of it, by circumstances: the manifestation of certain tendencies may never attain a visible importance; only looks and gestures, tones of voice, judgments and preferences revealing to the shrewd observer (or the recording angel) what the creature really was. In this the Writer is but as his fellow-men, and his potentialities are no more adequately used up than theirs. But between them and him there is a fundamental difference: that he has a possibility of manifesting his real personality where others have not. For the man who deals with words deals really with ideas, and his whole existence, as likely as not, is a perpetual reacting on what he sees, hears, reads of, nay, imagines. In his unnoticed way, perhaps in his solitary and detached existence, the

Writer is, like that personage of Browning's, more in the turmoil of life than his more seemingly active contemporaries. For of these, the practical man is oddly shut between the blinkers of his practice (note it in soldiers, politicians, men of business) and the creature of passion, be he sinner or saint, goes headlong towards the only satisfactions which exist for his nature, stumbling across, upsetting or trampling upon, everything alien to that dominant impulse. But the Writer is, by the nature of things, the contemplative man; and if the facts of life do not of necessity play havoc with his fortune, break his heart, or wear out his nerves, they abut upon his feeling, his thought, with no exceptions or impediments. This John-a-Dreams, often taxed with indifference or incapacity for action, is in reality for ever being subjected to impressions of pain or joy; his preferences and repulsions are called on, by what he witnesses, quite without ceasing; he is loving or hating persons and acts he may have only faintly guessed at; he is judging ten thousand things which practically do not concern him, weighing, turning over, going through all forms of suspense, doubt and resisted conviction; acting out stories back into the past, forwards into the future; he is in the whirlpool of life, and it is in him. This John-a-Dreams, whose name is Dante, Shakespeare, Goethe or Browning, may, indeed, not be living very noticeably in the modes of his particular station, situation or business. But he is living in those of fifty creatures in whom some day the world (reading of Francesca, Hamlet, Faust and those *Men and Women*) will recognize a life deeper, more concentrated, more essential than its own.

Such is my meaning when I repeat that the very great Writer must of necessity be a great man; a full-blooded type of some great class of men; and as such endowed with sensitiveness, passion, activities, *and experience* far surpassing that of other men.

And experience. I italicize these words and repeat them, because, superficially considered, this is what may oftenest seem lacking in one absorbed in contemplation, study and intellectual production. But experience is, remember, an inner phenomenon; and the mere accidental finding yourself in given circumstances does not necessarily give it. A man may have been in a battle or a shipwreck, and possess no real experience on the subject; even commoner things, being in love, losing nearest and dearest, health or fortune, seem, judging by results, by no means always to constitute experience thereof. And one of the disappointments of life is perceiving how extraordinarily little experience has been accumulated, very often, by those who have lived longest and most; Vanvenargues' saying, "*on tire peu des vieillards,*" being true of nothing so much as of experience. Whereas the Writer, if we chance to know him intimately, often surprises by the singular slightness of the facts which have given him abundant knowledge on certain points : a remark dropped, a word in a letter, a look sometimes, will be all he can point to as human document, and yet how wide, how deep he has reached into *our* hidden experience ! A grotesque proof of this is that Writers are sometimes taxed with indiscretion, almost libel, for having described real events which, at the time of writing, had not yet happened ; imagination in this case going straighter and quicker than facts. It may also be that a Writer, in some purely invented story, forestalled feelings which real circumstances awaken only later in him : his real self was there, truly ; and the imagined risk, loss or alternative, the imagined contact with a given other personality, will, by the logic of organic creation, have brought to his pen's tip the words he is one day destined to hear or speak. And it would be instructive (if such inquiries were not conducted mostly on the mere surface, all vanity and preconceived ideas, of authors) to inquire whether every great author has not, once at least in his existence, been astonished at meeting some real creature he had portrayed before knowing ; has not thrilled at the glance of eyes, the contact of nerves, which, in that seeming absence of real experience, he had felt and described long ago.

And here I would remark upon a misconception of literary talent. People, intelligent people, friends of mine, who should know better, have a way of talking as if the greater suggestiveness of a book or poem were due to superior literary endowment. "So and so, *with his literary talent*, of course, made the most of the subject." Not at all. So-and-so, my dear people, made most of the subject because he was more deeply, variously, richly *interested* than others; because, at the moment of writing, and probably at some half-unconscious, wholly forgotten, previous moments, that particular subject made a greater stir in a mind already filled with more items from more frequent past stirrings. To be more interested in the world, unselfishly, platonically, passionately; to understand more and more quickly; to feel things into their furthest ramifications, this is, indeed, the characteristic of the great Writer, but 'tis his human superiority, not, believe me, his literary talent. *That*, owing to the concordances of function which exist throughout life, will, very likely, be superadded: having an immense deal more to say, the special gift of speech will, nine times out of ten, have been evolved alongside of the gift of thought or feeling. But in the tenth case it may not: some of the greatest Writers, Browning, for instance, make one suspect an originally poor vocabulary, a defective sense of phrase, overcome by sheer necessity of saying, but of which traces remain here and there (like the seams in ill-compacted voices) in far-fetched, cumbersome or inappropriate expressions. But the man was full of things to say, of modes of feeling, leaps and rushes and quiet returnings on himself, movements backwards, forwards, upwards, downwards, weaving inextricably but intelligibly between those items; and, as they filled out every dimension of his own soul, enabling him to take the soul also of his Reader, and enclose it, worked upon, working, in the four-square edifice, in the eight-part counterpoint, of, say, *Abt Vogler* or *Galuppi*.

Literary talent: A thing most difficult of definition, because the order of the universe, finding it vain in itself, has on the whole not given it a chance when separated from the human worth of the Writer. Yet we occasionally get a glimpse of it; either when the mere poverty of thought and feeling, the vacuity of the *man*, as in Gautier, d'Annunzio and, I grieve to say, Swinburne and Landor, show it through rents and threadbareness; or, again, when other Writers, quite decently constituted human beings, like the brothers de Goncourt, fall to practising literary vocalizations, swells and shakes in public, desisting from singing a real tune out of sheer childlike solemnity of professional pride. *Literary talent*; a very wonderful, complex and scientifically interesting gift (like the vocal parts of a great tenor); and quite inestimable when used to some purpose, is, I want to repeat, so utterly useless in itself that Providence, the Cosmos, or Man's impatience has rarely given us the sight of it in its poor nakedness.

Closing this parenthesis, I may restate my conviction

that it is a mistake to scold, say, at Sterne or Voltaire because his works are not reliable certificates of his private behaviour; and that the great Writer's great humanity is real, because it really acts upon us through his works.

Moreover, the greatness of personality which underlies great writing must not be thought of as necessarily continuous. With Writers not of the first order the great inspiration is an exception, due to an exceptional strand in their nature, or an exceptional moment. It is an old remark that passion makes all men eloquent. I have verified its truth in the answers to letters of condolence; they are apt to have an eloquence contrasting sharply with the embarrassed conventionalities which call them forth. And a friend of mine has had the scheme of collecting such perfect pieces of literary expression from among the letters, published in the newspapers, of soldiers at the front. The psychological explanation of this sporadic eloquence is simple. A great emotion, when not so violent as to scatter everything, makes the human being live, for the moment, at higher pressure; morally and intellectually, and often physically, his temperature is higher, his circulation sweeps along swifter and fuller; and he breathes life into tissues shrunk and anæmic during the imperfect life of every day. Moreover, great emotion, and even more, that latent or continuous emotion we call *passion*, unifies the personality, deafens and blinds it to the appeal of irrelevant matters, forces all energies from vain competition into powerful co-operation, and establishes throughout the soul order and hierarchy. *Distraction*, in the truest sense of the word, becomes impossible, and frivolity vanishes; all words, gestures, movements not to that one purpose are sheer forgotten. And, for the moment, the creature, knowing of only one thing to say, says it to perfection; nay, feeling only one thing, thinks it with a fulness, a sudden illumination of remotest points and knitting together of most abstract connections, before which we outsiders feel as if suddenly in a prophet's presence.

Now such a state of intensified and co-ordinated feeling and thinking is the condition of all great artistic work. The ancients were not far wrong in comparing the inspiration of the poet with the demoniac possession of the priestess or the lover. We must not be misled by what we see, nay, what he himself remembers, of the great Writer's handicraft; much of which is but a critic's, an editor's, an imitator's or even a copyist's task: the labour, assiduous, weary, sometimes heart-breaking, of filling up the gaps and rents of flagging inspiration; of working up to the sample, as it were, of his lapsed genius. We are told that Mozart wrote most of *Don Giovanni* when so fagged at the day's end that his wife had to keep him awake by telling him stories. Taking this metaphorically, the anecdote is true; Mozart, we also know, invented his music when out of doors or playing at billiards, that is to say, in moments of excitement and concentration; and the scribe's or editor's work of those sleepy evenings had nothing to do with his genius. Similarly with the great Writer. The immortal thoughts come under the pressure of life vividly seen and felt; they grow, moreover (and this is a neglected side of the question), in the soul's silent leisure, but not in its laziness; gaining substance and taking shape in the moments, perhaps the seconds, of unrecorded, intensest life; for the incubation of genius should not be thought of as the sitting of a hen! A man has felt, nay probably thought, a thing a hundred times before it starts into his literary consciousness; even the meanest may be eloquent, like d'Annunzio, about his preferences and repulsions; and these imply habitual repetition of strong states of feeling. The preferences may be of humble, sometimes of base enough, kind, but they imply heightened vitality. Even the most rhetorical of Writers, those in whom we vainly seek a higher human quality, must have had an overmastering emotion, even if only for a half second, about a fountain in a garden, or an almond tree. All noble emotion is not exclusively for the benefit of wife and child, church or state, as we have a way of taking for granted. Moreover, in the specially gifted individual there is undoubtedly a special emotion: that of mere creation, the plunge into one's own element, the breasting of the sea of words and rhythms, the joy of effort mingling with divine facility. And it is this emotion, this emotion of trying, doing, succeeding, which probably accounts for the occasional splendours of Writers of the school of *art for art's sake*. Art happened to be their one passionate side, *their* piece of life and humanity.

XVI

The studies embodied in the foregoing and following notes have gradually convinced me that while literature answers to many and various needs of the spirit, it becomes an art through one great incidental characteristic : the momentary living in the *modes of eternity*, with its resultant bracing and clarifying of the soul. This is the central miracle, blessedness and blessing of all art.

That literature should ever compass it depends, in my opinion, not on the indefinable something called *literary talent*, but on the fact of this verbal gift belonging to a personage greater than the average of his audience ; greater at all events in connection with what he writes, and in that connection, feeling and thinking more; or, at the least, manifesting his moments of thought and feeling in more complete and more continuous fashion.

Before closing these chapters, let me recapitulate the elements with which the Writer works, and the psychological conditions under which he does so.

The Nature of the Writer

I have tried to show that the action of literature is different from that of real life, because the written word acts on the plane not of direct experience but of memory. Now the ways of memory are special to itself, and so, in a manner, is memory's logic. For memory means experience submitted to the disintegration, the elimination and addition, the chemistry, so to speak, of our whole human organism, and of the accumulated items of experience which it has previously altered and integrated in the mind. Memory is not a storage, but a selection;[1] and the fact of recollection implies already a certain suitability to our character and habits. Memory is not a helter-skelter gathering together, since everything new becomes at once connected by similarity or significance with something old. In memory, therefore, the items of experience, thus diminished, enlarged, and fused, come to exist in different dimensions, to move with different weight and pace, obeying no longer the rhythm of the outside world, but that of the inner one, and taking their meaning and power not from an alien universe, but from the individual human soul.

So much for the items of experience and the words, I am tempted to say the *nouns* and *adjectives*, which the Writer groups into patterns of almost magical power within the mind of the Reader. That magic is not merely inherent in those nouns and adjectives, due to

[1] I have tried to work this out in a preface to the English translation of Richard Semon's *Mnemic Psychology*. Allen & Unwin, 1925.

the community of experience of Reader and of Writer. Even more, in my opinion, its very mysterious essence requires to be sought in what I have alluded to as movement, as *pace and weight, impact and rhythm*. It is in these modes of activity that the individual Writer, like the individual artist, reveals and exercises his stronger, swifter, steadier, subtler and more harmonious life. This subject has received little or no attention, masked very considerably by the more obvious, but less essential functions of other kinds of movement applicable to words: prosody, alliteration, assonance, rhyme, in fact those audible peculiarities which make literature a poorer sort of music. What I am speaking of, and wish to see scientifically studied, is movement of a subtler and wholly interior sort, perceptible to one deaf or unacquainted with the pronunciation of a given language, and communicable, to a large degree, in every good translation. For it is simply the movement in the thinking and feeling of the Reader, obedient to the thinking and feeling of the Writer. It is the complicated pattern of stresses put not upon syllables, but upon suggestions; the pattern of insistence, of slurring, of hurrying, of binding together, of imperceptible approach or sudden attack, of dwelling on and drawing out, of letting go and breaking off, of reiteration and syncope; all woven together by a pace solemn or swift, lingering or light, but whatsoever it be, informed by some great unifying rhythm.

This it is, this quality of all great verse and all great prose, which answers to the higher moments of specially gifted individuals and generations and generations of individuals. And being such, through this mysterious soul-compelling quality of form, it is that literature can achieve the same result as do arts less seemingly hampered by practical, or less distracted by intellectual, needs: can make for the soul a habitation which is a mode of life.

Since such is the result of art, consciously and honestly striving to meet one of man's temporary wants, bodily or spiritual; the artist, drawing upon the stores of his own soul and his countless predecessors' souls, meanwhile frames such a combination of visible or audible, or intellectually apprehended, forms as imprisons in its nobility and beauty the feelings of the man who sees, or hears, or apprehends, the Reader who understands and makes the thing afresh.

And in this construction, whose material bulk or material duration may be that of a cup or a cathedral, a song or a whole opera, five lines of Pascal's or three volumes of Carlyle's—in this æsthetic construction the soul can dwell awhile and renew itself in active peacefulness, safe from the irrelevances of an imperfect world; and living, during those few seconds which have the value of eternity, the life intense, unified, ordered and universal; the life imposed not from the chaos without, but from the cosmos within.

XVII

How much greater is what man makes than what man is!

It was brought home to me, some years ago, at a reading, given at a theatre in Rome, of his Ode to Garibaldi by d'Annunzio.

The Writer was not morally suited to the subject, and the poem is by no means of his best. Yet watching the people in the theatre, and the author himself upon the stage, I felt the utter difference and immense superiority of the atmosphere of art as against that of reality. As the verses rolled out, sonorous and weighty, and the images surged up and receded in constant metamorphoses; as the whole poem advanced with the decision of course and the weigh-on of a great ship, it seemed as if none of these real people could have had a hand in the making of it, could belong to the same category of existence.

Yet the insignificant man holding the manuscript was the author; and these students in the pit, listless, vague, negligible, were, very likely, just like the youths whose heroic death on the Janiculum the poem commemorated. Had Garibaldi in his reality been present, he too, I almost think, would have seemed but another poor real ghost—or one taking on life only by poetic hyperbole—on that background of living artistic impression. For, when the hero of our enthusiasm appears, do we not robe his insufficiency in the pomp which is false to real life, but true to the demands of the spirit ?

In this way, being the response to man's organized and unceasing cravings for strength, clearness, order, dignity and sweetness, for a life intenser and more harmonious, what man writes comes to be greater than what man is.

V

STUDIES IN LITERARY PSYCHOLOGY

(A) The Syntax of De Quincey

IT was in examining some of the writings of De Quincey, with no other view originally than the improvement of my own English, that I first came across certain facts which led me to the notion that there may be some necessary connection between the structure of a man's sentences and his more human characteristics; and that style, in so far as it is individual, is but a kind of gesture or gait, revealing, with the faithfulness of an unconscious habit, the essential peculiarities of the Writer's temperament and modes of being.

This notion came home to me only gradually; so that these notes, which end as a page of literary psychology, begin, in all simplicity of heart, as an exercise in syntax and rhetoric. I shall leave them as they came, jotted down in the course of reading; for whatever truth there is in them will in this manner appear in its own plain way, not yet arranged to suit any theory.

The first thing which struck me during this analysis

of De Quincey, was that there was something very individual, something decidedly queer, in his management of *verbs*. I began accordingly to count the verbs in his writings, adding to them adverbs and active participles, as against the nouns and adjectives ; and, when I found a great preponderance of the latter kind, I did the like by two writers as dissimilar as possible from De Quincey—namely, Defoe and Stevenson, with an exactly opposite result. It now seemed to me that I had got hold of two categories of style : the one in which the chief part was given to action, as in Defoe and Stevenson ; and the other in which, so to speak, *mere being*, mere quality, was to the fore. And looking round, it seemed to me that style might be roughly divided into these two categories, with a third added, containing Writers, like Landor, in whom the elements of verb and of noun are very equally represented. But having established this, I continued to work at De Quincey, and found that there were other and more subtle and more important, peculiarities connected, apparently, with this one, and of these further peculiarities the following notes contain an analysis.

Here, to begin with, is one of the finest passages in the *Opium-Eater*, and, I should venture to add, in the whole of English Prose :

"Let it suffice, at least on this occasion, to say, that a few fragments of bread from the breakfast-table of one individual (who supposed me to be ill, but did not know of my being in utter want), and these at uncertain intervals, constituted my whole support. During the former part of my sufferings in . . . I was homeless, and very seldom slept under a roof. To this constant exposure to the open air I ascribe it mainly that I did not sink under my torments. Latterly, however, when colder and more inclement weather came on, and when, from the length of my sufferings, I had begun to sink into a more languishing condition, it was, no doubt, fortunate for me, that the same person to whose breakfast-table I had access, allowed me to sleep in a large unoccupied house, of which he was tenant. Unoccupied, I call it, for there was no household or establishment in it; nor any furniture, except a table and a few chairs. But I found, on taking possession of my new quarters, that the house already contained one single inmate, a poor friendless child, apparently ten years old; but she seemed hunger-bitten, and sufferings of that sort often make children look older than they are. From this lorn child I learned that she had slept and lived there alone for some time before I came; and great was the joy the poor creature expressed when she found that I was, in future, to be her companion through the hours of darkness. The house was large; and, from the want of furniture, the noise of the rats made a prodigious echoing on the spacious staircase and hall; and amidst the real fleshly ills of cold, and, I fear, hunger, the forsaken child had found leisure to suffer still more (it appeared) from the self-created one of ghosts. I promised her protection against all ghosts whatsoever; but, alas! I could offer her no other assistance. We lay upon the floor, with a bundle of cursed law papers for a pillow, but with no other covering than a sort of large horseman's cloak; afterwards, however, we discovered, in a garret, an old sofa-cover, a small piece of rug, and some fragments of other articles, which added a little to our warmth. The poor child crept close to me for warmth, and for security against her ghostly enemies. When I was not more than usually ill, I took her into my arms, so that, in general, she was tolerably warm, and often slept when I could not; for during the last two months of my sufferings, I slept much in daytime," etc.

In this page I have counted, of verbs, adverbs and active participles, about fifty, as against a hundred and fifty nouns, pronouns, adjectives and adjectival participles. But the difference in quality is far greater than that in mere quantity. The verbs are for the most part verbs of existence or of mere explanation, and many are in reality only fragments of adjectival sentences, which, in other languages, might perhaps have been replaced by actual adjectives. Whatever they are—" was," " ascribe," " begun," " call it " (in the sense of naming), " found," " learned," etc. etc.—they serve only to bind the nouns and adjectives into logical sentences, but do not bring any sense of action into the passage. Most of them, moreover, might be replaced by equally indeterminate words without altering the total effect. Look, on the contrary, at this list of nouns and adjectives: " Ill," " utter want," " uncertain interval," "whole support," "sufferings," "two months," "houseless," "London," "roof," "constant exposure," "colder and more inclement weather," "length of sufferings," "languishing condition," "fortunate person," "breakfast table," "large unoccupied house," "tenant," "household or establishment," "furniture," "table," "few chairs," "house," "single inmate," "poor friendless child," "ten years old," "hunger bitten," "sufferings," "children," "older," "child," "great joy," "poor creature," "house of darkness," "house," "large," "want of furniture," "rats," "noise," "staircase," "hall," "prodigious echoing," "spacious," "cold," "hunger," "forsaken child," "leisure," "ghosts," "protection," "floor," "bundle," "cursed law papers," "pillow," "covering," "horseman's cloak," "sofa-cover," "rug," "fragments," "articles," "warmth," "security," "ghostly enemies," "usually ill," "warmth."

Was ever such a catalogue of suggestions of gloom, terror and misery? The very reiteration, towards the end, of the word "warmth," after the string of words like "unoccupied house," "ghosts," "floor," "bundle," "horseman's cloak," "fragments," is of the strongest negative effect, even without the sequel or accompaniment of "security," "ghostly enemies," "ill," "hunger," and "sufferings." What a *study in black and wretchedness*, as Whistler would have put it!

But verbs are not merely unimportant in De Quincey;

they are also mismanaged, for his indifference to action becomes positive incapacity. Look at this passage from the *Opium-Eater*:

"Whatever is to become of poor Piranesi, you suppose, at least, that his labours must in some way terminate here. But raise your eyes, and behold a second flight of steps still higher, on which again Piranesi is perceived, but this time standing on the very brink of the abyss. Again elevate your eye, and a still more aerial flight of stairs is beheld: and again is poor Piranesi busy on his aspiring labours: and so on until the unfinished stairs and Piranesi both are lost in the upper gloom of the hall."

All through this passage there is confusion between the active verb and the passive, the two forms alternating quite without reason or connection. Now, as it happens, this accidentally coincides with the matter in hand, and heightens the impression of the whole thing being an opium-dream, almost a nightmare. But take a passage containing merely ordinary statements, and note the effect of this peculiarity, I should almost have said, this characteristic infirmity—of De Quincey's:

"I replied that, *as to the allegation of his enemies, as it* seemed to *be established upon* such *reputable testimony*, seeing that the three parties *concerned* all *agree in* it, it did not *become* me to question it; but the defence *set up* I must *demur* to. He *proceeded to discuss* the matter, and to *lay down* his reasons; but it seemed to me so impolitic to *pursue* an argument which *must* have presumed a man *mistaken* in a point belonging to his own profession, that I did not press him even when his course of argument *seemed* open to objection; not to *mention* that a man who *talks* nonsense, even though 'with no view to profit,' *is* not altogether the most agreeable partner in a dispute, whether as opponent or respondent. I *confess*, however," etc.

Here are twenty-eight verbs. Ask yourself what corresponding impression of movement, activity, they leave in you? But of these some are auxiliaries, employed as portions, often merely qualifiers, of ideas. Ten, characteristically enough of Latin origin, are distinctly abstract, savouring of jurisprudence and philosophical discussion—"reply," "establish," "concern," "agree," "question," "demur," "proceed," "discuss," "presume," "press," "mention." With this spuriousness of the words superficially denoting movement, go certain other peculiarities of the passage. Let us examine its structure. To begin with, one-half of the matter is presented, for the very first time, in the form of a parenthesis, or at least in a very parenthetical form—"as to the allegation of his enemies," etc., the second half making its appearance also in a somewhat similar, indirect, referential, shambling sort of way, "as it seemed to be established," etc. After this we have a real parenthesis, and no doubt of it. "Seeing that, etc. . . . agree in it." This parenthesis contains, moreover, two involutions, or what seem involutions, "agree in," and (by elision) "concerned." Closing the parenthesis we get the other half of the subject, "it did not become me to question it," presented negatively and itself a negation (to *question*). Tacked on, like an afterthought, comes the third main item, again presented negatively, "but the defence set up [De Quincey sets up the opponent's defence before having made his own attack] I must demur to." Remark that the chief verb comes so late that we are kept in suspense as to which it may be; it might have been "agree with." And so on.

On re-reading this sentence, the suspicion arises that it may be a joke, and intended as a caricature of polite discussion. But if this be the case (which nothing else leads one to suppose), it is merely the caricature, by De Quincey, of De Quincey's own style.

Let us take instead the last paragraph of *Levana*:

"Lo! here is he, whom in childhood I dedicated to my altars. This is he that once I made my darling. Him I led astray, him I beguiled, and from heaven I stole away his young heart to mine. Through me did he become idolatrous; and through me it was, by languishing desires, that he worshipped the worm, and prayed to the wormy grave. Holy was the grave to him; lovely was its darkness; saintly its corruption. Him, this young idolater, I have seasoned for thee, dear gentle sister of Sighs! Do thou take him now to *thy* heart, and season him for our dreadful sister. And thou—turning to the *Mater Tenebrarum*, she said—' Wicked sister, that temptest and hatest, do thou take him from *her*. See that thy sceptre lie heavy on his head. Suffer not woman and her tenderness to sit near him in his darkness. Banish the frailties of hope, wither the relenting of love, scorch the fountain of tears, curse him as only thou canst curse. So shall he be accomplished in the furnace, so shall he see the things that ought not to be seen, sights that are abominable and secrets that are unutterable. So shall he read elder truths, sad truths, grand truths, fearful truths. So shall he rise again *before* he dies, and so shall our commission be accomplished which from God we had—to plague his heart until we had unfolded the capacities of his spirit.' "

In this sentence a certain heavy jerkiness, very characteristic of De Quincey, seems to depend upon the needless reiteration of pronouns; and at the same time, the alternation, equally avoidable, of their cases, thus: " Him," " him," " his," " he," " whom," " he," " him," " him," " his," " he," " he," " him," " him," " him," and " I," " my," " I," " my," " I," " I," " I," " mine," " me," " me," " I," " thee," " thou," " my," etc. In ten lines we are given twenty-six pronouns, without counting two *ours*. And the fine movement of this passage begins only when this crowd of pronouns, with their wearisome fluctuations, at last comes to an end: " Banish the frailties of hope," etc.

The lack of movement, the nervelessness, of De Quincey's style is here manifest, not merely in that abuse of pronouns, in the redundancy of auxiliaries, and in the incapacity for dealing with the litter of small words, "to," "until," etc.; but very especially in this particular lazy and restless shifting which turns the same noun now into a nominative, now into an accusative, instead of keeping a steady course all through. One seems to feel the infirmity of the opium-eater's will. In a still finer passage, the same indecision (bringing with it extreme parentheticalness and marring all rhythm and cadence) is shown in a perpetual changing about from the active to the passive form, and *vice versa*:

"She it was that stood in Bethlehem on the night when Herod's sword swept its nurseries of innocents, and the little feet were stiffened for ever, which, heard at times as they tottered along floors overhead, woke pulses of love in household hearts that were not unmarked in heaven."

Note in this sentence the mismanagement of adverbs and prepositions and articles—"in," "on," "when," "which," "that." Each of these produces a change in our sense of place, time or person, a new adjustment like that of pulling out a register on an organ; and where there is no real movement in the subject-matter, we feel jerked about to no purpose. By this senseless shifting of case, turning from passive to active with reference to the same noun, the sword of Herod seems of a sudden to become the dominant subject of the sentence, while *She* in reality remains such. Then the little feet, first presented as accusative, become the nominative of the tottering and the waking of pulses; then, having been the nominative in the active form, they become the accusative in the passive form of the " marking in heaven."

But, in the same way as this incapacity for action turns De Quincey's experiences of that empty house into what they should be, terrifying dreams, with dreamlike vagueness of *how, when and why*, and dreamlike vividness of *what*; so also the same peculiarity and with it De Quincey's redundance and emphasis, unite in making the following into something of matchless grandeur. What a dream of sounds!

"A music of preparation and of awaking suspense; a music like the opening of the Coronation anthem, and which, like that, gave the feeling of a vast march, of infinite cavalcades, filing off, and the tread of innumerable armies. The morning was come of a mighty day, a day of crisis and of final hope for human nature, then suffering some mysterious eclipse and labouring in some dread extremity somewhere, I knew not where, somehow, I know not how, by some things, I know not whom—a battle, a strife, an agony—was conducting, was evolving like a great drama or piece of music. . . ."

This passage belongs to his eulogy of Sir Thomas Browne, and it suggests to me that we shall usually find not merely a key to an author's peculiarities in his criticisms, favourable or the reverse, of others; but that we may probably find that his own work is excellent or poor according as he is just or absurd in his judgments: efficiency of perception coinciding with efficiency of expression, and *vice versa*. Listen to De Quincey in the presence of his far greater predecessor:

"Where—he asks—shall one hope to find music so Miltonic, an intonation of such solemn chords as are struck in the following opening bar of a passage in the *Urn Burial*? 'Now, since these bones have rested quietly in the grave, under the drums and tramplings of three conquests,' etc. What a melodious ascent as of a prelude to some impassioned Requiem breaking from the pomps of earth and from the sanctities of the grave! . . . Time expanded, not by generations or centuries, but by vast periods of conquests and dynasties; by cycles of Pharaohs and Ptolemies, Antiochi and Arsacides! And these vast successions of time distinguished and figured by the uproars which revolve at their inauguration, by the drums and tramplings rolling overhead upon the chambers of forgotten dead, the trepidation of time and mortality vexing, at secular intervals, the everlasting Sabbaths of the grave."

Note how De Quincey has developed the "drums and tramplings" into a military requiem service, with its processions and its fugues; how he has used Browne's text as a theme for a great symphony of his own.

After this let us turn to De Quincey's eulogy of another of his idols, Burke, and see the alteration in his style, his judgment and his manners! These pages of his *Rhetoric* may be the more instructive that we shall have occasion to examine not only more of De Quincey's own writing, but a passage from Burke which he holds up for our admiration (*Rhetoric*, p. 57).

"*Fancy* in your throats, ye miserable twaddlers! as if Edmund Burke were the man to play with his fancy, for the purpose of separable ornament. He was a man of fancy in no other sense than as Lord Bacon was so and Jeremy Taylor, and as all large and discursive thinkers are and must be: that is to say, the fancy which he had in common with all mankind, and very probably in no eminent degree, *in him* was urged into unusual activity under the necessities of his capacious understanding. His great and peculiar distinction was that he viewed all objects of the understanding under more relations than other men, and under more complex relations. *According to the multiplicity of those relations, a man is said to have a large understanding, according to their subtility, a fine one,* and in an angelic understanding all things would appear related to all. Now, to *apprehend* and *detect* more relations, or to perceive them more steadily, is a process absolutely impossible without the intervention of physical analogy. To say, therefore, that a man is a great thinker, or a fine thinker, is another expression for saying that he has a *schematizing* (or, to put a plainer but less accurate expression, a *figurative*) understanding. In that sense, and for that purpose, Burke is figurative; but understood, as he has been understood by the long-eared race of his critics, not as thinking in and by his figures, but as deliberately laying them on by way of *enamel* or *after ornament*, not as incarnating, but simply as dressing his thoughts in imagery; so understood, he is not the Burke of reality, but a poor fictitious Burke, modelled after the poverty of conception which belongs to his critics."

There is in this passage a delicate piece of thinking, namely, the account of what one might call the relation-perceiving mind; and there is a daring, though perhaps not absolutely justified, connection established between it and the mind which thinks metaphorically. But in what truisms and repetitions is it not wrapped up! Or, rather, how this thought staggers about in irrelevant directions, and among useless provisos and distinctions, impelled (if I may speak like De Quincey) by the fitful wind of the critic's abusiveness! Here was something which wanted saying in the clearest, most abstract manner; yet how far less clear is it not than the far-fetched and romantically obscure train of thought of the criticism on Sir Thomas Browne. And now, having read De Quincey's encomium upon Burke, let us read the quotation which is intended to bring home to us the organic and inevitable quality of Burke's metaphorical thinking. This is it:

"Such are *their* ideas; such *their* religion; and such *their* law. But as to our country, our race, as long as the well-compacted structure of our Church and State, the sanctuary, the holy of holies, of that ancient law, defended by reverence, defended by power, a fortress at once and a temple, shall stand inviolate on the brow of the British lion; as long as the British Monarchy, not more limited than fenced by the orders of the State, shall, like the proud Keep of Windsor, rising in the majesty of proportion, and girt with the double bar of its kindred and coeval towers, as long as this awful structure shall oversee and guard the subjected land, so long the mounds and dykes of the low Bedford level will have nothing to fear from the pickaxes of all the levellers of France. As long as our Sovereign Lord the King, and his faithful subjects the Lords and Commons of this realm, the triple cord which no man can break; the solemn guarantees of each other's being and each other's rights, the joint and several securities, each in its place and order for every kind and every quality of property—as long as these endure, so long the Duke of Bedford is safe, and we are all safe together; the high from the blights of envy and the spoliation of rapacity, the low from the iron hand of oppression and the indolent spurn of contempt. Amen! and so be it, and so it will be.

"Dum domus Æneae capitoli immobile saxum
    Accolit; imperiumque pater Romanus habebit."

That is the quotation ; and this is what De Quincey has to say about it :

"This was the sounding passage which Burke alleged as the *chef-d'œuvre* of his rhetoric ; and the argument upon which he justified his choice is specious if not convincing. He laid it down as a maxim of composition, that every passage in a rhetorical performance which was brought forward prominently, and relied upon as a *key* (to use the language of war) in sustaining the main position of the Writer, ought to involve a thought, an image and a sentiment; and such a synthesis he found in the passage which we have quoted."

Now it happens, whatever Burke himself (with parental ill-judgment) may have thought to the contrary, that this passage is a model of the inefficacious, all, save the sudden, "Amen ! and so be it, and so it will be," and the Latin. Far from having an impression of stability, one has a feeling that all the various things in which digging and building come in, " well-compacted structure," " sanctuary," " fortress," " temple," " Keep of Windsor," " towers," " mounds and dykes," are not sitting still, as such heavy things should, but rambling vaguely all over the place. And this is due to the fact that the mind of the Reader, instead of being kept as quiet as the British Constitution, is hunted up and down a series of parentheses, and made, so to speak, to look round the corner of ever so many qualifying sentences. The result being (by the well-known psychological law) that the Reader attributes his own mental movement to the buildings. And this is made worse by the unnecessary use of the participle of so lively a verb as " defend." Had he said " guarded," things would have stayed just a trifle quieter. Then there is the equally unnecessary definiteness of " to stand " (where " to be " would have sufficed) ; and the negation " inviolate," bringing with it the suggestion its contrary " violation "; also the active verbs " limit " and " fence," " oversee " and " guard." The Windsor simile is thought *of*, not thought *in*. Had Burke actually felt, so to say, *in* the terms of Windsor and its connected images, he would not have spread out before it (as if he might Eton playground) the Bedford level, as though Windsor Castle and the British Constitution were at hand together to point guns at its invaders. Least of all, had he really seen the towers of Windsor arise as the symbol of British monarchy, would he have been able to think of Bedfordshire from the merely topographical and agricultural point of view, as " low " and " fat " ? What on earth could it matter to the monarchy whether the Duke of Bedford's estate was *low* and *fat* or high and thin ? Further, increasing thereby the sense of action which is already making the various solid structures to wobble uneasily in our mind, this same land is partially personified by the form. " have nothing to fear." But perhaps the crowning proof of this being a merely elaborately thought-out (and as happens in over-elaboration, bungled) piece of rhetoric, its irrefutable mark of rhetorical inefficacy is this meeting together of the pickaxes with the dykes and the mounds. Note the connection! Levellers of ideas—levelness of soil. Dykes and mounds naturally destructible—what by? Why, by those very levellers and pickaxes! But what the levellers would have made for would have been not the dykes, but Windsor Castle; the levellers of ideas do not destroy ploughed fields, fat or thin, they demolish Constitutions, monarchies.

It is quite probable that De Quincey was not only abnormally sensitive to the grandeur, the picturesqueness of the nouns in this passage (allowing them to evoke images in irrelevant fashion: "towers," "keeps," "dykes," "pickaxes," "levels," etc.), but that he did not feel the senseless quality of the action suggested by the accompanying verbs, simply because verbs had very little significance for him. I have already remarked that this incapacity for duly appreciating actions seems allied, in De Quincey at least, with certain other marks of a will-less and undiscriminating mode of being. These other characteristics are diffuseness, redundancy, a tendency to mix, quite irrationally, familiarity with grandiloquence, and finally a total lack of respect for others and of restraint upon his own vituperative faculties.

Here is a passage of which the items are placed so as not to coalesce :

"Again, at a coronation, what can be more displeasing to a philosophic taste than a pretended chastity of ornament, *at war* with the very purpose of a solemnity essentially magnificent ? An imbecile friend of ours in 1825, brought us a sovereign of a new coinage ' which ' — said he — ' I admire, because it is so exquisitely simple.' This, he flattered himself, was thinking like a man of taste. But mark how we sent him to the right-about. And that weak-minded friend," etc.

Here we have the long interrogatory passage about the Coronation followed instantly, when the mind is in a state of expectant attention and ready crammed with Coronation splendours, by the sudden and at first irrelevant introduction of "an imbecile friend," and his little feeble speech. Then follows De Quincey's criticism of the friend's speech, addressed not to the friend, but to the Reader, who is buttonholed by that sudden, " But mark ! " We have been shunted three times: from " Coronation " to " imbecile friend's point of view," and from that to De Quincey's critical *aparte* to us. Moreover, the "which I admire" of the friend is so placed as to suggest rather the previous sentence than the coin he is actually holding. The natural wording would have been " an imbecile friend," etc., " brought us a sovereign," etc., " saying he admired it because——" But this very simple and direct form contains a concordance of verbs of which De Quincey is frequently incapable. Let us look at this passage more in detail, for it is instructive to do so.

Its main fault is that of all De Quincey's bad passages, a senseless, flurried changing of point of view. Thus: "Pretended chastity of ornament," acts as nominative to "philosophic task," dative; then as nominative to (dative) "purpose of a solemnity," which is (by elision) nominative to "magnificent." The next nominative, to our astonishment, is the sudden "imbecile friend," who continues to be nominative of the verb "admire," although the really important noun is now the "sovereign of new coinage." Then "*he*" becomes the second accusative [the Reader having been made the first accusative by the sudden grabbing of him with that, "But mark!"]—and then "we"— *i.e.* De Quincey, becomes nominative to the "sending to the right-about." As a matter of common logic there are two chief nominatives—"elegant simplicity" and "sovereign of a new coinage," but they have got so jostled that we are scarcely aware of them. It is this jostling, this lack of order which gives De Quincey's style, for all its real magnificence, a certain vulgarity. We feel, however vaguely, that we are dealing with a man, occasionally subtle and frequently majestic, but unbalanced, ungoverned, without purpose or discrimination, self-important and self-indulgent, with the restlessness of egotism, and of whose breeding we are never sure.

The vulgarity is manifest in a tendency to talk big, and, at the same time, to mix slang with grandiloquence in situations where no humorous effect can be obtained by this proceeding. He might be describing himself in the phrases, "the very top of the tree among the fine writers" and "Birmingham rhetorician"; and here is a description in which, unwittingly, he has written himself down, matter and form:

"Undoubtedly he has a turgid style and mouthy grandiloquence (though often the merest bombast); but for polished rhetoric he is singularly unfitted, by inflated habits of thinking, by loitering diffuseness and a dreadful trick of calling names."

How sadly this applies to De Quincey himself is shown by his beginning his *Essay on Style* with—what would you expect?—an attack on "conceited coxcombs":

"Semi-delirious lords and ladies, sometimes theatrically costumed in caftans and turbans—Lord Byrons, for instance, and Lady Hester Stanhopes—proclaiming to the world that all nations and languages are free to enter their gates, with one sole exception directed against their British compatriots; that is to say, abjuring by sound of trumpet the very land through which they themselves, etc. etc. We all know who they are that have done this thing; we *may* know, if we inquire, how many conceited coxcombs," etc. etc.

And now we may take leave of this strange, ill-balanced mortal, with his incapacity for holding his tongue on irrelevant matters, which is a sign of intellectual weakness; his incapacity for keeping his irrelevant emotions (especially vituperative) to himself, which is a mark of moral vulgarity; and yet with such subtlety of thought, such tragic depth of feeling, and, occasionally, such marvellous power of seeing and saying! For in that self-same *Essay on Style*, where Mr. Snagsby and the modern paragraph Writer are both forestalled, we come upon this passage:

"The preparation pregnant with the future, the remote correspondence, the questions, as it were, which to a deep musical sense are asked in one passage and answered in another; the iteration and ingemination of a given effect, moving through subtle variations that sometimes disguise the theme, sometimes fitfully reveal it, sometimes throw it out tumultuously to the blaze of daylight; these and ten thousand forms of self-conflicting musical passion. . . ."

Self-conflicting musical passion! Is it not characteristic of De Quincey that to him music should signify self-contradiction, rather than order and harmony?

(B) The Rhetoric of Landor

I am the better pleased to have chosen Landor as the object of my random analysis, that he has been studied, as the type of the classical prose Writer, by so considerable a critic as Mr. Sidney Colvin. This coincidence will allow us, only the better, to examine in what manner even the most purely "artistic" writing is determined by the underlying temper of the man who writes; indeed, to what extent this same so-called *artistic* quality is in reality the result of very human qualities or defects.

Here is what Mr. Colvin tells us about the fundamental difference between what he calls *classic* and *romantic* methods in literature:

"The romantic manner, the manner of Shakespeare, and Coleridge and Keats, with its thrilling uncertainties and its rich suggestions, may be more attractive than the classic manner, with its composed and measured preciseness of statement. Nay, we may go further, and say that it is in the romantic manner that the highest pitch of poetry has assuredly been reached; in the perfect and felicitous specimens of that manner English poetry has given us something more poetical even than Greece or Rome ever gave us. But, on the other hand, the romantic manner lends itself, as the true classical does not, to inferior work. Second-rate conceptions, excitedly and approximately put into words, derive from it an illusive attraction which may make them for a time, and with all but the coolest judges, pass as first-rate. Whereas about true classical writing there can be no illusion. *It presents to us conceptions calmly realized in words that exactly define them, conceptions depending for their attraction not on their halo, but on themselves.*"

I have underlined the last sentence of this passage, because it defines the nature of what Mr. Colvin, quite justifiably but arbitrarily (since such names have never acquired more than a fancy value), calls by the name of *classic* or *romantic*. Now, my examination of Landor, and of my own feelings towards Landor, and of such items of literary psychology as I have been able to scrape together, seems rather to prove that these so-called classical ways of proceeding are more pretentious than efficient, that they are compatible with what is little better than verbiage, and that—one asserts it with awe—in Landor's own work they are indicative not of the great talent he really possessed, but of his melancholy limitations of soul and, therefore, lapses of sense.

The preference expressed for the classical manner appears to depend in great measure upon Mr. Colvin's notion that poetry (or prose in its artistic freedom) deals with *conceptions*, and that the words which best define such conceptions (and the more calmly defined apparently the better) allow us to realize most effectually whatever attraction these conceptions may have. There seems to be some underlying belief that the aim of literature is to tackle, so far as possible, the famous Kantian "thing in itself," stripping it of such purely phenomenal wrappers and disguises as its effects. The "halo" is evidently the value, the meaning which things occasionally take on owing to their relations with poor human souls. We have been referred to

Shelley and Wordsworth for examples of such "halo"; and the first lines of the "Ode to the Nightingale" might have been quoted in order to show us what *this halo* is like. There is something austerely attractive (if I may say so) in the renunciation of such halos, and it is very dignified, no doubt, thus to make all things equally uninteresting. But the power of literature upon the soul depends, oddly enough, on the soul's recognition of the massive or subtle connections between itself and the things the Writer is talking of. And, what is more curious still, there is in human nature such perverse hankering after relations between things and itself, that when the Writer, disdainful of halos, has stripped all things into isolation, he seems to be obliged to weave a new set of relationships, and these relationships are occasionally . . . well, you shall judge. I have italicized them; in this passage from one of Landor's finest dialogues, *Eugenius and Lippi*:

"The clematis *overtopped* the lemon and orange trees; and the perennial pea *sent forth* here a pink blossom, here a purple, here a white one; and, after *holding* (as it were) *a short conversation* with the *humbler* plants, *sprang* up about an old cypress, *played* among its branches, and *mitigated its gloom*. White pigeons . . . examined me in *every position* their *inquisitive* eyes could take," etc.

First of all, there appears to be no essential difference between the perennial pea and the pigeon; yet the one, speaking commonly, stays in its place and the other walks about, walks about, moreover, according to Landor, with a power of shifting the place of its eye, such as ordinary pigeons rarely display. And, excepting this ocular restlessness, Landor's pigeon gets through very much less business than his perennial pea. The classical Writer's refusal to tell us how the perennial pea affected Lippi, the stylist's horror of saying that the perennial pea merely *was*, has forced Landor, despite his singular sharpness of observation, into a number of amazing mis-statements, which I have underlined in my quotation, and can sum up as the transformation of so quiet, and one might fairly say, so passive, a thing as a garden corner into a dramatic entertainment, enlivened by circus performances. Perhaps Landor was bored by gardens; one might think so, and merely regret he should have chosen to speak of them; and pass to something else. But Mr. Colvin expressly tells us that "in images of terror no (what) other Writer has shown greater daring, or a firmer stroke." So I am acting fairly in taking another passage, from Mr. Colvin's own hand, as an example of the striking results of the desire for clearness, for logical elaboration, for what people call "objectivity," which distinguishes the *classic* manner.

Here is the passage :

"He extended his *withered* arms, he thrust forward the *gaunt links of his throat*, and upon *gnarled* knees, that smote each other audibly, tottered into the *civic* fire.

It, like some *hungry and strangest beast* in the *innermost wild of Africa*, pierced, broken, prostrate, motionless [I interrupt to remind the Reader that all this refers to a fire], *gazed at by its hunter in the impatience of glory, in the delight of awe*, panted once more and seized him."

Now, would you call all this story of lions and hunters on the one side, this anatomic plate of bony decrepitude on the other, a *vivid image*, a *daring and firmly rendered terrifying image* of an old hero throwing himself into a burning town?

[The malignance of my heart causes me secretly to rejoice at Landor's having called it the *civic fire*.]

Look, again, at this other sample given by Mr. Colvin, this time in verse :—

> I never pluck the rose; the violet's *head*
> Hath shaken with my breath *upon its bank*,
> And *not reproached me*; the ever-sacred cup
> Of the pure lily hath between my hands
> *Felt safe*, unsoiled, nor lost one grain of gold.

This passage might be called the carnival or dumb crambo of classicism, at all events of the method which refuses all mere subjective *halos*, and makes for the "conceptions in themselves." The lily was not allowed, of course, to stir Landor's fancy like those flowers, unseen at the feet of Keats, in the "Ode to the Nightingale." It had to be considered for what it was! So, in order to be in legitimate relations to a verb, it was made to *feel safe*; similarly, the violet was induced to refrain from reproach; nay, not the whole of the violet, which might have seemed exaggerated, but only the violet's *head*; the rest of the violet being presumably busy clinging to the *bank*, upon which, rather than upon the violet or than on to the owner of a sacred cup, Landor appears to have breathed. The lily, moreover, was turned into a *sacred cup*, filled, not, as is commonly the case, with *dust*, but with *grains of gold*. No one can complain that these flowers are presented through the halo of Landor's feelings, or that he had any feelings to present them through. But is Landor's method more really *direct* than, say, that of Keats, and does it give us more of the flower, or more of the Writer and his inkpot?

I want to run this matter to ground, because it will lead us, I think, to some important facts in the psychology and, I should almost call it, the *ethics* of writing. Here is a narrative (*Fate of a Young Poet*) of a simpler sort, and in which Landor is presumably aiming at interesting the Reader in his hero:

" It is said that he bore a fondness for a young maiden in that place, formerly a village, now containing but two farmhouses. In my memory there were still extant several dormitories. Some love-sick girl had recollected an ancient name, and had engraven on a stone with a garden nail, which lay in rust near it, Poore Rosamund. I entered these precincts and beheld a youth of manly form and countenance, washing and wiping *a* stone with a handful of wet grass; and on my going up to him, and asking what he had found, he showed it to me," etc.

What a struggle is here between reality and abstraction, and how in this confusion we utterly fail to know what to think, how to feel, fail utterly to receive the great Writer's word of command!

Now this *word of command*, or, if you prefer, this magician's spell, making our soul follow with docility, making it see, hear, feel solely what and in what manner the Writer chooses, can be given, I believe, on one condition only: that the Writer feel very distinctly the moods he wishes to impart, and see in a given light and in a given sequence the things he wishes us to look at. This very simple condition Landor by no means always fulfils. And when it is not fulfilled, nothing, not the clearest intelligence, the richest invention, the most faultless judgment, is a bit of good. All the powers of style are wasted if you do not care for what you are talking about.

And yet what powers of style are his! It is worth while examining and meditating on the merest technicalities of Landor's writings. His structure of sentences, for instance, is both musically and grammatically often a wonder. See how he breaks up long and repetitive movements with short abrupt ones; how he alternates nouns, verbs, adjectives, and even adjectives and particles at the end of members of sentences! Note also the skilful insertion of parenthetical passages. The lucidity of his successful phrases is perfect; you see, without ever having to look, along the whole passage, however intricate, and your mind is stimulated to such gentle yet vigorous exercise by the beautiful and constantly varied cadence, never putting you to sleep by one sort of repetition, nor giving you a headache by another. Compare, in order to appreciate Landor, that perpetual stress on the end of the sentence, or sentence's member, which makes De Quincey's fine passages often as harrowing to the nerves as the successive discharging of cartloads of stones. These are high triumphs of literary craft, but then everything, or nearly everything, in Landor is sacrificed to their attainment. One might imagine that he sometimes thinks his sentences first as grammar and syntax (as a poet may think a lyric as sound), and then fits in the items irrespective of their value as meaning.

He is full of mere mechanical dodges. Thus, the lucidity is often obtained by what I should call empty, transparent words: for instance:

"When he is present I have room for none (no reflections) *besides what I receive from him*."

The words italicized are idle, but they serve to *space* the sense. Elsewhere the clearness is got by an antithetical arrangement in places where, very often, there is no real antithesis ; thus :

"(Dashkoff) And when the one (the wife) has failed to pacify the sharp cries of babyhood, pettish and impatient as sovranty itself, the success of the other (*i.e.* the husband) in calming it," etc.

Here the impression of union which was required by the subject is absolutely marred by this futile structural opposition, but the syntax becomes wonderfully clear. And this antithetical arrangement, this introduction of the opposite for the easier apprehension of what is really being talked about, results in the peculiar kind of insipidity, of half-heartedness, which makes Landor such poor reading despite his very great qualities ; an impression is neutralized by its own negation before it has had time to solidify. Landor does not allow us to feel, so anxious is he that we should define and determine. For instance :

"Could she (Sappho) be ignorant that shame and fear seize it (love) unrelentingly by the throat, while hard-hearted impudence stands at ease, *prompt* at opportunity, and *profuse* in declaration ? "

In this passage lucidity is obtained by the distinction between *prompt* and *profuse*. But in the meantime poor Timid Love, who, after all, should have been the hero of the play, is forgotten !

All this is due, I think, to the fact that Landor did not really care for what he was writing about, but only for the fact of writing. This is proved by his metaphors being not expressive, but explanatory; he has not felt the subject in those, or indeed in any, particular terms, but cast about him for parallels for better apprehension. Thus, these metaphors are apt to be trite or slackly expressed, and they are (as we saw in the case of the old gentleman who flung himself into the burning town) very often carried on far beyond the needs of the subject. Whereas, on the contrary, if he had felt the metaphor, he might have expressed it more vigorously than the rest, but he would have let it go as soon as it ceased to concord with his chief vision and feeling. Let us look at one of his finest passages; and one of those in which the thought of death seems to have brought some genuine emotion—I mean Bossuet's speech to Mlle de Fontanges:

"This in which we live is ours only while we live in it; the next moment may strike it off from us; the next sentence I would utter may be broken and fall between us. The beauty that has made a thousand hearts to beat one instant, at the succeeding has been without pulse and colour, without admirer, friend, companion, follower. She by whose eyes the march of victory shall have been directed, whose name shall have animated armies at the extremities of the earth, drops into one of its crevices and mingles with its dust."

How clear and stately, yet how wearisome! Why? simply and crassly because there is no feeling in it at all. Eloquence there is, and in other parts of the dialogue, wit and humour in abundance. But it is all elaborately reasoned, planned out; and no man's reasoning and planning, however elaborate, can replace feeling. No Writer is able to shift his critical ruler and foot-measure quickly and subtly enough to adjust a whole effect, as does the mere sensitive eye, eye of body or of soul. See how even in this passage he leaves the essential behind in order to work out a mere detail— " animated armies at the extremities of the *earth*, drops into one of *its* crevices and mingles with its dust." Why, the earth has become the heroine of this passage, and the poor dying beauty is a mere adjunct to its extension, its battlefields and holes and dust. " So she is," Landor might answer. But not to her own feelings, nor to ours, nor to Landor's, if he had any!

Let us look at Landor's masterpiece, the dialogue of *Leofric and Godiva*:

" The beverage of this feast, O Leofric, is sweeter than bee or flower or vine can give us : it flows from heaven ; and in heaven will it abundantly be poured out again to him who pours it out here abundantly."

How complete is here the rhetorician's indifference! He is so little wrapped up in the dramatic situation that he wanders off after any pretty detail which is trailed across the path; he *must* be after the bee or the flower or the vine! But now he pulls himself together, having got to the tragic part of the business; we have come to the Famine, and, by all the gods of Pen and Ink, Landor will show us what a Famine is like!

Godiva speaks:

"There is dearth in the land, my sweet Leofric. Remember how many weeks of drought we have had, even in the deep pastures of Leicestershire; and how many Sundays we have heard the same prayers for rain, and supplications that it would please the Lord in His mercy to turn aside His anger from the poor, pining cattle. You, my dear husband, have imprisoned more than one malefactor for leaving his dead ox in the public way; and other hinds have fled before you out of the traces, in which they, and their sons and their daughters, and haply their old fathers and mothers, were dragging the abandoned wain homeward. Although we were accompanied by many brave spearmen and skilful archers, it was perilous to pass the creatures which the farmyard dogs, driven from the hearth by the poverty of their masters, were tearing and devouring, while others, bitten and lamed, filled the air either with long and deep howls or sharp and quick barkings as they struggled with hunger and feebleness, or were exasperated by heat and pain. Nor could the thyme from the heath, nor the bruised branches of the fir tree extinguish or abate the foul odour," etc. etc.

The first and most superficial thing which strikes me in this sentence is the constant see-saw of alternatives: if you are not going to be impressed by the *dead malefactor*, then try the *harnessed peasants*; if the *sons and daughters in harness* aren't enough, take the *fathers and mothers also*. Again, if the dogs *disturbed over the carcases* are not to your satisfaction, please note the *unfed* ones. Moreover, you may fix your mind, or your choice, either on the *sharp and quick barkings,* or upon the *long and deep howls*; in the same manner you are left free to attribute the dog's struggles either to (*a*) *hunger and feebleness*, or (*b*) *heat and pain*. After such a choice of evils it is not astonishing that you should require disinfection by two different disinfectants—namely, *thyme* and *fir branches*; nor need we wonder, after so many alternating possibilities, that the stench is neither *extinguished* nor *abated*.

During this examination a light seems to have dawned in me, a certainty far surpassing all considerations of Leofric and Godiva. I have watched Landor at work! Landor, even the mighty, severe demi-god of classic prose, has appeared to me in the semblance of a boy provided, by heartless teachers, with a theme, and obliged to produce a given number of lines thereon. Conscientiously, and with touching intellectual willingness, he has meditated, chin in hand, or hand in hair, upon the concatenated possibilities: the beginning of it all was a drought, that is to say, a scarcity of water (this suggests prayers for rain). The water supply being insufficient, there was no fodder; the cattle got none. Hence some died: hence carcases by the roadside; hence the employment of human labour in lieu of cattle; the sons and daughters harnessed—nay, in certain cases, the elder members of the family; nay, happy thought! the oxen have died of exhaustion on the way, and the family drags the wain homeward, for, of course, though carcases are left by the roadside, carts may always come in handy, and are worth taking home. Then the poor people couldn't feed their dogs any longer, hence the dogs eat the carcases, or else (for some dogs, though few, are confirmed vegetarians) died of hunger; and, as it was hot (for it is always hot when it is dry in England), occasionally also died of heat; and the dogs, very likely, fell to fighting over the carcases, and bit one another, or got lamed (perhaps by people throwing stones at them? Landor has forgotten this!) Such a state of things must have become positively dangerous, and there being danger, Leofric and Godiva required an escort, and being very great personages, had an escort of two kinds: namely, bowmen and spearmen, and the bowmen were skilful, for it is no easy matter to shoot with a bow, whereas the spearmen were only required to be brave, for it only requires presence of mind to run a spear into a dog. Meanwhile, of course, the unburied carcases stank, including those of the dogs who had died for so many reasons; in consequence, thyme and fir branches were provided; and here, I am sorry to note an omission, for Landor has indeed told us that the thyme was got from the heath, but has left us without due information concerning the place whence the fir branches were procured. This oversight is probably due to the excitement of perceiving what a fine opportunity this was of showing the unkind fussiness of Leofric. He not only clapped into gaol every person guilty of having left a dead ox on the thoroughfare, but frightened (though we are not told how) the poor peasants (even to the extent of making them run away) whenever he met them dragging their cart themselves, no doubt because his pedantic sense of propriety was offended by this innocent proceeding. . . . Here, then, in the course of learning every possible detail about a drought, we have had our mind prepared for a heartless and martinet Leofric.

At the end of the dialogue is an autobiographical note by Landor:

"The story of Godiva, at one of whose festivals or fairs I was present in boyhood, has always interested me; and I wrote a poem on it, I remember, by the *square foot* at Rugby. . . . May the peppermint be still growing on the bank in that place!"

How oddly simple, and how oddly like real poetry this is! Why? Because Landor was remembering his own past, and, once in a way, feeling genuine emotion.

I know nothing about Landor's private life, save that he lived a quarter of a mile from the house whence I am writing, and once threw his cook out of the window on to the violet bed, and made a *bon mot* at the time, or more likely, afterwards. And I have nothing to do with what Landor may have been capable, or not, of feeling under the stress of reality. But that he was an unfeeling wretch as soon as he dealt with pen and ink, his own or others', I will prove to you through his own words.

After telling us that Dante's lines about Ugolino are "unequalled by any other continuous thirty in the whole dominion of poetry," he hands them over "to whoever can endure the sight of an old soldier gnawing at the scalp of an old archbishop." Merely the bad taste of a man born, after all, in the eighteenth century? Perhaps. But he does not dismiss the other episode of Francesca, though it were better if he had, for he has furnished us with the following commentary:

"Then when she hath said, 'La bocca mi baciò tutto tremante,' she stops: she would avert the eyes of Dante from her: he looks for the sequel: she thinks he looks severely: she says 'Galeotto is the name of the book,' fancying by this timorous little flight she has drawn him far enough from the nest of her young loves. No, the eagle beak of Dante and his peering eyes are yet over her, 'Galeotto is the name of the book.' What matters that? 'And of the writer?' Or that either? At last she disarms him: but how?—'*That day we read no more.*'"

Nest of her young loves! There is something almost obscene, like the proceedings of a madman, in the intrusion of such Dresden china imagery into that place dumb of all light, and moaning as the sea in tempest moans, into the presence of a passion erring, but undying, of a tale which Dante ends thus: Whereas one of these spirits spoke in this fashion, the other wept so that for pity I swooned, like unto dying; and I fell, even as a dead body falls.

I said that I did not require to know anything about Landor's private life. There is enough, and too much, revelation of Landor in this notion of a Dante severely catechizing, of a Francesca all fright and blushes, and trying, vainly, to divert that sour prying pedant by talking of books and authors! And what unintended, perhaps unapprehended, self-revelations do authors sometimes consign to paper and print: "Galeotto," Francesca tells Dante, "was the name of the book, and the name also of the author!" What could be more interesting to a man of letters!

(C) CARLYLE AND THE PRESENT TENSE

Persuaded as I had become—and as I hope my Reader will also be after my analysis of De Quincey—that the greatest differences in literary effect are due mainly to different treatment of the verb, I set about an examination of the present tense, as it has been employed in our language.

It seems an idiotically obvious remark, yet one is apt

to feel a little shock of surprise when its truth is brought home to one : *the present tense makes things present;* it abolishes the narrative and the narrator. This can be verified, as the relation of relief and colour is best verified in pictures by a process of reversing, like standing a picture on its head. The ballad gives us this. For in the ballad the bulk of the telling is sometimes in the present tense, and the effects are obtained by a lapse into the past. For instance :

> He has gotten a coat of the even cloth,
> And a pair o' shoon of the velvet green;
> And till seven years were come and gone
> True Thomas on earth was never seen.

Here the ballad monger, like the uneducated folk of our own day, experiences a difficulty in following an action without actually witnessing it, hence he speaks in the present; but when he wants to sum up the result, he unconsciously employs the past tense, which makes an end of the business. And of course the alternation with the past tense produces by contrast an extremely lively sense of the present. In more artistic ballads the past tense is prevalent, and there is a jump into the present at the moment of passion and action, with a very solemn drop back into the past to give the result. Thus, in the *Braes of Yarrow* :

> Two has he hurt, and three has slain
> On the bloody braes o' Yarrow;
> But the stubborn knight crept in behind,
> And pierced his body thorough.

Again :

> She's ta'en him in her arms twa,
> And given him kisses thorough;
> She sought to bind his mony wounds,
> But he lay dead on Yarrow.

It is surely no mere coincidence that the past tense should here recur as soon as the action is finished.

I have said that the present tense abolishes the fact of narration. This has a most important result, that of doing away with the sense of cause and effect. For we cannot feel any causal connection without projecting ourselves into the past or the future. The present tense, constantly pushing us along, leaves no leisure for thinking about *why*; it hustles us into a new *how*. The present, in this case, never becomes a past, the thing which we can keep and look into; it simply drops off into limbo, vanishes entirely, as it probably does in the case of many children and of thoughtless, uneducated persons.

Moreover—and this is obvious—the present tense can bring the event before us, or us before the event, forcing us into a kind of sham belief. I say of *sham* belief, because this special kind of condition, that of dramatic illusion, is often totally different from the genuine kind of belief, what William James would probably call the " warm, familiar acquiescence " which belongs to the sense of reality. We may sit in a theatre and be hurried, bullied into interest and sympathy with something which we do not seriously believe possible. And here I should like to distinguish very clearly between this kind of realization, due to presentation on the stage, to presentation by the present tense and similar devices, and realization by such fullness and harmony, such organic synthesis of co-ordinated detail, as is produced by only the very greatest novels or poems. After watching a Sarah Bernhardt play, or reading a chapter of Dickens even with breathless interest, I am by no means haunted by a certainty that something is going on, that certain people are continuing to live, struggle and suffer, such as I have after reading Thackeray, or Stendhal, or Tolstoi; on the contrary, there is often, as one lays down the book or rises from one's seat, a feeling of abrupt breaking off, of turning off the lights. For once lapsed into silence, Lady Dedlock, Snagsby, Jo, Tulkinghorn, the wicked Chuzzlewits, cease to exist, cease therefore to develop, even like the personages of a Sardou drama after the curtain has fallen. But the Newcomes, the family of Del Dongo, and Katia, Levine, Anna, Wronsky, Natacha, Princess Mary or Peter Besukow are just as living and active when I am not reading about them as when I am; and the poisoning of Othello's mind takes place, as a matter of fact, *between* as much as *during* the acts. Why? Because all these great creations have an organic, inevitable existence of their own, and once in contact in our thoughts, they must alter and act on one another even like real things ; whereas the others are mere cleverly-painted puppets, whose movements catch and arouse our attention ; but which, once the band hushed and the lights out, collapse into heaps of wood and wire.

By this hangs the fact, often puzzling in the extreme, that " thrilling " stories are so often very poor and so often forgotten as soon as read ; also that pathetic effects can be produced by third-rate talent. The difficult, the unique thing to produce is such fascination as continues when the Reader is surrounded by different impressions, and submitted to contrary influences ; the fascination given by the life organic, which is also the life everlasting !

I have spoken of Dickens' use of the present tense. It is accompanied by several dodges converging towards the same effect. First, the dodge (the essential factor of theatrical illusion) of making the characters say their whole say, instead of telling us what they said ; with the result that the most unlikely thing is accepted because, in a way, you are made to hear it, and speeches are listened to with acquiescence which would revolt our sense of probability if their substance were merely retailed. Again, and more efficacious still, the dodge of undoing the wrappers one by one, taking the boxes one out of the other, and thereby producing, like the conjuror, a spurious belief in the reality underlying these deliberate proceedings. I will not lay un-pious hands on Dickens, whose greatness exists despite such glaring drawbacks; so I will invent a passage after his manner, burn him only in effigy. Listen! "In that street there is a house; in that house there is a room; in that room there sits a woman." Each affirmation (impossible to negative because there is no real connection with anything else) builds up a certainty in the Reader's mind. So that when we come to " and that woman is sewing a shroud," the certainty is positively crushing. How sceptical we should remain if the passage ran as follows: "In a certain house of a certain street, a woman sat sewing a shroud."

This undoing the wrappers is, as I hinted, a frequent accompaniment of the use of the present tense; it exists in most ballads, and in the popular recital (as one may still hear it in certain countries) of fairy tales. And all such processes—or all processes so employed: the present tense, the dialogued narrative, the reiterative development of unrelated facts (or, if you prefer, elaborate peeling away of one fact and showing the next), are substituted for the power of persuading the Reader by intellectual or emotional evidence that things really have happened in the way described. These processes have the advantage of saving, not merely the skill or intuition which the Writer has not got, but the intelligence and imagination, the sympathy, nay, the mere attention which the Reader may not be able or inclined to give. We are all of us at times too poor in spirit or nerves to meet the artist half-way, and help him to build his magic cities or plant his enchanted woods in our soul. It is on such occasions that a good thumping on the drum, or a good flaring of Bengal lights is highly welcome. And for this reason such aids to interest and to tears are indispensable to a large number of persons, those who happen to be intellectually inert, or never were anything else.

Now let us turn to a different aspect of the present tense and pass from depreciation to reverence. For amazing contrast to what, let us say, Dickens contrives by means of the present tense, is what Carlyle employs it to achieve. The contrast is between melodrama and the highest lyric, the lyric of prophecy. Here, say in *The French Revolution*, we become witnesses no longer of juggler's tricks, but of miracles. Let us watch and wonder.

The intellectual process is wholly different from the one we have been examining in Dickens. Carlyle's present tense does not oblige us to witness the taking of the Bastille or the death of Louis XVI. in the manner in which Dickens' present tense has obliged us to witness the death of the Man from Shropshire, or the interview of Lady Dedlock and Guppy. Louis XVI., Mirabeau, Danton, and the rest are seen but vaguely, as from a distance, recognizable on the whole by some constantly recurring attitude easily identified from afar : nay, by some quite superficial peculiarity like Dusky

D'Esprémenil, Gyrating Maurepas, or Sea-Green Robespierre, Carlyle's *Revolution* affording in this a curious contrast with Michelet's, where we learn so well the actual features, the marks of underlying temperament, the very visceral life, in many cases, of all the *dramatis personæ*. No ; in Carlyle the illusion is not in the least of the dramatic kind ; it is of the lyric. What the present tense does here is to transport us perpetually, to hustle us unceasingly, into the presence of Carlyle himself. It forces us, without allowing a pause to think or glance over our own shoulder, to look down on the revolution from the skyey post of observation where *he* sits, like some belfry gurgoyle overlooking a flattened city and a mapped out country, among storms and sunsets ; a kind of cosmic, archangelic dæmon, seeing the molehill-upsettings, the ants' processions and tumults of this world, and this world as but a tiny item of the swirling universe around him ; seeing it all with comprehension of the how and why, with pity and disdain. It sounds ridiculous to say (something like the anticlimax of a nostrum advertisement) that it is the present tense which allows Carlyle to do and be all this ; but that seems to be the case. For the present tense dispenses with all question and answer, all explanation ; and it gives continuity not to the things he speaks about, but to what he says about them, with the result that what we are witnessing is not the drama down below in streets and fields, nor even the drama in human hearts (there is wonderfully little fellow-feeling with any of his personages); but is the drama up here in the soul of this strange, marvellous prophet, Stylites-like among the forces of Nature, calling out what he sees in the little earth, in the vast infinity, like Jeremiah muttering and shouting of the past and future, "Therefore I am full of the fury of the Lord; I am weary with holding in. . . ."

There is no difference, save in length, in subject and in philosophic attitude, between the *Revolution* and a poem like "Abt Vogler," or the "Grammarian's Funeral." The doings of Jacobins and Girondins, the September Massacres or the War in Argonne, hold the same place as Browning's Illumination of the Cupola or Uphill Procession; they are episodes, illustrations, metaphors almost, bringing home the eternal laws of Being and Becoming, of Death and Renewal; and they are for Carlyle, as for Browning, what they were for the "Chorus Mysticus" : *alles Vergœngliche ist nur ein Gleichniss.*

Take a chapter of the *French Revolution* and transpose it into the past tense; you will get the same effect as by similarly transposing "Abt Vogler" or the "Grammarian" : all cohesion, all co-ordination will disappear; the transition from one subject to another will become senseless; the action, which is that of the Prophet holding forth, will come to a stop. But the consecutiveness of cause and effect, the intelligibility of history will not have been attained. For what will those sudden vocatives, invectives, prophecies become in a mere past-tense narrative of sublunary events ? And what connection will there be among those historical affairs, stranded in bits, if we no longer feel their connection in the travailing or transfigured spirit of the Seer ?

But I will take an example. I open the *French Revolution* literally at random, at the beginning of the fourth chapter of the last book. And, substituting the past tense for the present, I produce the following half-page :

" The Convention, borne on the tide of Fortune towards foreign victory, and driven by the strong wind of Public Opinion towards Clemency and Luxury, rushed fast ; all skill of pilotage was (or *being*) needed, and more than all, in such a velocity. Curious to see how it veered and whirled, yet had ever to whirl round again, and scud before the wind. If, on the one hand, it re-admitted the protesting Seventy-Three, it had, on the other, to consummate the apotheosis of Marat ; it had to lift his body from the Cordeliers' Church and transport it to the Pantheon of Great Men ; flinging out Mirabeau to make room for him. To no purpose : so strong did public opinion blow. A Gilt Youth-hood, in plaited hair tresses, tore down his busts from the Theatre Feydeau ; trampled them under foot ; scattered them, with vociferation, into the cesspool of Montmartre. His chapel was swept away from the Place du Carrousel ; the cesspool of Montmartre was to receive his very dust."

I should add that in making this slight alteration in a few verbs, I have found it inevitable to alter the pronouns also: it is impossible, for instance, to speak of the Convention as *we*: once it is a thing of the past it becomes *it* and thereby the interrogative passages become more or less childish.

This one travesty should suffice to show that in this book the present tense is not in the least a device (as people sometimes imagine) for making the narrative rattle on. As a fact the narrative never does rattle on; anything but that! The use of the present tense answers, on the contrary, to Carlyle's very personal attitude in what is really the world of contemplation; and it is, I believe we should find, only one of the inevitable literary expressions thereof; for no man's style was ever so organically personal as his, so intimately interwoven with individual habits of thought and feeling; at all events, I think, among English prose Writers. But if my Reader is not convinced we will try again, but this time purposely selecting one of the pieces of purest narrative, one, therefore, which ought, on the face of it, rather to gain than lose by transposition into the past tense. Here it is, made a hash of by that simple alteration of tenses:

"On the morrow morning, she delivered her note to Duperret. It related to certain family papers which were in the Minister of the Interior's hand . . . which

Duperret was to assist her in getting; this, then, had been Charlotte's errand to Paris? She had finished this in the course of Friday, yet said nothing of returning. She had seen and silently investigated several things. The Convention in bodily reality, she *had* seen; what the Mountain was like. The living physiognomy of Marat she could not see: he was sick at present and confined to home. About eight on the Saturday morning she purchased a large sheath knife in the Palais Royal; then straightways, in the Place des Victoires, took a hackney coach: 'To the Rue de l'École de Medicine, No. 44.' It was the residence of the Citoyen Marat! The Citoyen Marat was ill, and could not be seen; which seemed to disappoint her much. Her business was with Marat, then? Hapless beautiful Charlotte! hapless squalid Marat! From Caen in the utmost West, from Neuchâtel in the utmost East, they two were drawing nigh each other; they two had, very strangely, business together.... No answer. Charlotte wrote another note, still more pressing; set out with it by coach, about seven in the evening, herself. *Tired day labourers had again finished their work*; huge Paris was circling and simmering, manifold, according to its wont; this one fair figure had decision in it, drove straight, towards a purpose.... And so Marat, People's Friend, was ended; the lone Stylites had got hurled down suddenly from his pillar; *whither*? He that made him does know."

I have underlined the sentence about the workmen, because the result of the altered tense is particularly bad here; this sentence deals obviously with the general, the universal, the always happening, and that cannot be adequately given by the historic tense. For the same reason no large generalization can be formulated in the past tense. Compare the difference between " all men have died," and " all men are mortal ! "

The present tense, therefore, which is a rough and ready dramatic trick in the ballad, and a vulgar dodge for realization in a Writer (for all his genius) of the superficial psychology of Dickens, the present tense is also the natural form of the lyric or the prophecy. For men like Shelley, Browning or Carlyle, it is the tense of the eternal verities, which, from their very nature, have not *been*, but, like all divine things, always *are*.

VI

THE HANDLING OF WORDS

THE following studies are of the same general nature as my previous analysis of De Quincey, Landor and Carlyle; only they have been carried out on a more humble method, although I am apt to think, with more ambitious results. For a good deal has already been written, by everyone else and myself, about literary construction in the larger sense, and an incalculable lot about questions of rhetoric, whereas I seem to have been pursuing for the first time and in solitude the minutest elements to which literary style can be reduced, namely, single words and their simplest combinations.

Some years ago a letter to the *Times* from Mr. Emil Reich proposed that "statistical tests" should be applied to literature with the purpose of ascertaining in what Writers differ from one another. I do not know whether this suggestion was acted upon by anyone else; at all events I know of no results thereof except my own. Since, fired by that notion, I at once set about a census of the words contained in a page, respectively, of Defoe, Fielding, Stevenson, Pater and sundry other celebrated authors; extracting, classifying and counting up the parts of speech which they contained. By dint of this I came at length to find myself seated, metaphorically, in a circle of neat little heaps of nouns and pronouns, adjectives and participles, verbs and adverbs, and all the ambiguously named "prepositions," "conjunctions," even "adverbs," according to different grammarians and lexicographers, little words which receive least attention though they do so much of the work of a sentence. This last mentioned circumstance, as you shall see, had not so far dawned upon me. So there I sat, wondering why the numbers of nouns, verbs and adjectives were apt to be either so much the same in different Writers or so very different in the same one; and this quite irrespective of the likeness or unlikeness which I could not help feeling in their respective styles. Then I came to understand what I ought to have foreseen (but am glad I did not), namely, that the relative proportion of the more important parts of speech, the respective number of nouns, adjectives and verbs must depend in the first instance upon what the Writer has got to talk about, as distinguished from his individual propensities about how to say it. To get equal conditions for my statistical experiment, it would have been necessary to pick out specimen pages embodying exactly equivalent subject-matter, and who was to judge of that equivalence? Or else, to analyse pages enough—say all the pages he ever wrote—of each, turn about, of the authors under comparison in hopes of exhausting all the subjects he had ever written about, and thus arriving at an average classification of all the words which every one of the Writers under comparison ever employed. *The Statistical Test applied to Literature.* . . . Let me recommend the prosecution of this study to young gentlemen and ladies anxious to fit themselves out as general Reviewers.

Returning to myself, I found that though I was none the wiser for having counted the different kinds of words in a page of, say, Henry James compared with a page of Hardy, yet the course of these fruitless statistical labours had brought to light remarkable and suggestive differences in the use to which those words (and the small fry of auxiliaries, conjunctions, prepositions, etc., perhaps most of all), were put by the two Writers under comparison.

And with the gradual recognition of the pattern in which an individual author sets his words, connecting and co-ordinating them in a way peculiar to himself, there also became evident that every such pattern of words exerts its own special power over the Reader, because it has elicited in that Reader's mind conditions, or rather activities, similar to those which have produced that pattern in the mind of the Writer.

Writers and Readers. Here I was back at my old belief that literature takes effect solely by the co-operation, the interaction of him who reads with him who writes; a belief which had in the meanwhile been confirmed by my studies in the psychology of other arts.[1] As regards that of Literature, I had, as the foregoing essays show, long recognized that the Writer has always to draw upon the Reader's stored-up experience, and can tell him something he does not yet know only by evoking and rearranging what he already knew. The preceding parts of this volume embody one single inquiry; namely, which of the Reader's stored-up images and feelings are thus being drawn upon to produce a particular effect? Among which of those memories is the Writer compelling him to dwell and to move?

That had been, so far, my problem. The one I had now, almost accidentally, struck upon, was more elementary, more essential, more intimate, and certainly more recondite, and ran thus: What are the mental attitudes which the Writer forces upon the Reader? what are the mental movements he compels him to execute in that process of evoking and rearranging those past images and feelings? In short, not merely *what*, in the act of understanding, is the *Reader made to think about* by that particular Writer, but HOW is he made to think of it?

How, meaning: is the thinking to be done *easily* or

[1] Cf. *Beauty and Ugliness* (in collaboration with C. Anstruther Thomson); also my Cambridge Manual, *The Beautiful*.

with *effort*; *quickly* or *slowly*, *smoothly* or *jerkily?* How, meaning: in a *unified* way or a *scattered* way, *straightforward* or *intricate*? How also, in the sense of a horse's paces (is it an amble or a gallop?), or a man's gesture and action, leaning or supporting, leaping or stumbling, clutching, holding on or dropping. How, finally, in the sense of all those alternations of expectation, suspense, fulfilment or frustration, which make up not only the large and obvious drama of human life, but also this minute invisible drama of human thought.

Since, even in the few following analyses, we shall see the Reader following the steps of the Writer and mimicking his bearing while he is made to travel along level roads or steep or twisting paths; led straight to the subject's centre, or approaching it slowly and by stealth; made to rise and poise on steady wings with that eagle of the introduction to the *Ring and the Book*; or to go round and round the domestic lawn in the dark like Goldsmith's Tony Lumpkin. Neither is the Reader allowed to travel empty handed in the guiding (or misguiding) Writer's footsteps. Like him he must carry in his mind whatever he has been made to gather up on the way, holding its items asunder, or folding them over, or mixing them indissolubly with one another. . . . But the motions of our limbs, the acts we perform with our bodies, are few and simple and clumsy, compared with those of the mind, moving backwards and forwards in time as well as in space; and it is better to drop this inadequate metaphor of what, by his manner of disposing the parts of speech, the Writer, for better for worse, obliges the Reader to do. . . .

Since the name of that docile and active response, conscious in its results not its processes, is *Reading*. And having made all allowance for subject-matter and its detail treatment, the name of what determines the ultimate essentials of that response, so far as these lie with the Writer, is STYLE. *Style* when thus responded to by synthetic intuition. But when subjected to analysis, it turns out to be, as I hope I may prove, nothing but the Handling of Words.

(A) MEREDITH

Harry Richmond, chapter xxxvi., p. 55, of Heinemann's second volume. Five hundred words taken at random. Nouns and pronouns, 159 (of which half, roughly speaking, personal pronouns); verbs and verbal participles, 66; adjectives and adjectival participles, 25.

". . . Janet, liking both, contented herself with impartial comments. 'I always think in these cases that the women must be the fools,' she said. Her affectation was to assume a knowledge of the world and all things in it. We rode over to Julia's cottage, on the outskirts of the estate now devolved upon her husband. Irish eyes are certainly bewitching lights. I thought, for my part, I could not do as the captain was doing, serving his country in foreign parts, while such as these were shining without a captain at home. Janet approved his conduct, and was right. 'What can a wife think the man worth who sits down to guard his house door?' she answered with slight innuendo. She compared the man to a kennel-dog. 'This,' said I, 'comes of made-up matches,' whereat she was silent.

"Julia took her own view of her position. She asked me whether it was not dismal for one who was called a grass-widow, and was in reality a salt-water one, to keep fresh, with a lap-dog, a cook and a maid-servant, and a postman that passed the gate twenty times for twice that he opened it, and nothing to look for but this disappointing creature day after day! At first she was shy, stole out a coy line of fingers to be shaken, and lisped; and out of that mood came right-about-face, with an exclamation of regret that she supposed she must not kiss me now. I protested, she drew back. 'Shall Janet go?' said I. 'Then if nobody's present I'll be talked of——' said she, moaning queerly. The tendency of her hair to creep loose of its bands gave her handsome face an aspect deliriously wild. I complimented her on her keeping so fresh, in spite of her salt-water widowhood. She turned the tables on me for looking so powerful, though I was dying for a foreign princess. 'Oh, but that'll blow over,' she said, 'anything blows over as long as you don't go up to the altar'; and she eyed her ringed finger, woebegone, and flashed the pleasantest of smiles with the name of her William. Heriot, whom she always called Walter Heriot, was, she informed me, staying at Durstan Hall, the new great house, built on a plot of ground that the Lancashire millionaire had caught up, while the Squire and the other landowners were sleeping. ' And if you get Walter Heriot to come to you, Harry Richmond, it'll be better for him, I'm sure,' she added, and naïvely : ' I'd like to meet him up at the Grange.' Temple, she said, had left the Navy, and was reading in London for the Bar—good news to me.

" ' You have not told us anything about your princess, Harry,' Janet observed on the ride home.

" ' Do you take her for a real person, Janet ? One thinks of her as a snow-mountain you've been admiring.' "

The first thing striking me in this quotation from *Harry Richmond* is that these five hundred words have, among them all, only two semicolons, one of which does not even count, because it closes a quotation. Altogether the five hundred words constitute thirty sentences, counting everything closed by a full-stop as being a sentence. Of these thirty sentences, five have no comma in them ; only one, and that a quotation, begins with *and* ; not one begins with *but, for, therefore, consequently*, or any similar expression of logical separation or connection.

In the body of sentences, *but* occurs only once : " Oh, *but* that'll blow over—" : *and* occurs twelve times : five times as a mere link in an enumeration—" with a lap-dog, a cook *and* a maid-servant, *and* a postman," etc.—three times with a sense of consecutiveness, as in " At first she was shy . . . *and* lisped "—once only with the sense of connected thought : " Janet approved his conduct *and* was right." *For* is absent ; and so is *but*, the two causal particles, both differentiating, while they connect, and in so far betokening discrimination and logic. The absence of this class of words gives the quotation an irresponsible, unreasoning and impulsive air, and the lightness coming thereof. With this tallies the lack of weighing and analysing : the adjectives and adjectival participles and adverbs, " right—fresh—shy—wild," etc., being direct qualifiers designating the property of a noun, but never analysing it ; adjectives showing not so much what a substantive, a thing or person, *is*, as what the substantive *does*, how it affects others. As might be expected, in these same five hundred words I can detect only three parentheses : " I thought, *for my part*, I could not do as the captain was doing, *serving his country in foreign parts*, while such as these," etc., and "a grass-widow, *and was in reality a salt-water one*," etc., and neither of these parentheses reinforce the logical coherence.

It strikes me that in analysing style one should pay great attention to words like " of which "—" that," etc., because, referring back, as they do, implies a demand on the Reader's memory and constructive attention. There is no such demand made in this page of Meredith. If anything is claimed, is taxed, it is the

Reader's power of following short, rapid movements, and of "spotting," "twigging," their relation to one another. This is an interesting point. For, despite Meredith's habit of shooting out sentences without connection, and the impulsive impression given by his lack of causal words, the Reader finds himself called upon to synthesize, to judge and decide; more so, very often, than the less intellectual Reader at all cares to do. The fact is that he is told a number of things at whose meaning he must make a rapid guess, much as the sportsman decides on the nature of a bird or beast by a rapid series of suppositions, an argument, a synthesis.

Take this sentence: "Then if nobody's present," etc., said she, "*moaning queerly. The tendency of her hair to creep loose of its bands gave her handsome face an aspect deliriously wild*"—such a sentence is surely an unusual demand on a Reader's intuition and experience: it is the flight of a bird, and he must decide what shape and habits that flight implies. It is this odd selection of what he tells and does not tell, this omission of links, which makes Meredith a sealed book to careless or unintelligent Readers. While his style runs on without causal marks or logical forms, the choice of items is perpetually forcing us to spot and to conjecture. We are made to be intellectual in default of himself: to supply what his impatience and impulsiveness denies. Probably much of his wonderful vividness arises from this; we are never allowed to sit still and wait to be told; we must watch and decide while the words fly past, very much as we do in the case of certain real people, who, laconic and detached, work themselves into our soul by dint of the effort of understanding which their reserve, their lack of formula, imposes upon us. There is about Meredith some of the swiftness, unclutchableness, and mystery of reality, just because there is so little of the connection, analysis, synthesis of contemplation.

Connected with this is the singular similarity and straightness of direction of his sentences and half-sentences, as, most typically, in the following saying: " I always think in these cases that the women must be the fools." There is no reason given for thinking thus; it is direct and inevitable; in fact, it is thought because the *I* happens to think so. In Meredith everything seems to be whatever it is *because he thinks so,* no other possibility existing in the presence of this vivacious, headlong, delightfully egotistic mind. Remark that instead of the sentence just quoted, most people would have written: " In these cases I think that the women must be the fools," or rather, " I think the women must be the fools in these cases." The first arrangement would have qualified the women being fools by *my* way of thinking, whence a chance of error; in the second case the foolishness would have been limited to the cases in point. But, as Meredith has put it, the " in these cases " has been tucked away so close, so small, that what stands out is " I think—women fools." As a fact the literal meaning of Meredith's syntax, " I always think in these cases that the women must be the fools," is not what he conveys to us, which is: " I always think that in these cases." Yet, despite his placing of the *that*, the sentence prances on to its unqualified and unjustifiable conclusion. Probably the habitual way of expressing such a thought would be " It always seems to me that " ; but Meredith, judging by this page, eschews two forms : the oblique and the passive or deponent (false passive). The sentence after this seems an attempt, and an awkward one, to break this monotony of too many transitive verbs. " Her affectation was to assume a knowledge of the world." No one surely ever thought in such a form except for literary purposes. Meredith's meaning is " she affected to assume " ; while the *literal* meaning of this form implies something more, namely, that every one has affectations, and that this particular one was Janet's ; or that we had been given to expect an affectation from Janet, and this, sure enough, was it.

This remark leads me to think that there is great importance in the proportion, first, of passive forms to active ; secondly, of what I may call *deponent* or false passive forms, " seems," etc., to transitive forms ; thirdly, of oblique (dative or locative) forms to direct ones with accusative or possessive. In this quotation I can find only one oblique statement (since the sentence about Janet's affectation is misleading, but, as syntax, quite direct) : " The tendency of her hair to creep loose of its bands gave her handsome face an aspect deliriously wild." Here the obliqueness of the thought is further marked by the introduction of " the tendency." There is something *cryptic*, if I may be allowed such jargon, in this very plain statement, as if more were meant than meets the ear. It is as if this oddly straight-flying creature suddenly dived and disappeared. I fancy that it is such sentences which give Meredith an affected air, but also one of knowing more than he cares to tell. They must make the Philistine pause, or kick them aside as lumber. It would be interesting to examine such *cryptic* or enigmatic utterances, and the impression they leave of our dealing with unusually intuitive persons, bringing up marvellous fragmentary knowledge out of their suddenly dived-into depths ; an impression due to such sudden rupture of ordinary modes of speaking. The peculiarity exists as a positive nuisance in that very gifted *poseur*, M. Barrès. In Meredith, as in Stendhal, it is doubtless genuine and temperamental.

This analysis will, I hope, serve to suggest to my Reader and fellow student what such studies are beginning to make clear to my mind, namely, that the degree of life in a Writer's style depends upon the amount of activity which he imposes upon his Reader. If this activity is disconnected, discursive, of the rapidly *spotting, twigging* kind, the style will be living and active, but disjointed and a little enigmatic as in Meredith ; if this activity is logical, we shall have the sense of orderly and harmonious energy we shall see presently in Stevenson ; certain other modes of activity, as revealed and as communicated by syntax, we shall have occasion to analyse in Henry James and in Hewlett.

(B) KIPLING

Kim. Five hundred words taken at random, only choosing a page without dialogue, p. 118. Nouns, 157 ; verbs, 59 ; adjectives and adverbs, 53.

". . . Who would have bid him learn. But had it not been proven at Umballa that his sign in the high heavens portended war and armed men ? Was he not the friend of the stars as of all the world, crammed to the teeth with dreadful secrets ? Lastly—and firstly as the undercurrent of all his quick thoughts—this adventure, though he did not know the English word, was a stupendous lark, a delightful continuation of his old flights across the housetops, as well as the fulfilment of sublime prophecy. He lay belly flat and wriggled towards the mess-tent door, a hand on the amulet round his neck. It was as he suspected. The sahibs prayed to their god ; for in the centre of the mess-table —its sole ornament when they were on the line of march —stood a golden bull fashioned from old-time loot of the summer palace at Pekin—a red gold bull, with lowered head, ramping upon a field of rich Irish green

To him the sahibs held out their glasses and cried confusedly.

"Now the Reverend Arthur Bennett always left mess after that toast, and, being rather tired by his march, his movements were more abrupt than usual. Kim, with slightly raised head, was still staring at his totem on the table when the chaplain stepped on his right shoulder-blade. Kim flinched under the leather and, rolling sideways, brought down the chaplain, who, ever a man of action, caught him by the throat and nearly choked the life out of him. Kim then kicked him desperately in the stomach. Mr. Bennett gasped and doubled up, but, without relaxing his grip, rolled over again and silently hauled Kim to his own tent. The Mavericks were incurable practical jokers; and it occurred to the Englishman that silence was best till he had made complete inquiry.

"'Why, it's a boy,' he said, as he drew his prize under the light of the tent-pole lantern; then, shaking him severely, cried: 'What were you doing? You are a thief.'

"His Hindustanee was very limited, and the ruffled and disgusted Kim intended to keep to the character laid down for him. As he recovered his breath he was inventing a beautifully plausible tale of his relations to some mess-scullion, and at the same time keeping a keen eye on and a little under the chaplain's left armpit. The chance came; he ducked for the door-way, but a long arm shot out and clutched at his neck, snapping the amulet-string and closing on the amulet. 'Give it to me, oh give it me! Is it lost? Give me the papers ? ' The words were in English, the tinny, saw-cut English of the native bred, and the chaplain jumped.

" ' A scapular ! ' he said, opening his hand—' no, some sort of heathen charm. Why—why do you speak English ? Little boys who steal are beaten. You know that ? ' "

The first paragraph contains several *changes of grammatical direction* : a passive form " had it not been proven " turning into an active " that his sign portended." Moreover, we have a nominative which is a whole phrase ; the *it* which was *proven* becoming the *that* of the " that his sign," etc. After this a simple past—" was he not a friend of the stars," etc.—and a perfectly direct interrogation with *he* as nominative and " friend of the stars also." Both these two first sentences are interrogative, and that is their only formal connection.

Next we get a sentence with a double parenthesis, which, however, makes it only the clearer, and seems to put on weight. " Lastly—and firstly as the undercurrent of his quick thoughts—this adventure," etc. Weight is also put on by the sort of drum tap call on the attention of the *firstly* and *lastly*. The impact of this sentence is due to the damming up of the meaning by those two parentheses. The Reader is made to expect something by that *lastly* ; his attention is restrained violently by the " firstly as the undercurrent," etc.—

The Handling of Words

which, although parenthetical, is in no way an *obiter dictum* slipped in, but, on the contrary, a reduplication of that call on his expectation, a sort of multiplier of the movement. Only after these two strong pullings-back of the meaning do we get the beginning of it with *this adventure*. But the impact is heightened again by a new stoppage: "though he did not know the English word." Then only is the meaning let go, with a snap—"was a stupendous lark." There can be no doubt after this of the truth of the assertion that the chief importance of the thing from Kim's point of view, was *its being a lark*. Compare, in order to realize the mechanism of tension and restraint by which Kipling has obtained this effect, the very clear and proper, but absolutely nerveless sentence in which I have just paraphrased it! After the sort of radiating crash of that word *lark* (something corresponding to the high note of an intricate Mozart *Cadenza*), comes a sort of developing *Coda*, as, in some of Beethoven's Sonatas, symmetrically uniting the two ideas: "a delightful continuation of his old flight across the housetops as well as the fulfilment of sublime prophecy." After this elaborate and very dynamic passage describing Kim's consciousness, we pass abruptly to his bodily condition, considered objectively: "he lay belly flat and wriggled towards the mess-tent door, a hand on the amulet round his neck." Here also, after an analysis of motion, *i.e.* of abstractly considered moods, we get a very vivid image of bodily position and movement, almost an instantaneous snapshot. We have a feeling as of the boat having been finally shoved off from shore. This whole arrangement is extremely efficacious. It may, no doubt, degenerate into a trick. If such arrangements are frequent in Kipling, this would explain much of his popularity; on the other hand a sensitive Reader might resent their repetition and thereby wreck their efficacy: the fatal suspicion arising *of the thing being cheap, i.e.* perfunctory, shoddy.

This suspicion of *cheapness* happens here to be borne out by the sequel, which is evidently neither inspired by continuous interest nor revised by habitual care; this sequel is a deviation of meaning. Let us look at it. Here is the passage:

" It was as he suspected." Here the Reader's attention is twitched, and ordered suddenly back to Kim's consciousness. Now comes a logical elision, a showing to us of the thing which Kim had had in his mind, while showing us, at the same moment, its counterpart in reality (instead of saying " *he had expected that the sahibs,*" etc., " *and it appeared that they really were doing it.*"

Such sudden rolling into one of the expected thing and the actual thing has the vivacity of a conjurer's trick, of any kind of summation of two modes of calling on the attention. It is the " you are going to see," said at the instant of pulling the thing out of the hat; we get the total of two (what I must call) *movement values*, and the additional value of their comparison. So far, so good.

But now we come to the slack part. The slackness of attention, I may remark, by the way, betrays itself by the use of a wrong tense : " It *was* as he suspected. The sahibs *prayed* to their god "—the logical development requires the concordance *were praying*, because the two items cannot be on the same *plane of thought*, the first sentence telling us about Kim, the second about what Kim was telling (or had told) himself. Such a difference of what I call *plane of thought* is more important even than a difference in the *plane of time*, and, in most cases, it implies the latter. The praying of the sahibs did indeed go on contemporaneously with Kim's suspecting. But it was a continuation ; and the part of their *praying* which was going on was not the same part as the one he *suspected*, since it was a part about which a tense is used showing that the suspicion was verified by the praying, consequently must have existed apart and before. This slackness of realization of the relations in time and in logic between the two verbs, accounts for an actual and quite unintentional deflection from the meaning really in Kipling's mind. For the substitution of " prayed " for " were praying " in that juncture gives the past tense, the *prayed*, the meaning of habitual doing of the thing instead of doing it at that moment. " It was as he suspected. The sahibs prayed to their god "—means, according to English grammar and usage, that Kim was borne out in his suspicion that the sahibs *were in the habit of praying* ; whereas the true meaning is that what the sahibs were doing at that moment answered to Kim's suspicions. I fancy that the transition from Kim's consciousness to the external reality has been too much, at this moment, for Kipling's attention or lack of attention.

Let us look further at this which I might call the slackening of Kipling's grasp. "For in the centre of the mess-table—its sole ornament when they were on the line of march—stood a golden bull from old-time loot of the summer palace at Pekin—a red gold bull, with lowered head, ramping upon a field of Irish green."

Now the sentence, "the sahibs prayed to their god" represents what Kim thought, not in the least what was really happening. And the *for* of the succeeding sentence most distinctly connects its contents with this notion of Kim's; we expect to be told something to justify Kim's view about the praying to a god. We expect to be told it, moreover, *in terms of Kim's thought*, since no indication has been given that we have done with Kim's suppositions. From this point of view it is a pity to speak of a *mess-table*; for to Kim, most probably, it was only a *table*. Then Kipling tells us that the object he is about to describe was the mess-table's sole ornament when they (*they* can only refer to the sahibs, thus connecting back to Kim's imaginary people praying to an idol) "were on the line of march"—a piece of information which could scarcely have been understood by Kim, even if it had been suggested to him. For what could Kim, thinking of *idols*, understand about the regulation-ornamenting of mess-tables at one moment rather than another? Kipling, notwithstanding, continues to abound in information respecting this messtable ornament: it had been fashioned "out of oldtime loot of the summer palace at Pekin"—and it had, he tells us, "a field of Irish green," while of all this information the only piece Kim could have grasped (even had he, instead of us, been told) is that the thing in the middle of the table was a "red gold bull, with lowered head."

We have left Kim and his head full of suspicions a good way behind! Yet the next moment we jerk back to it, and look at the table no longer in the light of Kipling's information, but in that of Kim's imagination, for the ensuing sentence states, not that the officers were drinking toasts round that golden bull, but that "*to him* the *sahibs* held out their glasses and cried aloud confusedly."

But, you may say, was Kipling not to tell us the reality which had erroneously confirmed Kim's suspicions? This is just the *hic*. My contention is that had Kipling's consciousness been full of the subject, he would inevitably have seen the two orders of facts, the objective in the mess-tent, the subjective in Kim's mind, in their real relation of importance to the Reader, that is to say, the objective strictly subordinated to the subjective. He would have told us, because he would have thought of, the details of the mess-tent, etc., *only in so far as they explained Kim's ideas* and his consequent action. The mischief in all this, the origin of the faulty construction, even of the misuse of tenses, lies, I fear, in the slackness and poverty of the thought. Where ignorance of the habits of a language cannot come into account, I believe that bad syntax, bad grammar, bad rhetoric can be traced to a lapse in the power of feeling and thinking a subject. Literature, more than any other art, is a matter of intellectual and emotional strength and staying power. Let us see whether, in our five hundred words, Kipling recovers himself after this lapse.

He has been talking of Kim, so far. He now requires to talk about the chaplain. Instead of turning clean to his new point of view, he lurches over to it across that self-same sentence in which irrelevant information about the mess-table was given alongside of Kim's impressions. He has so little the feeling of having made a mistake that he builds upon it. "*Now* the Rev. A. B. always left mess after that toast." Here we are again going to meet, if not an absolutely incorrect concordance of tenses, at least a very slack employment of them. Listen! "... *always left* ... and, *being* rather tired by his march, his movements *were*," etc. To put the tenses right it would be necessary to slip in " and to-day "—or " on this occasion "—so as to connect the general statement with the particular one. Moreover, the pronouns are so placed that the verb "being tired"—is either without a nominative or governed by "his movements." Such a lapse, doubtless common enough among eighteenth-century Writers, has come to represent a real confusion of thought, at least a stumble in thinking, nowadays that grammatical habits have acquired more precision and stability.

The next sentence begins with *Kim*, as the preceding one did with the Reverend Arthur; and our attention being drawn to him and his "slightly raised head . . . staring at the totem," we are as surprised as he when "the chaplain stepped on his right shoulder-blade." After that we have first Kim as governing the action, then the chaplain; two *leads* made more conspicuous by Kim beginning with an intransitive verb and another making him passive to the Reverend Arthur's boot ("Kim flinched under the leather and . . . brought down the chaplain——"), and the chaplain deflecting from the passive into the active with the parenthetical information "ever a man of action." What would this exchange of nominatives have looked like without that parenthesis? Let us try. "Kim flinched under the leather, and, rolling sideways, brought down the chaplain, who caught him by the throat and nearly choked the life out of him." The sentence, reduced to this, is weak, without solid middle on which to articulate it; and the two nominatives strike out confusedly like puppets whose strings have got mixed up. The " ever a man of action " serves as supporting body to these disjointed members. It steadies the rest, and makes the continued exchange of nominatives in a way rhythmical; for the interchange continues. But there comes a sudden break, showing that this seesaw of nominatives has been accidental and the result of disorder. For after "silently hauled Kim to his tent"—we get this other thing, "The Mavericks were incurable practical jokers." After this comes the second half explaining this sudden introduction of the regiment—" and it occurred to the Englishman that silence was best till," etc.

It is an odd proof of deficient logical feeling, and (in so far, perhaps also, of real sense of consecutive action), that Kipling should not have written: "*for* the Mavericks were," etc. As it is, this whole sentence is chaotic; and although the verbs employed are consecutive in their meaning, " Kim kicked "—" Mr. Bennett gasped and doubled up . . . rolled over . . . silently hauled Kim," etc.—the lack of logical connection makes them into a series of ill-understood jerks, *as they no doubt would have seemed to bystanders.*

The lack of causal clearness continues; perhaps I might add, Kipling's satisfaction with an imperfectly stated causal relation. " His (the Reverend Arthur's) Hindustanee was very limited, and the ruffled and disgusted Kim intended to keep to the character laid down for him." This follows upon two Hindustanee words, which this unstrung sentence explains in retrospective fashion. It is possible that such logical slackness may lighten the trouble of some Readers, those who don't care to follow the *hang of an action*, and are satisfied with staring at mere movement. If so, I am not sure whether this way of writing may not be a kind of *impressionism*, a deliberate trick on Kipling's part. For note the sequel: "The chance came; he ducked for the doorway; but a long arm shot out and clutched at his neck," etc.

If impressionism, however, it is unsuccessful; because all impressionism, literary as much as pictorial, depends upon *a fixed point of view* whence unity and intelligibility are obtained. Now this elision of the man to whom the arm belonged does not go with a point of view. Not Kim's; for to Kim the central occurrence would not be the nominative *arm* actively shooting out from the inexplicable, but a nominative *Kim* suddenly collared [hence become passive] by a very well guessed-at chaplain. And if not Kim's point of view, then whose? The absence of words denoting the *causal attitude* (and all words save nouns, adjectives, verbs, and their satellites are words deciding the Reader's attitude) is conspicuous in the next sentence also: "The words were in English—the tinny, saw-cut English of the native bred, *and* the chaplain jumped."

And? the chaplain may be said to jump also over this connecting link. This gives vivacity, but also a sense of emptiness and superficiality. The effect is

increased by the spasmodic speech of the chaplain—
"A scapular," he said, opening his hand. "Why—why—do you speak English? Little boys who steal are beaten. You know that?" I have no doubt the chaplain actually did speak like that. But it affects me as Reader exactly like a snapshot leaving the *how* of a movement unintelligible. A certain scamping of the passage is shown by not altering the *why*, which may also mean "*for what reason*," and which by no means announces itself at once as an interjection.

I am sorry that accident should have furnished me with so poor a page from what is, in many ways, a great and charming book. But having trusted to mere chance in my selections from Meredith, Henry James, Hardy, Stevenson, and Hewlett, I had no right to pick and choose when it came to Kipling. Of course there must be, in even the most inspired or the most careful Writers, a certain amount of work in which inspiration or care has been insufficient, work done in moments of their being, intellectually, *below par*; or else work done at the beginning of a day before the mind has warmed to the task. On the other hand, it is in such less fortunate work that we can judge of what I should call the Writer's *constitutional tradition*, of the habits and standards which operate in re-reading and revision; and I think it is probable that Kipling is among the most unequal and hasty, and in so far the least disciplined, of contemporary English Writers.

(C) STEVENSON

Travels with a Donkey in the Cévennes, p. 151. Five hundred words. Nouns and pronouns, 138; verbs, 70; adjectives and adjectival participles, 41.

"All was Sunday bustle in the streets and in the public house, as all had been Sabbath peace among the mountains. There must have been near a score of us at dinner by eleven before noon; and after I had eaten and drunken, and sat writing up my journal, I suppose as many more came dropping in one after another, or by twos and threes. In crossing the *Lozère* I had not only come among new natural features, but moved into the territory of a different race. These people, as they hurriedly despatched their viands in an intricate sword-play of knives, questioned and answered me with a degree of intelligence which excelled all that I had met, except among the railway folk at Chasseradès. They had open telling faces, and were lively both in speech and manner. They not only entered thoroughly into the spirit of my little trip, but more than one declared, if he were rich enough, he would like to set forth on such another.

"Even physically there was a pleasant change. I had not seen a pretty woman since I left *Monastier*, and there but one. Now of the three who sat down with me to dinner, one was certainly not beautiful—a poor timid thing of forty, quite troubled at this roaring table d'hôte, whom I squired and helped to wine, and pledged and tried generally to encourage, with quite a contrary effect; but the other two, both married, were both more handsome than the average of women. And *Clarisse* ? What shall I say of *Clarisse* ? She waited at table with a heavy, placable nonchalance, like a performing cow; her great grey eyes were steeped in amorous languor; her features, although fleshy, were of an original and acute design; her mouth had a curl; her nostril spoke of dainty pride; her cheek fell into strange and interesting lines. It was a face capable of strong emotion, and, with training, it offered the promise of delicate sentiment. It seemed pitiful to see so good a model left to country admirers and a country way of thought. Beauty should at least have touched society; then, in a moment, it throws off a weight that lay upon it, it becomes conscious of itself, it puts on an elegance, learns a gait and a carriage of the head, and, in a moment, *patet dea*. Before I left I assured *Clarisse* of my hearty admiration. She took it like milk, without embarrassment or wonder, merely looking at me steadily with her great eyes; and I own the result upon myself was some confusion. If *Clarisse* could read English, I should not dare to add that her figure was unworthy of her face. Hers was a case for stays; but that may perhaps grow better as she gets up in years.

" *Pont de Montvert*, or *Greenhill Bridge,* as we might say at home, is a place memorable in the story of the Camisards. It was here that the war broke out; here that those southern Covenanters slew their *Archbishop Sharpe*. . . ."

The whole first page gives the sense of ponderation. We get, in close sequence, two sentences of appreciation of circumstances, nay of supposition. The two first sentences had been direct affirmations : *All had been Sabbath peace among the mountains. There must have been near a score of us at dinner,* etc.; the reference is to something which is not the Writer. In the second half of the second sentence we suddenly double back to Stevenson—" and after I had eaten and drunken," etc.—not for his own sake, however, but merely using him as a sort of fixed point of view whence to see the real object under discourse. Then we get " as many more came dropping in." His slipping in here of " I suppose " (when the objective meaning could have been got equally by " *about* as many more ") prepares one for a perpetual give and take between the told thing and the teller, which is very characteristic of Stevenson's mode of exposition.

In the very next sentence—" In crossing the Lozère I had not only come among new natural features," etc. —the *I* returns, the mere statement turns into personal narrative. The last sentence of this paragraph—" They had open telling faces, and not only entered thoroughly into the spirit of my little trip "—sums up this interplay of the traveller and the journey with the reference to the proper " entering into the spirit of my little trip." The whole of this paragraph is active ; even in a place where a passive might be expected, Stevenson makes himself the nominative of *supposing*, while the *people* remain nominative of " *dropping in.*" The seesaw in the subject-matter is given by a seesaw between nominatives of different parts of the sentence.

[Note meanwhile the direction given to the sentences and half-sentences as indicated by their initial words: "*All; there; and after; I suppose; in crossing; these people; they had; they not only.*"]

Let us go on with the verbs; I fancy we shall find the same variety, but variety coherent and co-ordinated. First, "*all was*"; then, "*all had been*"; this pattern of simple and reduplicated past is continued: "There *must have been*"—"I *had* eaten and drunken"—and this is further complicated by the combination of the simple past and present participles: "*had* eaten, *sat* writing." Again we have the same structure—"In *crossing* the Lozère I *had* not only *come*," etc.—only reversed, the participle coming first, and this time with a compound past "had come."

These changes in tense are, so to speak, *dimensional movements in time*, and their variety and intricacy enlarges it, as variety of movement in space enables us to feel an object as cubic. The next sentence, "these people, as they hurriedly despatched . . . questioned and answered me," etc.—somehow leaves an impression of the *presentness* then, of that past.

In the next paragraph, I find no passive form, nor even one of those apparently passive forms, which, from Latin analogy, we may call *deponent*. "I had not seen a pretty woman since I left Monastier, and there but one. Now of the three who sat down with me to dinner, one was certainly not beautiful," etc. At the outset there is a *chassez-croisez* between two nominatives; the accusative *woman* of the first sentence becoming the nominative of the next. Let me note a lapse of grammar—alack, ye pedants!—for we had *woman* in the singular, and now, behold, have " of the three." But, as I think we should find also in Sterne, this lapse, so far from seeming awkward, has a cavalier grace, as of a hat a little askew. To return to our actives and passives: there is, as we shall see by continuing the quotation, only *one* deponent, and of this the real quality is that of an adjective: " And Clarisse? What shall I say of Clarisse? She waited at table with a heavy, placable nonchalance, like a performing cow; her great grey eyes *were steeped* in amorous languor ";—and this apparent deponent breaks agreeably through the series of active verbs governing more obvious adjectives: " Her features . . . *were*, her mouth *had* a curl; her nostril *spoke* of, etc.; her cheek *fell* into," etc. All this is not merely variety, it is movement.

Stevenson, by introducing verbs of movement about things which are motionless, supplies that sense of activity which we get from the fact of the person spoken of being in movement (the woman, remember, was waiting at table), and which he could not keep on reiterating. I feel certain that writing is largely an art of such substitutions of effect, one set of items being made to furnish an impression required for another. Hence the utter mistakenness of criticizing single expressions, as in the case of Carducci's famous *Silenzio verde*, of which pedants repeated, that silence, being unappreciable by the eye, could not be *green*; overlooking that the greenness and the silence produced equivalent impressions, and converged in our consciousness.

Again, let us return to Stevenson: we are now no longer hurrying across provinces, but in a dining-room, looking about us leisurely. And the sentences, hitherto short, have now expanded into much complexity of clause. I would point out that the sudden breaking in with a question which is in reality an interjection (—" And Clarisse? What shall I say of Clarisse? ") gives the page not merely a lyrical (or mock lyrical) vivacity, but, by association with certain eighteenth-century forms, a certain gallant affectation, an archaism transfiguring what would otherwise be mere eyeing of a waitress in a restaurant: 'tis the opening of a bag of graceful, old-world associations. This little interlude prepares us (being in fact the expression of the already existing attitude in Stevenson) for the order of thought in the next sentence :—" Beauty should at least have touched society; then, in a moment, it throws off a weight that lay upon it; it becomes conscious of itself, it puts on an elegance, learns a gait and a carriage of the head, and in a moment, *patet dea*"—ending with that Virgilian phrase (which also takes us back to the eighteenth century of "And Clarisse?"—so purely literary): *Patet Dea*.

By this time we are just prepared for "If Clarisse could read English, I should not dare to add that her figure was unworthy of her face. Hers was a case for stays, but that may perhaps grow better as she gets up in years." The sentence—" Hers was a case for stays "—acts, I think, to bring us back to homeliness, and especially to the individual, *narrative* reality.

Remark how in examining this whole passage I have passed, continually, from the *form* to the actual *contents*; in literature they are closely intermeshed in the effect on the Reader. It is *form* to think in this and not a different, succession of *items*; and it is *realization* of the items to produce such forms. Note that we get a consistency and co-ordination in Stevenson's mood (*i.e.* the subjective matter under discourse) exactly answering to the co-ordination in the mere words, as explained before. Let us examine into one or two other points:

The passage thus accidentally selected begins with a deliberate symmetrical repetition: "*All* was Sunday bustle in the streets . . . as *all* had been Sabbath peace upon the mountains." It is a figure of symmetrical comparison: *Sunday—Sabbath*; *bustle—peace*; *streets —mountains*. But we do not again get any such symmetrical form, at least in the five hundred words under examination ; and there is a looser logical tie at the end of the paragraph : "*not only* entered into the spirit of my little trip, *but* more than one declared," etc. Persistent use of such symmetrical exposition, as we get it in Johnson, Gibbon, and Macaulay, awakens, in a Reader at all sensitive, the suspicion of perfunctoriness on the part of the Writer, of a curtailing and twisting of facts for easier exhibition ; since facts do not exist in this neat form, nor feelings either. Whence the inference that Writers, who see or show things in this convenient but mendacious manner must be either pedants or charlatans.

Nothing could be further from Stevenson's practice. Besides, this passage is extraordinarily full of logical forms ; loose but not the less effective. In the sentences under examination I find a great number and variety of expressions denoting intellectual processes and stimulating them : " I suppose "—" or "— " not only "—" but "—" not only "—" but " (second time)—" Even "—" Now of the "—" other two "— " although "—" It seemed "—" I own." This means that the Writer (and the Reader of course also) discriminates, separates, calculates, compares and draws conclusions. Moreover, the short initial phrase of the second paragraph, " Even physically there was a pleasant change "—forestalls the summing up the Reader is going to be made to make, even as the previous paragraph contains a longer forestalling of the same kind. " In crossing the Lozère," etc. And, although the whole passage is perfectly clear, it is remarkably complicated : full of turns and superpositions, however frankly and carefully pointed out. So that I can easily imagine that although this degree of logical activity is a pleasure to the intelligent Reader, an actual enhancement of the adventurous and fanciful subject-matter, it may represent to the stupid or tired Reader an exertion which will make him prefer something " more straight to the point," meaning thereby something vaguely intelligible despite inattention.

Looking at these five hundred words in the spirit of a graphologist, one may generalize as follows : first, great balance, what in the contemporary French pseudo-physiological jargon would be noted as belonging to a *magnifique equilibré*; second, richness of modalities ; third, steady and lively activity without ups and downs, promising in moderation and always achieving ; fourth, equally keen perception of outer things and of human qualities ; fifth, active imagination always returning to the starting point (*vide* Clarisse) ; the same *coming back on itself*, the very same completion, as regards feeling and logical processes ; sixth, wonderful, I will not say *self-restraint*, but natural discipline, co-ordination of functions. No exaggeration, no watering down ; no false starts, no loose ends. A humane, many-sided, well-compacted, singularly active, willing and unegoistic personality : a creature in whose company our soul loves to dwell, because we receive much, and are made to give more and better than usual.

(D) HARDY

Tess of the d'Urbervilles, p. 42 (cheap edition). Five hundred words. Nouns, pronouns, and nominal words, 108 ; verbs, 62 ; adjectives and adverbs, 62.

" However Tess found at last approximate expression for her feelings in the old Benedicite that she had lisped from infancy, and it was enough. Such high contentment with such a slight initial performance as that of her having started towards a means of independent living was a part of the Durbeyfield temperament.

" Tess, it is true, wished to walk uprightly, while her father did nothing of the kind ; but she resembled him in being content with immediate and small achievements, and in having no mind for laborious effort towards such petty social advancement as could alone be effected by a family so heavily handicapped as the once powerful d'Urbervilles were now. There was, it should be said, the energy of her mother's unexpended family, as well as the natural energy of Tess's years, rekindled after the experience which had so overwhelmed her for the time.

" Let the truth be told : women do as a rule live through such humiliations, and regain their spirits and again look about them with an interested eye. While there's life there's hope is a conviction not so entirely unknown to the betrayed as some amiable theorists would have us believe.

"Tess Durbeyfield, then, in good heart, and full of zest for life, descended the Egdon Slopes lower and lower towards the dairy of her pilgrimage. The marked difference, in the final particular, between the rival vales now showed itself. The secret of Blackmoor was best discovered from the heights above; to read aright the valley before her it was necessary to descend into its midst. When Tess had accomplished this feat, she found herself to be standing on a green-carpeted level, which stretched to the east and west as far as the eye could reach. The river had stolen from the higher tracts and brought in particles to the vale all this horizontal land; and now exhausted, aged, and attenuated, lay serpentining along through the midst of its former spoils. Not sure of her direction, Tess stood still upon the hemmed expanse of verdant flatness, like a fly on a billiard-table of indefinite length, and of no more consequence to her surroundings than that fly.

"The sole effect of her presence upon the placid valley so far had been to excite the mind of a solitary heron which, after descending to the ground not far from her path, stood with neck erect, looking at her. Suddenly there arose from all parts of the lowlands a prolonged and repeated call. From the furthest east to the furthest west, the cries spread as if by contagion, accompanied in some cases by the barking of a dog. It was not the expression of the valley's consciousness that beautiful Tess had arrived, but the ordinary announcement of milking-time, half-past four o'clock, when the dairymen set about getting in the cows.

"The red and white herd nearest at hand which had been phlegmatically waiting," etc.

This passage forces me to examine into the nature of the words I have counted in my several analyses. For whereas the other Writers analysed give from 132 to 159 nouns, Hardy gives 108; while verbs rise to 62, higher, that is, than Kipling and Hewlett, and adjectives to 62; that is to say 9 more than Kipling, 8 more than Hewlett, who was highest on my list. First let me see how I account for those additional adjectives.

At first sight, on re-reading the passage from end to end, I am not struck by many adjectives and adverbs to omit. It does perhaps seem unnecessary that the river should be both "exhausted, aged, and attenuated." But on reconsidering the sentence it is difficult to decide which of these adjectives is the superfluous one. *Exhausted* is not implied in attenuated, nor is either *exhausted* or *attenuated* implied in *aged*, nor *aged* in the two others. The expression tallies with the thought; and it is the thought itself which is redundant and vague. We are being *told all about* the locality, not what is necessary for the intelligence of the situation. For instance, in these five hundred words we are twice given points of the compass—that is to say, information which has nothing to do with the subject in hand, and which the Reader neither needs, nor, as a fact, is able to apply. Since points of the compass can add to the meaning of a passage only if: (1) We already possess the geography of the region, and require to feel in which direction on the map the traveller is going; thus it is of consequence to know that Stevenson drove his donkey, say, south-east or south-west; it is of consequence if I say, "forests lying north of Paris" or "the seaboard west of Rome," etc. (2) Points of the compass can be mentioned to some purpose if they imply a peculiarity of light or warmth or the time of day; we learn something when we are told that "the sun was now in the west," or that a room "faces north."

But what do we learn when Hardy tells us that a particular valley, whose name is imaginary, *stretched to the east and west as far as the eye could reach*? The only movement in one's mind is a faint question, "Was the valley so very narrow as not to stretch at all north and south; and, if it was so narrow, is the word *stretched* very applicable to its east and west direction?

We get a reference to this detail of orientation further on—"from the furthest east to the furthest west the cries spread"—and, since we perceive no reason for this dragging in of points of the compass, we imagine one, and get a vague idea that the sounds rose in the east in some sort of connection with the sun. At least this is my experience; and I feel annoyed at finding that that east and west really implies nothing about the sounds.

I therefore suspect that all this talk of orientation is a mere mark of irrelevant writing, of saying everything there is to be said about the subject, as we have seen about the river. It is a soliloquy of Hardy's about two valleys and their contents, without reference to the story or the Reader. Listen to him! "The marked difference, in the final particular, between the rival vales, now showed itself "—" The secret of Blackmoor was best discovered from the heights around; to read aright the valley before her it was necessary to descend into its midst."

Now, we can quite imagine a passage in Stevenson comparing two valleys much in this manner; but then the valleys and his journey, the genius of the place, so to speak, would be the chief personages; and the points of comparison would be such as the Reader, who had never been in that neighbourhood, could visualize in fancy. But here we are not merely listening to Hardy's recollections poured out without reference to us, but we are, while doing so, interrupted in our attempt to follow the adventures and the inner vicissitudes of Tess. All this detail about the geological formation, " the river had stolen from the higher tracts and brought in particles to the vale all this horizontal land—" all this orientation and comparison of lie of land is subject to the sentence: " Tess Durbeyfield then . . . full of zest for life, descended the Egdon Slopes lower and lower towards the dairy of her pilgrimage." And the sentence of comparison between the two valleys is suddenly succeeded by "when Tess had accomplished this feat she found herself to be standing on a green-carpeted level," etc. After which we again leave Tess in order to remark on the geological history, as noted above.

After disposing of the river in the prehistoric past, we revert to Tess, who "was not quite sure of her direction." And this lack of certainty is in Hardy as well as in his heroine.

Notice how he tells us the very simple fact of how Tess stops to look round: "Tess . . . stood still upon the hemmed expanse of verdant flatness, like a fly on a billiard-table of indefinite length." "*Hemmed* expanse," that implies that the expanse had limits; it is, however, compared to a billiard-table "of indefinite length." Hardy's attention has slackened, and really he is talking a little at random. If he visualized that valley, particularly from above, he would not think of it, which is bounded by something on his own higher level (*hemmed*, by which he means *hemmed in*), in connection with a billiard-table which is bounded by the tiny wall of its cushion. I venture to add that if, at the instant of writing, he were feeling the variety, the freshness of a valley, he would not be comparing it to a piece of cloth, with which it has only two things in common, being flat and being green; the utterly dissimilar flatness and greenness of a landscape and that of a billiard-table.

We are surely in presence of slackened interest, when the Writer casts about for and accepts any illustration, without realizing it sufficiently to reject it. Such slackening of attention is confirmed by the poor structure of the sentence, "a fly on a billiard-table of indefinite length *and* of no more consequence to the surroundings than that fly." The *and* refers the "of no more consequence" in the first instance to the billiard-table. Moreover, I venture to think that the whole remark was not worth making: why divert our attention from Tess and her big, flat valley, surely easy enough to realize, by a vision of a billiard-table with a fly on it? Can the two images ever grow into one another? is the first made clearer, richer, by the second? How useless all this business has been is shown by the next sentence: "The sole effect of her presence upon the placid valley so far had been to excite the mind of a solitary heron, which, after descending to the ground not far from her path, stood, with neck erect, looking at her." Leave out all about the billiard-table, and the sentences coalesce perfectly and give us all we care to know. Such as Hardy has left them they give us a good deal more; not indeed of items, but of words. "The *sole effect* of her *presence,*" etc. Here are two nouns, both abstract, and an adjective not of quality but degree. Then "so far" — with the tense "had been"—giving the notion of far longer time than Tess probably stayed looking about. Moreover, her presence excited not the solitary heron, but the *mind* of the solitary heron. And the heron, we are told, "descended to the ground *not far* (why not *near*?) from her path," etc. How all the action of the heron's downward flight and sudden inquisitive stopping is lost in all these circuitous phrases! We scarcely see the heron at all.

After all these meanderings the next sentence fairly startles us, and since it tells us of something startling it is right it should startle us. But it does so merely by contrast with the vagueness of the preceding sentences; for in itself it is weak and vague. "Suddenly there arose ... a call" is the only active element in it; "*from all parts* of the lowland" is again feeble, for the meaning is simply "from all around," and the reference to *parts*, the reiteration of *lowlands* (as if by this time we hadn't been told often enough that we were in a valley!) is mere padding.

The next sentence is largely a repetition of this, with the added and useless orientation, "from the furthest east to the furthest west—the cries spread." But Hardy must needs add "as if by contagion." This adds something, undoubtedly, to the meaning; but the idyllic impression of the pastoral cries waking each other as they spread does not gain by suggesting the spread of a malady! Nor is Hardy even now satisfied: "accompanied *in some cases* by the barking of a dog." He has given us an orientation, he has explained that the cries arose in echoing succession; why bring in "some cases," why say "accompanied by," when the meaning is simply "and here and there the bark of a dog."

But Hardy has started on further and even less necessary information, for he tells us: "It was not the expression of the valley's consciousness that beautiful Tess had arrived"—who in his senses would have thought that it was? Meanwhile we have got two abstractions and a personification, in a cumbersome attempt to weld together the disjointed items about the valley's origin (old exhausted stream), its orientation, flatness, greenness, billiard-table, etc., with Tess's journey. I can only surmise that Hardy has become suddenly aware of having left Tess in the lurch and wants to make up for it. Then he is afraid lest we should take this poetico-mythological "expressions" of the valley's consciousness too seriously. It wasn't that in the very least, he hastens to tell us, it was "but the ordinary announcement of milking-time," and he adds "half-past four o'clock, when the dairymen set about getting in the cows."

This page is so constructed, or rather not constructed, that if you skip one sentence, you are pretty sure to receive the same information in the next; and if you skip both, you have a chance of hearing all you need later on. This makes it lazy reading; and it is lazy writing.

Lazy reading is not without attractions, for we are

often lazy; and I can conceive that some of Hardy's popularity, despite certain great qualities of fantastic imagination, tragic feeling, and a certain almost pantheistic or mythological spirit—all of them rather caviare to the general—may be due to this indulgence of the Reader's indolence. But it is bought at the price of the Reader's indifference.

There are moods when we prefer to read a novel, skipping whole phrases and passages and moving in slow and somnolent fashion; but in more wakeful moments our energy, seeking for employment, resents these heaps of useless words to be thrown aside; and it demands of an author that he direct it along definite ways, at definite speeds. Our attention, when we really give it, wants to be made to move briskly, rhythmically, to march, nay, as Nietzsche puts it, *to dance*.

Now marching and dancing are done in literature, as in all art, by the awakening of the activities of measuring, comparing and unifying. Furthermore, all these analyses of mine have persuaded me that the *active quality* in literature is not due so much to a richness of words—of verbs—expressing action, as to the presence of words, and arrangements of sentences, *forcing the Reader to think*. *To think*; for literature, let us remember, deals exclusively with thought and its modes, and constructs its patterns, not of sounds or lines, but of impressions and inferences. To *think*, not in the sense of thinking whether a thing is true or false, the subject of a sentence put back, as it were, from the sphere of words into that of real experience; but to *think* in the sense of following, realizing the relations in which, by the placing of words, this subject is put. The intellectual activity of the Reader is called forth in realizing the comparative importance of the different items mentioned, their dependence upon one another. He is forced to pass from side to side, seeking equivalents and differences, backwards and forwards, identifying causes and effects, all round, in front and behind, getting at things at their proper angle of vision: he is made to construct the meaning, as the sentence is constructed, in a more or less elaborate logical architecture, or, if you prefer, counterpoint; and made to do so at a pace, with an accentuation, imposed by the Writer.

Now this activity of the Reader, when he makes a sufficiently complete response, is stimulated and kept alive by the swiftness and certainty demanded of it, and by the constant need for perceiving and co-ordinating a variety of items. A page of literature, whatever its subject-matter, gives us the impression of movement in proportion as it makes *us* move: not forwards merely, but in every direction; and in such manner as to return back on the parts and fold them into unity.

All this is mainly a work of logical thinking. To begin with, there is the general distribution of the subject-matter, the amount of cause and effect, of similarity and dissimilarity, which the Reader is made to perceive. In this page of *Tess*, such distribution can scarcely be said to exist. The five hundred words I have analysed begin with psychological remarks on the state of mind of Tess, on the hereditary characteristics of her family, with an *excursus* on the peculiarities of the feminine mind. All this, loosely but sufficiently, put together, should constitute the end of a chapter; we ought to be allowed more than a mere new paragraph before passing from this inner landscape to the outer one; or else the two ought to be interwoven, as we find it, even trickily, in Zola and other French Writers, by attempting to show how the new scenery affected Tess's mood. Hardy has neither broken off and paused, nor worked the two subjects into one another. He has connected them by one little word only, the word *then*. "Tess Durbeyfield *then*, in good heart, and full of zest for life, descended the Egdon Slopes." This might be sufficient, the *then* standing vaguely for all the foregoing, and loosely connecting the past with the present, if only we continued to talk of Tess; if, for instance, the passage continued, "Crossing the hill, Tess saw the new valley before her and noted its difference from the one she had left behind her." But Tess is simply dropped; not even set about some action which should feel as continued behind our backs, and which we should find at a further stage, when we revert to her. Tess is forgotten; and, instead, our attention is called, without anything denoting deliberate intention, to all those details of lie of the land, and geological structure. Then suddenly Hardy would seem to have remembered Tess, and felt that she ought not to have been neglected. But so perfunctory is his co-ordination, so slack his realization, that he reverts to her with an expression which is utterly unsuitable. Having introduced the two words "*before her*" quite irrelevantly into the sentence, "the secret of Blackmoor was best discovered ... to read aright the valley *before her* it was necessary to descend into its midst," he finds no more appropriate allusion to Tess's walk down than to call it *a feat*, and describe it as "accomplished."

I mention this singular inaptness of expression, because I regard it as a sign of the general slackening of attention, the vagueness showing itself in the casual distribution of the subject-matter; showing itself, as we shall see in lack of masterful treatment of the Reader's attention, in utter deficiency of logical arrangement. These are the co-related deficiencies due to the same inactivity and confusion of thought.

I will not go over the subsequent passages again; my Reader can verify at a glance this lack of coherence, of sense of direction, particularly if he will bear in mind, for comparison, Stevenson's marvellously constructed account of his descent from one Cévennes valley into another, and of their respective physical and moral characteristics. The two passages — Hardy's and Stevenson's—represent, within the limit of endurable writing, the two extremes of intellectual slackness and intellectual activity. Having pointed out so much, I will proceed to the words and sentences which, in this page of Tess, are of the class which directs, or rather ought to direct, the Reader's attention.

The intellectual movement I have alluded to is not imparted to sentences by the mere preponderance of verbs as such; it depends mainly upon the complexity of verbal concordance; upon the arrangement of different tenses with reference to one another, by which the Reader, passing from present to future, from more remote to less remote past, from the historic past to subjunctives and gerunds, is forced at once to realize very definitely the exact import of each grammatical form and to connect them swiftly with one another, thus establishing a kind of *intellectual space* in which the logical concatenation is held, and a series of *planes of action*, more central (*i.e.* present) or more back (*i.e.* past), or more forward (*i.e.* future), and in various positions of mutual dependence, along which the Reader's attention shifts the nouns and adjectives obedient to the Writer's behest and thus grasps the exact meaning. Here again I would refer to that page of Stevenson's for an example of richness and clearness of verbal concordance, and also to the coming page of Hewlett.

236 The Handling of Words

Bearing this contrast in mind, let us examine the quoted five hundred words from *Tess*. There is a distinct preponderance of the direct narrative tense. In the first sentence it is complemented with its co-relative and with the auxiliary: "Tess *found* in the old Benedicite . . . that she *had* lisped." Here are, so to speak, two *planes* of past. After this come over a hundred words with nothing save the narrative tense, "was — wished — did — resembled—effected—were" — with only two, and only slightly accentuated correspondence of other tenses (I leave out the present of "it is true," which does not belong to the story), namely "resembled him in being and having," these participles introducing a sense of presentness into that narrative past; and "having no mind for . . . effort towards such . . . *as could . . . be effected* by a family so heavily handicapped as . . . now *were*."

This sentence, without much accentuation, is constructed in a clear and logical interchange of reference to present and to future, while remaining in the past. And it is undoubtedly the most braced and active sentence of the whole quotation.

Let us examine the terms in the succeeding one. Here there is variety: "*was* (narrative past); *it should be said* (present with future involved); *rekindled*—had *overwhelmed* (remote past); *let* the *truth be told* (imperative); women *do . . . live*; regain; *look about; while there's life there's hope; is a* condition; *would have us believe.*" There is even considerable variety; but quite insufficient co-ordination.

The present tense particularly and the imperative "*let the truth be told, women do live,*" etc., is a mere chatty interruption. So far from feeling that we must attend, we have the sense that the author is pleasantly divagating into generalities, whither we may, but need not, follow him.

Instantly after this we get the historic tense again, with its concording tense—" Tess *descended* "—" The difference now *showed* itself "—" The secret was best *discovered* "—" to *read* . . . it was necessary *to descend* " —" had *accomplished* "—" found herself *standing* "— " *stretched* "—" could *reach.*" But this concordance, so far from being rigorously logical and impelling our thoughts in a definite direction, leaves the impression of utter perfunctoriness. For one does not expect to hear these unchangeable topographical peculiarities treated in narrative style; and there is an aimless emphasis in " the secret of Blackmoor was best discovered from the heights around; to read aright the valley *before her* it was necessary to descend into its midst "; and that member, "*before her,*" slipped in for conscience' sake (Tess having been left in the lurch), gives a wrong personal meaning to the perfectly general statement about *descending into its midst*; and contrasts with the extreme generality of the previous statements.

As already remarked, all this dropping and taking up

of Tess like a puppet, sometimes plopping her into the landscape and sometimes withdrawing her, entirely confuses the *planes* on which we think out this information. The remote past "*the river had stolen*"—coming as it does immediately after "Tess *found herself standing*"—appears to be concordant with it, and suggests that the river had done its *stealing*, not as Hardy means, in prehistoric ages, but *while Tess was standing there*, or only just before. Substitute for the river "shepherd," and we see the whole thing happening alongside, a little behind, so to say, Tess's standing.

From word 350 to 500, approximately, the historic tense continues: "Tess stood"—with very simply concorded, remoter pasts—"*had* been to excite . . . a heron . . . after descending stood—then arose . . . the cries spread . . . accompanied. . . . It was not"— few verbs, and so connected that scarcely any variety of what I must call "planes in time" are established.

It is, so to speak, all on the flat; and the attention is not called upon to understand when or why.

There is thus very little of the first item which determines a sense of activity in literature. There is still less of the other, namely, correlation in time and space of the words and arrangements implying logical processes and forcing the Reader to measure, compare (therefore to recollect), and see cause and effect. In the very first sentence of all, which we have had occasion to find the best in other ways also, there is a comparative wealth of the words implying different modes of intellectual movement : "*However—at least—it is true—while* her father—*but it should be said—let the truth be told.*" These words diminish significantly as we pass to the second half of our quotation, where the slackness of writing becomes conspicuous ; a change so great that I venture to think that with the words " Tess Durbeyfield then "—there begins another day's work, betraying the listlessness of the resumption of a daily task, and that difficulty of warming to the subject which often obliges more careful Writers to write afresh the sentences with which they have, so to speak, merely got their pen under weigh.

But to the lack of complexity of tense and logical form (meaning as these do activity of realization, memory, foresight, comparison, and causality on the Reader's part) we must add, if we are to explain the weakness and vagueness of this page, also the number of unnecessary qualifications.

A word which qualifies will undoubtedly arrest the attention and set up a movement of intellectual weighing on the part of the Reader. But not if he recognize that it is due to mere non-committal and habit of adding a *rather* or an *at least* when not needed. *Then* it comes to express mere hesitation, lack of energy of the Writer ; and the Reader passes it over as he would any other form of mental stammering.

Now in these five hundred words a large proportion

of the statements are qualified where no qualifying is needed. We have " at least approximate expression " —" such a *slight initial performance* "—" *immediate* and *small* achievements "—" *laborious* effort towards *such* petty social advancement *as could alone* be effected " —" women do *as a rule* "—" not *so entirely* unknown *as* "—" the *marked* difference in the *final* particular " —" *exhausted, aged*, and *attenuated*, lay *serpentining* "— " not *quite* sure "—" the *sole* effect."

Such superfluous qualifications account for the preponderance of adjectives and adverbs ; and to them is due much of that impression of slovenliness and lack of interest to which I have already so often adverted.

But these faults may also lend themselves to that dominant impression of lazy, dreamy, sensual life among lush vegetation and puzzled rustics as slow as their kine (when not stirred by sudden gusts or wellings-up of animal love, rage, or devotion), which Hardy's genius has put before us. Trees, grass, and haystacks do not move about ; sheep, cows, and bulls do not think ; the pale moon nights, the long, sultry noons, are made for dreams. And Stevenson, Meredith, or Henry James would scarcely be what is wanted for such subject-matter.

The woolly outlines, even the uncertain drawing, merely add to the impression of primeval passiveness and unreasoning emotion ; of inscrutable doom and blind, unfeeling Fate which belong to his whole outlook on life. And the very faults of Hardy are probably an expression of his solitary and matchless grandeur of attitude. He belongs to a universe transcending such trifles as Writers and Readers and their little logical ways.

(E) Henry James

The Ambassadors, p. 127. 500 words. Nouns and pronouns, 137; verbs, 71; adjectives and adverbs, 48.

"Our friend had by this time so got into the vision that he almost gasped 'After all she has done for him.' Miss Gostrey gave him a look which broke the next moment into a wonderful smile: 'He is not so good as you think.' They remained with him, these words, promising him, in their character of warning, considerable help; but the support he tried to draw from them found itself, on each renewal of contact with Chad, defeated by something else. What could it be, this disconcerting force, he asked himself, but the sense, continually renewed, that Chad was—quite in fact insisted on being—as good as he thought? It seemed somehow as if he couldn't *but* be as good from the moment he wasn't as bad. There was a succession of days, at all events, when contact with him—and in its immediate effect as if it could produce no other—elbowed out of Strether's consciousness everything but itself. Little Bilham once more pervaded the scene, but little Bilham became, even in a higher degree than he had originally been, one of the numerous forms of the inclusive relation, a consequence promoted, to our friend's sense, by two or three incidents with which we have yet to make acquaintance. Waymarsh himself, for the occasion, was drawn into the eddy; it absolutely, though but temporarily, swallowed him down; and there were days when Strether seemed to bump against him as a sinking swimmer might brush against a submarine object. The fathomless medium held them—Chad's manner was the fathomless medium; and our friend felt as if they passed each other, in their deep immersion, with the round, impersonal eye of silent fish. It was practically produced between them that Waymarsh was giving him then his chance; and the shade of discomfort that Strether drew from the allowance, resembled not a little the embarrassment he had known, at school, as a boy, when members of his family had been present at exhibitions. He could perform before strangers, but relations were fatal; and it was now as if comparatively Waymarsh was a relative. He seemed to hear him say 'strike up then,' and to enjoy a foretaste of conscientious domestic criticism. He had struck up, so far as he actually could; Chad knew by this time in profusion what he wanted; and what vulgar violence did his fellow pilgrim expect of him, when he had really emptied his mind? It went somehow to and fro that what poor Waymarsh meant was 'I told you so—that you'd lose your immortal soul!' But it was also fairly explicit that Strether had his own challenge, and that, since they must go to the bottom of things, he wasted no more virtue in watching Chad than Chad wasted in watching him. His dip for duty's sake, where was it worse than Waymarsh's own? For he needn't have stopped resisting and refusing; he needn't have parleyed, at that rate, with the foe."

I begin with the first sentence virtually not dialogue: "They remained with him, these words, promising him, in their character of warning, considerable help; but the support he tried to draw from them found itself, on each renewal of contact with Chad, defeated by something else." Here I find *they—these—their—them—him—him—he*—besides an *itself*. Surely an unusual dose of pronouns, that is to say, of words decidedly *personal*. And here I ask myself why I have written this word *personal*? Am I under the suggestion of the fact of Henry James being a "novelist of personality"? Perhaps. But also it seems to me, that pronouns, used like this, have something more personal than nouns: they here become a sort of personification. There is, at all events, an extraordinary circling round these pronouns. I feel that, had they been *nouns*, they would have undergone some transformation, not remained this selfsame something we circle about.

Circle about and among; for we penetrate between them (one almost forgets what *they* really are, feeling *them* merely as something with which one is playing some game—pawns? draughts? or rather adversaries?), finding them now as a nominative, now a possessive, now a dative. It is noteworthy that this shifting of the *case* of these pronouns gives the sentence an air of movement, more than would be given by the presence of verbs. In the two next sentences I have again the impression of an unusual abundance of pronouns, perhaps because of the *two its* : " What could *it* be, he asked himself," etc., and " *It* seemed somehow," etc. Evidently the use of pronouns implies a demand on the Reader's attention : he must remember what the pronoun stands for, or rather (for no one will consent to such repeated effort where only amusement is at stake) the Reader will have to be, spontaneously, at full cock of attention, a person accustomed to bear things in mind, to carry on a meaning from sentence to sentence, to think in abbreviations ; in other words he will have to be an intellectual, as distinguished from an impulsive or *imageful*, person. In this sentence we get the equivalent as subject-matter of this singular intellectuality and judicialism of form : " What could it be, . . . but the *sense* that Chad was . . . as good *as he thought*." What I mean is that the thing we are watching with Strether, almost hunting, indeed, is not a human being nor an animal, neither is it a locality we are trying to discover ; not even a concrete peculiarity we want to run to ground ; it is the most elusive of psychological abstractions : a *force*, a *belief*, in other words an intellectual residuum of experience, which, being defined, involves a comparison. The question is not : Did Chad do this or that ? but : Did Chad come up to a conception which

Strether had formed? Remark also the logical form (*by elimination*) of " what could it be, but," etc.

In the next sentence we again have a comparison of degrees; and an affirmation of logical necessity—" it seemed *somehow* as if he couldn't but be as good from the moment he wasn't as bad." I have underlined the *somehow*. For it denotes a scientific habit, accepting a fact with the reservation that at some future time an obscure part of it will be understood; it is a sign of careful classing of known and unknown.

In the next sentence we have an acknowledged parenthesis, a forestalling of a logical objection or question: " There was a succession of days, at all events, when contact with him—and in its immediate effect, as if it could produce no other—elbowed out of Strether's consciousness everything but itself." Indeed the parenthesis is a double one, for inside the fact of being told that it was the immediate effect of the contact we are also assured (lest we should stray off to other possibilities) that " it could produce no other." Nay, in the beginning of the sentence there is another clause: " at all events."

Let me stop to say that I quite understand that such qualifying sentences may, at the first glance, seem padding, like the " he said "—" says I "—of uneducated people; mere attempts to gain time to deal with disorderly thought. But I believe that here, on the contrary, they betoken, and provoke, a subdivision of meaning, an act of intellectual care and prudence. Similarly, take note of the expression "*succession of days*": a less analysing and classifying Writer would have been satisfied with "there were days." In the next sentence we have: "Little Bilham pervaded the scene"; Little Bilham being thereby volatilized into a thin essence; the elision meaning "the fact or existence or idea of Little Bilham pervaded," etc. With, however, a proviso, "*but* Little Bilham became," etc. Is this proviso going to restore to Little Bilham any of his forfeited concreteness? You little know Henry James if you think that! For the proviso proceeds to make Little Bilham into "one of the numerous forms of the inclusive relation"; nay, he grows into a complex abstraction "in a higher degree than he had originally been." What nouns we have here! *Form, relation, degree*! And for adjectives and adverbs, *numerous, higher* (meaning more intense) and *originally*. And if we go on to the full stop we add, "a consequence promoted, to our friends' sense, by two or three incidents with which we have yet to make acquaintance." In all this sentence only two words, "Little Bilham," have a concrete meaning, give a visual image; and even Strether becomes "our friend," that is to say, gets considered not as anything tangible or visible, but as a relationship. Meanwhile we have added to the nouns of the first half-sentence, "*consequence, friend, sense, incidents*, and *acquaintance*," but to the adjectives, nothing! And to the verbs *promoted* and *make*, which merely represent alterations of intensity and valuation in these abstract nouns. I almost believe that my analysis is less abstract than this sentence out of a *bona fide* novel! But now comes a change. The next sentence is not only concrete but picturesque: " Waymarsh himself, for the occasion, was drawn into the eddy, it absolutely, though but temporarily, swallowed him down; and there were days when Strether seemed to bump against him as a sinking swimmer might brush against a submarine object." Here we have an *eddy*; the eddy *swallows* Waymarsh; and he and Strether are *sinking swimmers*, bumping against *submarine objects*. But even this is qualified with abstractions; it is "for the occasion" and "absolutely, though but temporarily," and it is governed, if not grammatically, at least in intention, by the verb *seem*. For in the next sentence, " The fathomless medium held them," etc., we learn that "Chad's manner was the fathomless medium"— sufficiently abstract in all conscience!

There is once more a curious concreteness in the continued metaphor: "they passed each other, in their deep immersion, with the round, impersonal eye of silent fish." Of course it only *felt* like this to Strether. But it feels like this to the Reader; and this thoroughly carried-out picture is probably what enables the Reader to live on through more abstraction. If I may talk in an Irish manner, we seem to take a provision of breath in that concrete metaphorical world (even though a submarine one) sufficient for a continued walk in the rarefied atmosphere of the real story. This deep-sea metaphor is a master-stroke. It has awakened a sense of the concrete; and he caps it with a comparison, that of the exhibition at school, " and the shade of discomfort . . . resembled not a little the embarrassment he had known, at school, when members of his family had been present at exhibitions. He could perform before strangers, but relations were fatal," etc., a concrete image actually rising to the dramatic point where Waymarsh, transformed into the schoolboy's relative, seems to cry " Strike up ! " The tendency to concrete thought continues : " He has struck up, so far as he actually could ; Chad knew by this time in profusion what he wanted ; and what vulgar violence did his fellow pilgrim expect of him when he had really emptied his mind ? " Not only a repetition of the *striking up* which is now metaphorically done by Strether ; but we get " profusion," an expression singularly referable to concrete things ; then " vulgar violence," then " fellow pilgrims," then " emptied his mind."

In the next sentences we get " bottom of things," " wasting virtue "—" dip " (in the sense of dipping in water), and finally so definite an image as " parleying with the foe." But all this concrete metaphor does not prevent our having, in these hundred words or so, had "so far as he actually could"—"wanted"—"expect"—"really"—"somehow"—"fairly explicit"—"at that rate." And it is quite proper that the most conspicuous sentence of these five hundred words should be, "I told you that you'd lose your immortal soul!" For the whole business is one of souls and nothing but souls.

What the people *do* has no importance save as indicating what motives and what spiritual manners they have, and how these affect the consciousness of their neighbours. And, in this quotation, a considerable amount of extremely vivid feeling of concrete things becomes merely so much metaphor, illustrating purely subjective relations.

"Alles *Tangible*," one might say, paraphrasing *Faust*, "ist nur ein Gleichniss."

Let us now ask ourselves how it is that all this is not vague, *swimmy*, and merely wearisome? How is it that we have not to clutch on to the meaning as on to that of a metaphysical treatise?

I think because of the splendid variety, co-ordination, and activity of the verbal tenses.

In the first sentence, "They remained with him, these words, promising him, in their character of warning, considerable help"; there is the passage from one real nominative (*these words*) to another (*their character*), through the "promising him," followed immediately by a change of active into passive, "but the support he tried to draw from them found itself . . . defeated by," etc. Then the sudden interrogation—"What could it be," etc.—and the concatenation of parenthetically placed verbs, pressing on each other, "but the sense, constantly renewed, that Chad *was*—quite in fact insisted on being——" etc. Here the parenthetical holding back merely hurls the meaning along with accumulated force. The immediately following sentences, "It seemed somehow as if he couldn't but be," etc., "There was a succession of days," etc., "Little Bilham, once more," etc., seem to me perfect models of clearness and cogency. The sense is abstract, far-fetched; but how the fine ordering of the verbs forces us to go right through, with no gaping or wondering, no shirking of any part of the meaning! It is useless to review the whole five hundred words, because the remark I have to make would always be the same. With what definiteness this man sees his way through the vagueness of personal motives and opinions, and with what directness and vigour he forces our thought along with him! This is activity, movement of the finest sort, although confined to purely psychological items. And it is in virtue of this strong, varied, co-ordinated activity forced on to our mind, that we fail to feel the otherwise degrading effect of what is, after all, mere gossip about an illicit *liaison*.

These are storms in teacups; but under the microscope of this wonderful Writer, what gales, currents, eddies, whirlpools, Scylla's seadogs ready to tear, and Charybdis yawning! We may wind up by repeating that we, like Strether, "waste no virtue in watching Chad."

(F) MAURICE HEWLETT

Richard Yea and Nay, p. 8. Five hundred words. Nouns and pronouns, 132; verbs, exclusive of auxiliaries, 56; adjectives and adverbs, 54.

"In Paris Richard repaired to the tower of his kinsman, the Count of Angoulesme, but his brother to the Abbey of St. Germain. The Poictevin herald bore word to King Philip Augustus on Richard's part; Prince John as I suppose bore his own word whither he had most need for it to go. It is believed that he contrived to see Madame Alois in private; and if that great purple cape that held him in talk for nearly an hour by a windy corner of the Pré-aux-Clercs did not cover the back of Montferrat, then gossip is a liar. Richard, for his part, took no account of John and his shifts; a wave of disgust for the creeping youth had filled the stronger man, and, having got him into Paris, there seemed nothing better to do with him than to let him alone. But that sensitive gorge of Richard's was one of his worst enemies; if he did not mean to hold the snake in the stick he had better not have cleft the stick. As for John and his writhing, I am only half concerned with them; but let me tell you this. Whatever he did, or did not, sprang, not from hatred of this or that man, but from fear or from love of his own belly. Every Prince of the house of Anjou loved inordinately some member of himself, some a noble member nobly, and others basely a base member. If John loved his belly, Richard loved his royal head: but enough. To be done with all this, Richard was summoned to the French King hot-foot, within a day or two of his coming; went immediately with his Chaplain Anselm and other one or two, and was immediately received. He had, in fact, obeyed in such haste that he found two in the audience chamber instead of one. With Philip of France was Conrad of Montferrat, a large, full, ruminating Italian, full of bluster and thick blood. The French King was a youth just the age of Jehane, of the thin, sharp, black-and-white mould into which had run the dregs of Capet. He was smooth faced like a girl, and had no need to shave; his lips were very thin, set crooked in his face. So far as he was boy he loved and admired Richard; so far as he was Capet he distrusted him with all the rest of the world. Richard knelt to his suzerain and was by him caught up and kissed; Philip made him sit at his side on the throne. This put Montferrat sadly out of countenance, for he considered himself, as perhaps he was, the superior of any man uncrowned. It seems that some news had drifted in on the west wind. ' Richard, oh Richard,' the King began, half whimsical, half vexed, ' what have you been doing in Touraine ? ' ' Fair Sir,' answered Richard," etc. . . .

One has, at the outset of this quotation, the impression of being presented with a very straight narrative and little else. Taken superficially one might skip certain words, and read it thus: " In Paris Richard repaired to the tower of his kinsman, the Count of Angoulesme . . . his brother to the Abbey of St. Germain. The Poictevin herald bore word to King Philip Augustus on Richard's part; Prince John . . . bore his own word whither he most needed it to go." The words I have omitted are only five, and not important ones; and it is only on continuing the page as it really stands that one feels these words *have been there*, and that they have acted, what we call "unconsciously," in such a way as to convey a gesture, an intonation, wholly different from that of my altered version. The *but* turns the mere consecutive account of where the King and his brother respectively lodged into the beginning of a comparison of their respective proceedings.

After the straight statement about the herald's carrying Richard's news comes a statement, at first sight not much more complex, to the effect that " John bore his own word whither he had most need for it." This might mean simply that the author is not concerned with John, if the Reader had not been invited by that continuous symmetry (Richard does this, John that, Richard's message on the right, John's on the left) to a constant comparison, accentuated by that *but*; we understand that if Hewlett does not specify to whom John sent word of his coming, the " whither he had most need for it," is not a passing over John's proceedings as unimportant, but a pointing at them as suspicious. It does not mean " I know that Richard sent the herald and to whom; it doesn't matter what John did." It means " Richard acted openly and officially, with the perfunctoriness, perhaps, of official proceedings; John in secret, and in secret because he was up to something." This suspicion is thrown on to John with redoubled strength by slipping in the " I suppose." It is Don Basilio's " Ah del paggio quel ch'o detto era solo un mio sospetto." It is stronger than a direct statement, by the impact of all the author's untold reasons; we feel in the presence of a man with facts up his sleeve and who has thought it all out; hence we are unable to disregard even innocent-looking statements of his. By this time we are quite prepared for the " it is believed that he contrived to see Madame Alois in private "—the belief, treated apparently as a mere *on dit*, converging apparently with the suspicions of the author. It is not only Hewlett who suspected John, but the public at large. After this comes a statement which does not surprise us, that John had a more or less marked meeting with Montferrat; a statement put in form of supposition—" and if that great purple cape that held him in talk . . . did not cover the back of Montferrat "—which by passing it, so to speak, through our own and the Writer's judgment, makes it infinitely more cogent: it is turned into a logical necessity, not a mere observed fact capable of misinterpretation. And it is closed by the author openly taking sides, calling additional witnesses, "then gossip is a liar." In short, this, which has looked like a plain narrative, is in reality a lawyer's summing-up, a lawyer's putting things in his own light, an accusation. John is condemned in our opinion, and we are quite prepared to find that Richard had long judged and condemned him; moreover, that our future dealings with him will be as with such a condemned person. In the sentence following: "Richard, for his part, took no account of John and his shifts; a wave of disgust," etc.,—we leave the apparently objective narrative, the "for his part" making us look at things from Richard's point of view. And now let me leave for a moment the minute analysis of this page to make an observation which adds to its interest. Reading Hewlett's more recent novel, the *Queen's Quair*, I felt more and more, as I expressed it to myself, that Hewlett had somehow applied to the Past, and to a story of violent tragedy, the methods invented by Henry James in his later books for the treatment of the teacup storms taking place in well-bred and peaceful modern souls.

This impression, which I had not then leisure to analyse, was due, so far as I could guess, to the manner in which the items were thrown down before the Reader in apparent confusion, until, with his help, they slowly sorted themselves into certainties far more compact and cogent, far more difficult to shirk, than those conveyed by any clear and straightforward narrative. The Reader, to paraphrase the other James (William, the psychologist), was bombarded with impressions out of which he had to make something intelligible. Make it, but how? Can mere pelting with random facts force upon the Reader an overwhelming sense of coherence? Surely not. I have not the *Queen's Quair* by me; but the explanation of the point is furnished, I think, by *Richard Yea and Nay*. I had remembered this book as a strange mixture of the heroic and the extremely intimate; the nature of the subject making it very unlike my recollection of the *Queen's Quair*. But now, on looking at this page, I see that instead of a narrative we are really having a discussion of motives, neither more nor less than in Henry James; and a discussion of motives (also as in Henry James) from the point of view of one person at a time. Now applying this fact to the question, "Why should bombarding with random impressions as in the *Queen's Quair* and the *Ambassadors* result in leaving the Reader, after a period of utter confusion, with convictions which are irresistibly cogent, especially the conviction *that things had to be like that*," I have come to the conclusion that this element of cogency must be due to the perpetual enlisting of the Reader's logical sense. It is all those sentences of comparison: " A, *on the one hand*, B, *on the other*, Richard, etc. etc., *but* John," etc. etc., which set the Reader comparing, measuring, weighing. And it is the " I suppose "—" it is believed," all those references to gossip, which set the Reader supposing, believing, and sifting gossip. Otherwise stated, the depth of the Reader's conviction comes from the logical activity forced upon him. For logic has the imperative in belief, the *must*; whence it comes that we see *what must be* (*i.e.* what we have ourselves calculated and foreseen) far more intimately and insistently than *what merely is*. Hewlett and Henry James both catch us in the meshes of the Writer's and the various personages' views, which become our own by our effort to follow them; whereas Writers like Meredith and Kipling pass their magic-lantern figures across the blank screen of our fancy. For, paradoxical though it may sound, *to think a thing out is to live it out*; we stretch our real attention parallel to those dead facts, we clasp them with our living thoughts, and thereby make them ours, since our *thought* of a situation is a part of ourself; while the mere outer situation itself is—well, no situation at all, a mere bodiless phantom.

Hence (odd as it appears) there is a fundamental resemblance between Henry James and Hewlett; the resemblance revealed (as by some graphological detail) by those words " but "—" then "—" if "—" on his part " —those forms " I suppose "—" it is believed "—which signify that the situation is an inner, not an outer, one. The interest in both cases is in the attitude of the various persons towards one another, not in the "actions" which reveal or suggest that attitude; both novelists are subjective and logical and judicial. Henry James is the judge studying the case quite impartially; Hewlett, the advocate preparing a very partial special pleading. Both say to the Reader not "Look what happened"— but "Think what *must have* happened"—and the *what has happened* (or rather, what we infer must have happened) has value, not in itself, as a source of further outer happenings, but rather as producing certain inner conditions of the *dramatis personæ*. The incident at the river-side inn (in the *Ambassadors*) is not made interesting in itself, but in the altered conception of Chad and Madame de Vionnet, which it brings about in Strether's mind, just as the murder of Rizzio (in the *Queen's Quair*) is not made interesting in itself, but in the added fear and hatred in the soul of Queen Mary. The drama for both novelists is an *inner* one. *Inner*, undeniably; but *inside* what? The answer is easy, so far as Henry James is concerned: *in* refers to the *mind*, the *soul* of the *dramatis personæ*, in which (and evidently not in the streets, the fields or even in a drawing-room or garden) the real action takes place. An intellectual and moral revolution is happening in Strether's nature: what we watch are his impressions, suspicions, surmises, certainties, the fluctuation and alternation of his standards, and the emotional ups and downs and upsets accompanying them. . . . What is he going to think of the relations between Chad and the French lady? Will he condemn, condone, perhaps even come to secretly rejoice at them? That is the drama of the *Ambassadors*, and its scene is Strether's *mind*. I repeat this over-obvious statement, the better to bring out the difference between Henry James and Hewlett by previous insistence on their points of likeness. For, as we have already noticed, with Hewlett also the drama is mainly an *inner* drama. Only the *inner* refers to something quite different. My impressions on this subject are so vague, although so pervading (gathered from other of his works also, besides *Richard* and the *Queen's Quair*), that it is fairer not to set them down at once in black and white, but convey them by examples to my Reader. Well then! In these five hundred words, selected quite at random, we have five references to bodily peculiarities. John is a "creeping youth"— Richard "the stronger man"—John is "writhing"— Montferrat is "large, pale, ruminating, full of bluster and thick blood." The King of France "thin, sharp, of the black-and-white mould into which the dregs of Capet had run." Remark that the adjectives, so sparse with Hewlett, follow on each other thick when it is a question of what I must call *physiological* peculiarities. The first of these passages is to tell us of a "wave of disgust for the *creeping* youth"—and of Richard's "sensitive gorge." And the core of the matter is in the remark: "Every prince of the house of Anjou loved inordinately some member of himself, some a noble member nobly, and others basely a base member. If John loved his belly, Richard loved his royal head." This summing-up is the more striking, that however natural it may be to think of the *creeping, writhing* John as " loving his belly," the *contents* of the head, a man's thoughts, standards, and volitions, are so bodiless that we rarely think of them as being his *head*; so that this forcing of spiritual things into bodily terms becomes suggestive of a very strong bias on the author's part to feel and think with reference to bodily temperament. Now this is what differentiates Hewlett's subjectivism from that of Henry James. Hewlett's personages exist towards one another, not as human beings whose temperamental difference culminates, transmuted by intellectual activity, in an intelligible idea, but rather as creatures in whom the element of thought and purpose is but the fitful result of their physiological constitution, and who exist towards each other with the obscure attractions which animals may feel, and the constant, deep, mysterious, blind, dumb hostilities of their animal nature. I know, of course, that underlying all our feelings and thought and action is the deep-seated mystery of temperament, are the sympathies of flesh and blood, the incompatibilities of nerves and viscera, the purely bodily selection of prey, of mate, of enemy. But with the ordinary human being all this appears in consciousness as something different, transfigured for the benefit of reason into reasonable motives and judgments; and we are not conscious of the bodily temperament making us love and hate, even as the man in health is unconscious of the inner functions through which he lives, and of the muscles, thanks to which he moves; the clarified, precise data of intellectual consciousness driving the bulky, vague knowledge of our fleshly constitution into the background.

This is not the case with Hewlett's personages. Of them we must repeat that "they loved inordinately some member of themselves——"; or rather, let me alter the formula, loved, not " some member "—but " *with* some member of themselves; loved *with* a noble member nobly, or *with* a base member basely." Certain it is that we are always made to feel the bodily phenomenon at the bottom of all their emotions. Thus, in the passage which I have paraphrased, we are told of Richard's " worst enemy," his *wave of disgust*, his *sensitive gorge*; likewise that John was a thing not merely *loving his belly*, but using it to move with " creeping, writhing "—a belly mainly. Moreover, that Montferrat was not merely blustering, but "full of thick blood," and " ruminating "; that the King of France was a half degenerate, almost sexless creature, a child when he should already have been a man, and with a child's calf-love for this *strong* Richard of the ready disgusts. Nay, even in the mode of address of Philip to Cœur de Lion there is an odd bodily tremulousness given by the queer placing of the interjection: "Richard, oh Richard"—which is the beginning of a sob, as distinguished from "O Richard, Richard" which, in English, is the usual form for conveying reproach. Temperaments made conscious to themselves and to one another; that is the formula of Hewlett's personages: stirring of blood and viscera, shrinkings of cuticle and muscle directly conveyed to the creature's mind and to the Reader's; the garment, nay, rather the outer skin, of thought, motive, habit, stripped away; and the creatures moving, through an odd penumbra, in the quivering, half-flayed nakedness of their physiological nature. When it is that of Richard, of the magnificent, solemn and magnanimous feline, we feel the uncannily quiet animal movements as so much dignity and charm. And this, with the heroic surroundings, the constant open air and open sea of *Richard Yea and Nay*, and its tragic tale of adventure and devotion, leaves an impression of exotic grandeur, a relief after our reasoning and talking modern world. But the work presented by the Writer represents the equation of his tendencies of treatment and of the subject he chooses to treat. And while in *Richard*, Hewlett gets the subject which corrects, checks, and purifies his tendencies, he gets the subject which intensifies them in the *Queen's Quair*. With Cœur de Lion we are safe on the adventurous mountain paths and stormy seas in the rare atmosphere of the epic; we watch the great lonely beings who, in their

The Handling of Words

simplicity and struggle, seem so much finer than our poor selves : the lion, the hunted antelope, the eagle, made noble by centuries of heraldic symbol. But with Queen Mary and her rout of wenches and pages and cut-throats, we come to obscure creatures whose inner workings move to disgust more even than to tragic horror ; and Hewlett's handling, magnificently efficacious, turns those tortuous and stuffy palaces of Valois times into the burrowing places of mere human vermin. It is just because we are made to realize so well the longings and the fears and rages of his murderers and his wantons, that we cannot do with them ; and that, instead of pathos or terror, we feel only the faintness of nausea. Feel it, at all events, *in remembering* the book.

For here we strike upon a curious point in the psychology of Readers, if I may judge other Readers by myself : it sometimes happens that my remembrance of a book is accompanied by feelings different from those which I recollect having had at the moment of reading that same book. This does not always happen. In the case of the *Ambassadors* (as in that of Stevenson's *Cévennes*) the feelings accompanying the remembrance tally exactly, become fused, with the feelings I remember having had while reading. But in the case of other Writers, notably Hewlett, there is a discrepancy. The reason must be that while there are books whose subject-matter and style are homogeneous, so that whatever you remember of them must always affect you in the same manner, there are other books which are heterogeneous, a dualism of HOW the Writer makes his Reader think and of WHAT he makes him think about. I take it that when the actual wording of this latter kind of book is forgotten, the subject-matter may be remembered, and instead of being neutralized, clarified, purified by the style, that subject-matter left to itself, may remain in our mind as insipid or villainous dregs.

And now, having given some examples of the physiological information which constitutes the subject of so much of Hewlett's discourse, let me return to my quotation and show even more clearly the peculiarity of his style I find so oddly at variance with that subject-matter of his. This will further bring out his unexpected points of resemblance with Henry James, the novelist who lets us least into the secrets of that *mortal coil* which even his heroes and heroines had not entirely shuffled. For, like the style of Henry James, Hewlett is elaborately, intricately, inexorably intellectual, nay logical. The Reader is drilled to infer rather than to accept. He is ordered to put two and two together and draw conclusions. He is coerced by *whiles* and *thens* into going only a certain distance along one line, in order to turn back and judge the distance compared to the previous one. He is compelled to pause and look round by *buts* and to start afresh by *ands* ; to turn aside by *as fors* ; to crane into the beyond by *ifs* and *whatevers*. He is forced to pull items together for himself simply by their being left unconnected. Put briefly, this Reader of Hewlett's is made to exert himself, to live actively and attentively. He is made to be highly intellectual and highly judicious while reading about deep-seated and inarticulate mysteries of temperament and unbridled, unreasoning impulses. He is made to live with his brain, indeed perhaps more literally than psychology as yet ventures to suggest, with his *motor centres*, while dealing with the *creeping belly* of John and the *thick blood* of Montferrat. Now such intellectual activity is comparatively rare ; it is braced, balanced, and noble ; and the Writer who calls it forth, *because he possesses it himself*, is in so far, and whatever his subject, whatever the substances which stain and befoul his thoughts, *noble also*.

I think I have already alluded to a belief which seems to prevail among literary critics, meaning thereby, such of us as generalize and codify our own quite un-criticized personal likings and dislikings—the belief that *nobility*, indeed, *virility* of style is a question of abundance of verbs and paucity of adjectives. I suppose I am a literary critic myself ; and at the beginning of these psychological exercises I certainly started with that belief. This examination of one single passage of Hewlett will, I trust, have shown that things are less simple ; and that such qualities as nobility and virility are really due to the variety and co-ordination of the verbal tenses, and to the cogency of the logical parts of speech ; which means to the degree of activity elicited from the Reader, and the economy and efficacy thereof. Take, for instance, the beginning of the sentences which I have been analysing ; you will find that the initial word betokens an almost constant change in the direction of the thought, but a change of direction which is congruous, in other words, an unusual amount of varied but co-ordinated intellectual movement. Let us look into it : " But that sensitive gorge of Richard's was one of his worst enemies," etc. *But* firmly deflects the attention, forces us to attend to something quite different, forces us to face round to another standpoint. *That* employed instead of *the* before " sensitive gorge " makes us look back on the foregoing, and carry along one of its items with the *sense of the item having come out of the direction we have left*—" was one of his worst enemies "—a general statement, reminding us by a movement towards something already known that Richard was surrounded by enemies. And now we come to a very particular statement : " *If he did not mean to* hold the snake in the stick, *he had better not have* cleft the stick." We get, moreover, a future combined with a *more than perfect past*, a looking forwards and a looking backwards, but not merely straight backwards as in the case of *the perfect pass*, a looking across one past into a remoter, deeper down past. We have, in this concordance of tenses, two *planes* in time as well as two directions in subject. "As for John and his writhings, I am only half concerned," etc. Here is a sudden, but perfectly intelligible and connected leap from the merely objective position "Richard and John were or had been"—to the subjective position of the Writer; a change therefore from a narrative of past and gone things to a pleading in the present. "But let me tell you this," etc.—and now even *we* are dragged in; we feel that the narrative is becoming a play within the play, or a picture inside a picture (like the Bible Histories of the Sixtine Ceiling, framed in the architecture of Sybils, Prophets, and Genii). "Whatever he did or did not"—a general statement in symmetrical shape and with the extra cogency of the negative form (which often acts like a spring)—"sprang *not* from hatred *but*," etc. What perpetual shifting and adjusting of our attention, backwards, forwards, laterally, etc., in this sentence!

Now look at the words which do the marshalling of our thought: "*But, if, not; not, this, that, but, from, or, from, own*"—they are all words telling us nothing at all except how *we are to think and feel in this matter*.

Again we get a general statement: "Every prince of the house of Anjou loved inordinately some member of himself," with a symmetrical division of attention, "some a noble member nobly, others basely a base member——"; the noble—nobly, basely—base, forming a couple to the right and a couple to the left, and accentuating the symmetrical arrangement. Then the sudden pulling up short: " But enough." After which a rapid turning round to the general statement: "to be done with all this "—a present which is a future; and a plunge back into what promised to be the smooth, straight current of the past: " Richard was summoned to the French King," etc.

The next sentence, however, " he had, in fact, obeyed in such haste that he found two," etc., is a return to the explanatory mode: we are to attend to a *why*, not merely to a *how*. " With Philip was Conrad "—this plain statement of fact is tacked on to the preceding argument, just by reason of its isolation: in the frame of mind induced by the " in fact "—of the previous sentence, the Reader, so to speak, stoops and picks up the isolated statement about Conrad, recognizing in it, thus detached and dropped, the thing he has been made to expect by that rather mysterious " he found two in the audience-chamber instead of one." The fact is not insisted on; it gains the more significance by the swift and secure transition to plainer statement of things: " The French King was a youth . . . of the thin, sharp, black-and-white mould into which had run the dregs of Capet." Hewlett, it may be remarked, puts unusual trust in the nimbleness of his Reader's wits. The first sentence gives us the genealogy and the moment, tells us what to expect. In the light of the " dregs of Capet" information, we see, without need of explanation, that the beardlessness, the crookedness of Philip's face, are signs of racial degeneracy. The next sentence divides Philip in two "so far as he was boy, etc.—so far as he was Capet," and by this symmetrical placing of his two tendencies, we are prepared for his ambiguous treatment of Richard; ambiguous, but now intelligible to us. After all this preparation for the future we again quietly return to the Past.

"Richard knelt," etc. Note the feeling given by the sudden change from active to passive. We might thus, keeping the contents, rewrite the sentence but altering the movement—"Richard knelt to his suzerain, and Philip caught and kissed him"—instead of "Richard knelt to his suzerain and *was by him caught up* and kissed," as Hewlett has it. Hewlett's version keeps Richard as the important person, the nominative of the passive as well as of the active. We have to look sharp to understand what has happened; but we find Richard in the centre of the stage as before. Then, suddenly, Philip is the nominative, making Richard sit on the throne. This is necessary to change the movement and take our attention in the direction of Montferrat, who was left standing. This sentence is splendidly inclusive of much past and future. "For he considered himself (as perhaps he was) the superior of any man uncrowned." So much tacked on to one small FOR, thanks to the steadying power of that parenthesis ("as perhaps he was"), which gives it a firm basis of pause. And then our interest is stirred by the sudden introduction of the narrator's opinion: "it seems that some news had drifted in on the west wind." Rewrite that sentence, "It happened that some news," etc.—and note the way in which the point gets lost by this alteration.

POSTSCRIPT

And now, having got to the end of my allotted five hundred words of *Richard Yea and Nay*, and also of the batch of contemporary Writers whom I analysed when in pursuit of "Statistical Tests," let me sum up the results of these examinations. Or rather let me enlarge upon the fact that there may or may not exist a concordance or a discrepancy between what a Writer is thinking about and the manner in which he compels his Reader to follow his thoughts. This seems a mere platitude when we are in the presence of verse, where you cannot help being aware that the rhythm and rhymes and other audible elements are mysteriously compelling you to keep step with them; a step which, you are also keenly aware, is suitable or not to the argument in hand, as, for instance, a hop, skip and jump is unsuitable to a funeral. Everyone knows that, besides the subject, there is, in all verse, something which is called the *form*. What seems less universally recognized is there being a form also in prose (and in as much of any poetry as can be rendered into prose). Since this latter kind of form, such as constitutes the *style* of prose, does not appeal through the ear to the moving and *miming* arms and legs, but in more modest and subtle, yet quite as imperative a manner, through our hidden organs of silent speech to . . . well! the rest of that invisible totality which, in a merely psychological sense, we may as well call our *Soul*. FORM is not merely something we perceive; it is something which determines our mode of perception and reaction. And, naturally, nowhere so imperatively and categorically as in what is meant by Art, implying as that word does a pause in real life's pursuing and being pursued; a moment of safe comtemplation (no "hungry generations treading us down," or we them), a leisurely space of time wherein we surrender our liberated activities to the biddings of the artist. This explains why literary *form* or *style* means a lot in a novel or essay, and little or nothing in a manual we are cramming for an exam.

As to the nature of this thing, *prose style*, and wherein its various potentialities and imperatives reside, that is precisely what we have been trying to run to ground. Incidentally to so doing we have come upon the fact that the individual qualities of a Writer's style may constitute either a unity or a dualism with the other qualities which that Writer has accepted as inherent to his subject, or, owing to individual affinities, has found especially attractive in that subject. In the case of the *Ambassadors* (and probably much of Henry James's later work) the unity between subject and style was, we found, complete : we got a soul's drama exhibited in the most intellectual and imaginative (*e.g.* the metaphorical) terms. In *Richard Yea and Nay* no such unity could be discovered. And in that other great novel of Hewlett's, which we glanced at without any analysis, I will take it on myself to state that the dualism between subject and wording was absolute, the two elements of the *Queen's Quair* falling completely asunder in *this* Reader's recollection of the book.

Now what I should like to point out before closing this particular set of studies—for the point is much to the credit of this great art of prose writing—is that, although such a dualism, or if you prefer, contradiction, may diminish our literary happiness in one way, it may safeguard it in another ; or save our own self-respect and our esteem for an author. Such a discrepancy may, indeed, mar our profit from that Writer's virtues ; but when the virtues are rare and commanding, like those of Hewlett's style, they will (if we have the right literary sensitiveness) oblige us to forgive, and what is more, even forget, that drawback. Not, mind you, merely tolerate it slackly, blinking feebly and, as that Elizabethan put it, "shutting our apprehension up," ourselves remaining by so much the less keen and clean in consequence. Not tolerate—and every Reader is thus indulgent to some favourite Writer (if not Hewlett why, maybe, Dickens !)—but really forgive and forget. Since here comes in the sovereign miracle of all great art, that, in the radiance of what we love it blots out what we do not like; the overwhelming nobility of high æsthetic enjoyment making us, by what Karl Groos has called the mind's "monarchical constitution," incapable of taking offence at less noble details; just as the full-fledged musical listener does not realize or even believe in the morbid or intoxicating effects of Wagner's music on hearers incapable of following its marvellous musical complexities.

Having thus touched upon the unity or dualism constituted by a Writer's style, his *handling of words* with his subject-matter, let us call to mind once more that there is another kind of concordance possible in these matters, and another kind of discrepancy, namely, between him who writes and him who reads; without which concordance, or happy coincidence, between the native constitution and the traditions of writer and Reader, no amount of genius can save the situation. This is the undeniable truth at the bottom of that so apparently disheartening remark, *De Gustibus*. You cannot (or had better not !) *dispute* of tastes; but you can amply *account* for them. And accounting for them, you need not be disheartened, since the same diversity of temperament and training obtains among Writers as among Readers. And since writing, like all other art, varies in character according to the time, the place and the individual, there will always be a good Writer for every good Reader. Whether there will always be found a good Reader for every good Writer is another matter, leading us into questions of printing, publishing, reviewing, and, generally, of Gray's "Churchyard" and the "Mute inglorious Milton" buried therein.

That there will always be forthcoming a bad Writer to suit a bad Reader, is an article of my belief in the Harmonies of Creation. There are also less *a priori* grounds for asserting it to be the case.

VII

"IMAGINATION PENETRATIVE"
APROPOS OF MR. LUBBOCK'S *CRAFT OF FICTION*

I

AS happens when one lives alone in the country, I have been spending my winter evenings, for all company, with a novel. Sometimes a very good novel; oftener indifferent poor, though always accepted with gratitude; names shall be neither here nor there. Latterly there has been the accompaniment also of random meditations on Mr. Percy Lubbock's charming little *Craft of Fiction*. Now, as may happen when thoughts are coming and going round about a subject, a sentence, indeed only a couple of words, have been knocking about in my head: *Imagination Penetrative*. They are Ruskin's, remembered across years and years, but with no recollection of the precise sense himself connected with this very noble phrase. So that around it my own meaning has freely shaped itself in various groups of impressions and analyses.

It happens that the person who, of any I ever came across, had most intuition (shall we say " Imagination

Penetrative " ?) on the subject of pictures, used to point out that second best painters, while giving their figures any amount of detail and of *projection forwards* (knees, elbows, bosoms, paunches, indiscreet rotundities, hitting you in the eye), are quite unable (just because they *are* mediocre people) to make the beholder realize that their figures, if real, would have a back view, that there would be space, space full of other things, if you explored into it, *behind them.* Now it seems to me that, quite similarly, the second-rate novelist, indeed the mediocre anybody you choose, has little or no sense of, no interest in, the unseen; that he is aware, or, at any rate, able to make *us* aware, only of the contingent; that he is without instinct for the *beyond*, for what I call in my mind *otherness*, and is therefore also without the understanding of change which comes of there being *otherness* and *beyond.* Such a novelist, or such an anybody, lacks " Imagination Penetrative "; which comes to saying that he has no surplus thought, vision or feeling. And what I should like to see investigated—though I can scarcely hope Mr. Lubbock will undertake the investigation, and I shall presently say why I don't think he will—Lubbock or no Lubbock, what I should like some ardent young critic to inquire into is a notion I have long entertained *a priori*, and shall set forth as a duly modest query—namely, whether the Novelists with what I have called *no back, no beyond*, to their *dramatis personæ*, are not also the Novelists dealing preferably in *situations*, while the Novelists I should call the *three-dimensional ones*, those whose personages possess sides, qualities, besides the ones we are told about, are the Novelists dealing preferably in *character*. "Three-dimensional" I have called them, because like every human activity related to time and space, Imagination (whether Penetrative or merely superficial) can be expressed in terms of dimensions, of movement of thought or feeling beyond the present aspect or present interest.

Perhaps I should explain what I mean by *novels of situation* or *novels of character*? But, no! I should be merely paraphrasing those words whose meaning is just that and no other.

I don't know what questions young writers may be discussing nowadays; but when I was young, such discussions raged, usually without much practical result or theoretic conclusion, around the respective method and status of *novels of situation* as against *novels of character*; turning over which sort one would aspire or condescend to write, although one usually grew old without writing any novel at all. I imagine these discussions must have been imported from Paris, revolving as they did round Stendhal, Flaubert and Maupassant. And indeed I find them renewed (or shall I say *renovated*?) by Mr. Lubbock under the supreme auspices of *Mme Bovary*. I can appreciate, because I can remember, the superior attractiveness of the "Novel of Situation." You felt cleverer, or felt you would feel cleverer if you also were a novelist, in plotting out " if A happens to B, then C will happen to D." Such processes shared the intellectual prestige of arithmetic or chess, neither of which I ever mastered ; they had the elegance of the first five problems of Euclid, at which my geometry stopped short. *Situation* was eminently neat, at all events when conceived by a novelist. *Character*, on the contrary, had a tendency to loose ends and hopeless knots ; it was *not* neat, and unless one condescended to horrid Dickensian caricature, one couldn't feel masterly about it, surely. Because *Character* seemed to have a way of its own. Hence in stories where *Character* was the chief interest, there seemed no obvious imperative why anything should happen as it did, or indeed happen at all ; the action, as well as the actors, was not quite definite and coherent. Whereas, in the novel of *Situation* there was definiteness, coherence and a quite irresistible causal imperative ; things *couldn't* have happened any differently from how they did.

Thus I felt and argued in the distant ardent Eighties. Nor did it strike me till the Eighties and such discussions had long been left behind, that the reason why, in novels of *Situation*, everything thus behaved according to definition and programme was that, as a matter of fact, none of it had ever happened at all ; the exquisite fitness of such representations of human existence being referable to the same cause which makes clothes sit so accurately, with never a crease or a bagging, on the dressmaker's doll.

And now let me return, after this biographical illustration, to "Imagination Penetrative," and to those qualities of fiction for which I have developed an exclusive and doubtless unfair preference, those which I find in the other kind of novel, that of *Character*. The main difference between the two schools is that one of them intuitively, *i.e.* from a feeling left by repeated but unsifted experience, makes allowance for the potential and changing, for what the novelist is not certain or clear about, the unknown of which he knows only that it exists. While the other School of novelist is interested only in such qualities and probabilities as are needed for his little—or perhaps his magnificent !—scheme. This *Constructive* novelist, perhaps like all other *Constructive* persons, thinks of the universe only as brick and mortar, or lath and plaster, for his august temple or pleasing gazebo. And just as the practical man throws away everything he has no use for, and marks his passage through time and space with rubbish-heaps alongside monuments, so also, methinks, this constructive novelist is occasionally overtaken by the Nemesis of the thus discarded and disdained elements of human reality. Speaking without metaphor, I am beginning to suspect that the novelist of *Situations* frequently invents a situation which is impossible and even absurd, like that of the *Altar of the Dead*, whose introductory page is perhaps Henry James's very loveliest. Even worse may happen, and, alas! did happen to that same noble and exquisite Master. I am alluding to his *Turn of the Screw*. Only the inveterate habit of working out situations as if they were chess-puzzles can account for the anomaly of a man so tenderly and reverently decorous having come by the abomination of such a story. The very title of it seems to hint at a sense of having put himself into the grip of a logical mechanism every turn of whose relentless winch forced him deeper and deeper into hideous innuendo. For once that situation hit upon, it could be made plausible only by suggestions he would never have entertained had he shrunk from the first contact of those obscene ghosts of servants and of that (one hopes) neurotic governess. That he did not shrink came of the lack of *Imagination Penetrative*, such as reveals the further potentialities of whatever the artist looks at, and thereby stirring his irresistible human preferences and aversions, preserves him from the temptations which beset mere constructive ingenuity in the novelist.

Some of its lesser dangers also beset the critic, as witness Mr. Percy Lubbock. Does he not arraign Tolstoi's *War and Peace* as shapeless; and fall foul of all details and episodes *which do not conduce to a plan*, just those which express the Writer's, and awaken the Reader's, intuition of what I can only call *otherness*, of that third dimension in which alone change can take place and life expand.

II

With this, perhaps only personal, preference in the way of novels, there hangs together my conception of how works of fiction can act for good or evil in the abstract; and even the notion I form of how a particular work of fiction may be acting on a particular Reader. This latter notion is at times curiously vivid, and itself constitutes a little romance occupying my own mind for, maybe, a few minutes. Let me give an instance of this, no doubt, quite fallacious fantastication, since it did in this case lead to reflections which are not fanciful, but reasonable, and, I think, not unimportant. Thus: it happens that a young man has told me he is promised a place as tutor in a foreign family; and then, the conversation passing to quite different subjects, and turning on famous novels, he comes to mention Stendhal's *Rouge et Noir*, of which, of course, the hero happens to be a tutor. Instantly the thought, unspoken, arises in my mind: if he gets that place, will the story of Julien Sorel not suggest, nay, does it not suggest already, that the mother of his pupils may become for him a Mme de Rênal? I seem to see the thought forming in his mind, while it is really forming, perhaps solely, in *mine*. I continue thinking; and pass out of the realm of fantasticating. May there not have been in the mind of Julien Sorel, or rather of Stendhal when he created him, some lurking reminiscence of a Rousseau's *Julie*, or some less famous eighteenth century fair frail one, succumbing to a tutor . . . ?

I have, of course, never entered a family in such a capacity, nor, for the same reason, come into the presence of a Mme de Rênal except by hearsay. Indeed, perhaps because we writers turn our potential day-dreams (as Dr. Varendouck suggests in his recent book) at once into so much copy—I have little or no experience of such romantic imaginings as I just now attributed to my would-be young tutor. But I know that as a child I spent weeks in the hope of lighting upon a Pictish Camp like the good little boy in . . . could it have been *Sandford and Merton*, or some of Miss Martineau's stories? And even more certain is it that several early years of mine were spent in the company less of my flesh-and-blood playmates than in that of the *Swiss Family Robinson* (a fifth son thereof myself!) and of Jules Verne's scientific argonauts. Is it not in this manner, I mean thanks to such (perhaps gratuitously supposed) romance between that real young tutor and Stendhal's fictitious lady, or as my own *bona fide* childish dreams of Pictish Camps and Desert Islands—is it not thus that the novelist helps us through lives and along walks (my own at the heels of my elders) which might otherwise be but a weary, dreary drag? . . .

Of course it is also in this manner that fiction may warp us, as indeed it warped Flaubert's *Mme Bovary*; as Stendhal's Julien was warped, poisoned by a fiction in historical guise but acting as fiction does, the *Mémorial de Ste Hélène*, which you remember he hid inside his seminary mattress. But moralists have never ceased falling foul of the dangers of every kind of reading, philosophers arraigning novelists, and novelists accusing philosophers. Thus did not our eminent contemporary M. Bourget delight *bien-pensant* France with his pious invention of the agnosticism of Herbert Spencer and Taine leading an innocent DISCIPLE (*vide* the novel so called) into seduction of young girls and eventual murder? When, in the meanwhile, each and all of his own novels must have incited callow French Readers to expensive adultery in elaborately inventoried *entresols*. All of which dangers, and some more obvious ones, constitute nevertheless, to my thinking at least, a very trifling drawback to set against the immense benefit of bringing new currents into thoughts and feelings silted up behind the many breakwaters of civilized existence. Nay, the horrors and vulgarities of up-to-date cinemas, no less than the monsters of old-fashioned fair-booths, probably constitute what is nowadays called a *biological advantage* to hidebound toilers and moilers; anyhow, whether or not biologically valuable to the race, a mitigation of the lot of poor individual souls. And, after all, what is a *race* except an aggregate, a series, of individual souls, mostly rather to be pitied? So I should hesitate about discountenancing even the most sensational and subversive suggestions in novels and plays. They are probably the less of two evils (modern psychiatry tells us some of the greater!) even when they are not real blessings in questionable disguise. I am also unable to make up my mind *a priori*, indeed only further progress of abnormal psychology will enable us to do so, whether such leniency should be extended or not to " immoral " and even to " brutalizing " readings. One would surely have to know more, and with scientific certainty, about the previous mentality of those who enjoy them before deciding whether such (to our noble selves!) unsavoury enjoyment should be condemned as an incitement to evil courses or be condoned as some kind of Aristotelian *Catharsis*, bringing to a crisis the latent infections of the soul and purging them away by application of that classic remedy called terror and pity.

But while thus unable to judge in similar cases and inclined to suspect that " horrors " may be a necessary condiment for savages and no-better-than-savages, I am in no manner of doubt concerning the mischief they do to those who are not, and need not be, savages at all. Because unless we are blinded by our own respectability, we can sometimes watch in our own persons the nightmares, or at least the moral dyspepsia and infectious eruptions due to the spreading, to what is technically called the *proliferation*, of certain ideas in our mind. Such ideas may be decorously summed up under the French rubric, "Du Sang, de la Volupté et de la Mort," which is the rather self-slandering title of a volume of Barrès's stories, and might more justifiably be the sub-title of so much of d'Annunzio's even finest work. We are informed by psychiatry of the unclean and sterile merging of the various items of that title: Volupté, which ought to stand for "the procreant bed and cradle," being made to preside over the torture chamber and the charnel, to the mind's monstrous pollution. Nor is this danger limited to *bona fide* fiction. The avidity, scarcely explicable by mere patriotic and humanitarian righteousness, which met the Bryce and *Matin* Reports of enemy atrocities, and the output of lewd and sanguinary myths which marked the War Years in every belligerent country, should warn us civilized persons that "terror and pity" are not always purifying passions. We high-minded readers of newspapers and of history read as a newspaper, need not grudge our meaner brethren the life-enhancing and possibly even life-sustaining thrills of such literature as *we* avert our eyes from.

Indeed the need for thrills, for stimulation of our torpid attention and thick-skinned sympathy, and for narcotic production of blissful dreams, is at the bottom of all such art as Nietzsche aptly called *Dionysiac*. And it is only little by little, as Man emerges from brutish darkness to some far-between moments and places of safe and lucid life, that art sheds its Dionysiac emblems and instruments, becoming, instead, *Apollinian*. Now to bring about that change, while itself that change's effect and symbol, is largely the work of what I have called, adopting Ruskin's beautiful expression, " Imagination Penetrative " ; since such imagination is indeed as the light of the Sun-god, of the divine musician and healer. Penetrating through our surroundings, it lets us see more and more of the universe whereof we are a trifling little portion ; and dispelling, for a moment, the dark fumes of our animal instincts and our visceral life, it allows us to witness even the drama of our own life as if it were the drama of others.

VIII

CAN WRITING BE TAUGHT?

A QUARTER of a century and more ago, as I had ended a lecture, one of the first in this volume, upon Literary Construction, there came up from among my audience a young and intelligent lady, who, after the compliments suitable to the occasion, asked me to tell her *where she could learn the value of words*.

Some poet, I forget which, would have answered, as he did on a similar occasion, that such knowledge must be looked for in her heart. My own answer was quite in that style, with the addition (only not spoken out loud) of calling her, as the poet had called his interviewer, a fool. And then I went on through the years —and the fool was myself—imagining that had settled the question.

The fact is that the increasing, and by this time inveterate, habit of looking at such matters from the psychological rather than the biographical point of view, led to my forgetting how I myself had learned to write; nay to my almost taking for granted that the individual writer teaches himself in the course of his practice; or at the utmost finds whatever can be taught embodied in the practice of other writers. I recognize having thought so much about the relation between Writers and Readers as to overlook the relations between teachers and pupils, and tacitly almost to deny their importance. Now that is absurd. So, having collected these studies of the literary art, I am trying to apply my mind to this side of the subject.

A priori, there is no reason why, instead of being left to find it all out for himself, a writer should not be taught (though, alas! there are often concrete reasons why he should never learn) that sundry literary proceedings, whereunto the natural creature is evidently propense, are far better avoided.

All education, all progress, we are told, is carried on by such forestalling of individual experience and consequent setting free of human effort for something new. Neither is it sufficient to be set imitating good models, since no model is good all through, just as no saint is entirely saintly, and it is just as well to be told, "Do this but don't do that." Ninety-nine times out of a hundred it is the case for "Don't do that." Not because our hearts and our taste are originally bad, but because (at least so I incline to think), whether in dealing with *bona fide* children or with the metaphorical undying Child called *Man*, inculcation of virtue and wisdom is unimportant by the side of dissuasion from evil courses; nay, I suspect that our indulgence in such conduct as jeopardizes self, neighbours and whole nations, is often proportionate to the admonitions we receive to become heroes, sages and saints. As regards Literature, at all events, what beginners require are not treatises on the Sublime and Beautiful, but rules of thumb against such practices as they would naturally fall into with self-complacency. Let me illustrate this by an example taken, as our fathers would have said, from a Sister-Art, since it is sometimes easier to be brief and incisive when talking about what one knows less about. Of all the Rules of Thorough Bass I vainly attempted to master in my salad (or rather mustard-and-cress) days, one only has remained indelible in my memory, namely: Never, under any circumstances whatsoever, to commit Consecutive Fifths in the Bass. What these are I prefer not to be asked nowadays; suffice it that they are forbidden. Well! I would put my hand in the fire, or, [like the famous contrapunctist, Fenaroli, when correcting a pupil's *figured basses*] put a thumb into the inkstand, to testify that a vast amount of the genius of Bach, Handel, Haydn and Mozart (I am more cautious about Beethoven quartets after Opus 122) was saved by their having been taught as little boys (like the octogenarian *maestro* from whom I had that inky anecdote), taught maybe by that terrific dripping black thumb drawn across the consecutive fifths of their exercises—anyway *taught* during infancy, to avoid that and all similar sequences, instead of learning from individual experiences of the wry faces of excruciated hearers.

Such is my intimate conviction with regard to music, about which I know but little; and it applies *mutatis mutandis* to Literature, about which I know quite a lot. However, having a suspicion that Consecutive Fifths may become, or already are, the sole *basis* as well as *bass* of modern harmonies, I do not hold by the eternal validity of any particular set of rules about them or about anything whatever, but only the validity of rules of one sort or another as requisite for art's essential play of habit, acquiescence, expectancy and surprise. Which opinion, when applied to the art of letters, admonishes me to take example by the immortal M. Bergeret, and murmur, "Serait-ce un nouveau style?" while admitting that I am too far advanced in years to have any use for such new-fangled delights and sublimities. Is not all life a to-and-fro between stability and change, a metabolism (as biologists would put it) between law-respecting and law-discarding?

All of which comes to saying that I withdraw any remarks which might imply that you cannot be taught by other persons how to write, and especially how *not to write*. Only adding the proviso: that you must be a writer-born before you can learn these things to any purpose.

So, taking for granted (as all who write must do) that I too was a "born writer," let me stretch out across the dark solid years since anybody taught me anything, and lay hold of a few reminiscences of how and by whom I was made a writer after having been duly born one.

First, however, there are sundry other memories to be dealt with, but under the heading "how one teaches oneself." For in such matters, indeed perhaps in all matters, what one is taught—taught in the sense of deliberate tuition—can take effect only if applied to an incessantly shifting continuity of one's own trying and repeating; indeed, as I have already remarked, such teaching by others is mainly a "don't do that," and consequent selection and adaptation of one's own process of doing, trying and repeating. I suppose one may fairly generalize from one's own experience that every "born writer" is possessed by the demon of scribbling, sometimes at an age when that demon has to commandeer the hand and spelling of some elder, bored but proud. Since it is evident that a "gift for writing" means a tendency to think in words rather than in visual or any other imagery, as indeed what one deems one's best writing comes spontaneously in verbal form, without there seeming to have been a meaning pre-existent to those words; without, in short, an act of translating one's thoughts. Moreover, all the effort and grinding and gnashing of teeth comes in working up to that spontaneously generated sample, in translating (and this time it *is* translation and no doubt about it) whatever has presented itself in non-verbal form, say as sequences of inner pictures or wordless impulses and moods, into arrangements of words such as may pass muster alongside the—shall we say ? —*verbally thought* passages; neither more nor less than when a translator from a foreign tongue works at making his translation read as if it were an original. But to return to the self-teaching processes : Persons possessed of, or rather *by*, this queer facility for thinking straight off in words (and *words* imply a complicated perspective of their own), and possessing also the capacity for translating their *other* thought so that it reads as if it originally were verbal, persons, in short, with the " gift of writing," presumably have it to the extent of an unruly instinct forcing them to scribble. And also, though here I am generalizing from my own case—pushing them to exercise this gift with the pertinacity and deliberation which others put into learning tennis, golf, chess or any other game. Since, to the " born writer," there is no game comes up to writing, none so full of the enthralling ups and downs of hope, triumph and desperation, nor with such ineffable joys of moments of facility, *Mozartian*, triumphant, heart-melting, heavenly. . . . The gift of writing thus comes to be developed by spontaneous, but also by deliberate exercise. I suppose that with many this takes the shape of abortive verses and stories, or, less agonizingly, letters and diaries. With others, as happened with myself, a habit may arise of forcing into words all that passes through one's head and under one's eye, or what is taken for all such, since I daresay the literary selective faculty already hoodwinks us into disregarding what does not fall into verbal forms or verbal perspective. Which latter remark leads to a very important but neglected truth, namely, that the literary gift implies a rapid, unhesitating, often quite unconscious choice of what items to present, indeed of what attitude to take up, towards the matter in hand; in what succession to exhibit its various aspects, let alone which of those potential aspects to shut out altogether, creating and obeying a scale of "values" purely literary and often oddly at variance with the values of real life. For what else is the art called *rhetoric*?

These natural processes are, of course, fostered by certain educational habits, especially making young people compose on given themes; a habit, by the way, which accounts for the superior verbal and logical nimbleness of one's French friends, but also for their intolerable ratiocination (*ergoter* they call it!) and amplification, let alone their speech being petrified into *clichés*; or rather their very judgments and sensibilities cramped by reach-me-down formulas made, like their soldiers' clothes, in three sizes only. . . .

Having let myself go to this unjust tirade—due to the retrospective terror of having in my teens hesitated between becoming a French or an English writer—let me atone for this unmannerly outburst (and incidentally let me push on in our discussion) by expressing the deep conviction that reach-me-down phrases, or perferably the readiest-made, threadbarest, second-hand ones, are the natural, legitimate, irreplaceable, spiritual raiment in which a writer can learn to explore the universe and his own soul; one might almost add, in which any human creature learns to think and feel humanly at all. Modern man, moreover, is a reading as well as a speaking creature. And no one is more primarily a reading animal ("animal benigno," as Dante's Francesca so justly calls him who pays attention to her story) than is the creature who writes. And the chief result of reading, the first and foremost use of the Writer, is that we are helped to recognize whatever exists, whether in the macrocosm or the microcosm, by being shown it drawn, painted and perspectived with words, made easy and pleasant for our comprehension, just as we are taught by the Painter to notice shapes and effects in nature by having them isolated and focused and emphasized on his canvas. Perhaps it is only by having learned other folks' valuation that we can get a scale of what is valuable ourselves; at least once we have got beyond the snatchings, lungings and cowerings of mere appetites and fears; once we proceed erect, with our eyes on the skyline as befits Homo Sapiens, and especially the *Reader and Writer* variety thereof.

And now, thanks to having indulged unjust prejudice

against the over rhetorical and pseudo-logical training of our Latin cousins, I have come to a very important stage in this disquisition, namely, the statement that all art lives and develops by our first tackling whatever we want to say or show by the use of the formulæ of our predecessors. Which, when it comes to literature, means that ninety-nine hundredths of all teaching resides in the works of other writers; and that it is while reading that we learn most and best how to write.

The very revolts of new schools prove this to be the case. There would be none of the topsy-turveying of all the old habits of seeing, feeling and saying, unless these innovators, romanticists or futurists of whatever epoch, had not been bored to death or impotently exasperated by doing what their elders had done, or trying to do it or being admonished to do it. So true it is that, as Hegelians teach, nothing is closer akin to an assertion than its negation, nothing more conducive to the use of furs or fans than feeling cold or hot; or, as Freud puts it, that our virtues are but inverted vices and (this is surely a case for adding?) *vice versa* . . .

There are doubtless temperaments which are naturally docile; also epochs ruled rather (as Tarde pointed out) by tradition than fashion. So it is possible that my Mid-Victorian self may have been of slower growth and more stolid acquiescence than my juniors and betters. Nevertheless critical investigation of the works of authors taken at random would, I think, confirm my own experience: that it is the rarest thing in the world for a writer to be, so to speak, himself from the very outset. Among my own contemporaries, especially in the one I know best, I can recognize long preliminary stages of being *not oneself*; of being; *being* not merely *trying* to be, an adulterated Ruskin, Pater, Michelet, Henry James, or a highly watered-down mixture of these and others, with only a late, rather sudden, curdling and emergence of something one recognizes (even if there is no one else to recognize!) *as oneself*. Whether that *oneself* is better or worse is neither here nor there. What I am driving at is only the fact that writers learn most from what they read, because the mind is not a Pallas Athena bursting full grown and in full dress from even the most Olympian brain, but takes its substance and shape mainly from what it feeds on. Or, if you prefer a biological simile such as fashion requires, that our mind observes a law of heredity unlike that of our bodies, whether those be obedient to Lamarck or Weissmann or Dr. Semon or Mr. Bateson.

I spoke of *ninety-nine hundredths*. The hundredth part of what has taught us to write in the way *we do* write and not otherwise, is precisely what is merely meant by *teaching*, similar, for instance, to the prohibition of *Consecutive fifths in the Bass*. Such teaching as this doubtless makes a difference, since even the hundredth ingredient of a mixture conduces to its total character. It is influential, as every negation must be, by producing a different kind of assertion, as is shown by the well-known harmonic effects (whatever they may have been which I do not know) of avoiding those consecutive fifths instead of building up one's bass out of nothing else. At all events I can vouch for an endeavour to avoid certain literary courses which I was told were wrong; even though perhaps, because no temptation thereto had arisen in my so distant infancy, I may not have avoided split infinitives and "slangy expressions" as rigorously as latter-day reviewers have admonished me. What is surer still, and a great deal more important in my own eyes, is that an inborn desire to make quite sure what others and even myself happened to be talking about was fostered to the utmost by the lessons I received. And whether that hundredth fraction, meaning what *was taught*, be of much importance or not as against the ninety-nine parts of imitative self-teaching, this hundredth is very dear to remember. For it means the Past and those who are past, including one's dead and gone self, and so many dead and gone places, backgrounds it would be impossible to recognize.

I was taught most of that negative part of writing which, after all, is merely the application to literature of common sense and good manners, by my Mother. She was, almost in proportion as many of her views and ways would have been called "advanced," decidedly old-fashioned, as belonging to a West Indian family and brought up in a remote district of Wales. Thus she clung, even in the seventies, to certain eighteenth century words and pronunciations, and to heresies which I later identified as Voltairian, or derived from Rousseau and Tom Paine; and her politics were those of Charles James Fox. She had never heard of Browning, who was her exact contemporary, nor of George Eliot; nor apparently of Darwin, though when his views were brought to her notice she spoke as if all reasonable persons must have held them. I remember her speaking of Shelley, whose "subversive" notions were quite according to her heart, as "rather morbid, my dear"; and would have added, had she not deprecated applying such a word to poetry, decidedly new-fangled. Like our latter-day lovers of French literature, she had read little of Racine, but liked him only the better. She was very strong on grammar; acquired an exhaustive (and to my childish mind exhausting) knowledge of the fourteen cases (including *avec le peu*) of the French past participle. Also she had great faith in Euclid, of whom she had mastered up to and inclusive of the fifth proposition of the first book, besides the *definitions* and *postulates*, all of which she endeavoured to convey to me during our walks, always by word of mouth, and without allowing me to glance at a diagram or even to draw one furtively in the road's dust, deeming as she did that relations of the sides and angles A, B, C, and D were most properly dealt with by the logical faculty or "Causality," located by phrenologists half-way between the brows and ears (alongside of *Ideality* and *Veneration*); and deprecating the intrusion into such subjects of the bodily eye which she kept almost entirely for reading, although she had a poetic taste for scenery, specially of lakes and mountains. This mathematical education of herself and of me pursued, like her study of pianoforte and guitar fingering, with indomitable application and on self-devised methods, was interrupted after a couple of years by the urgent need for guiding and curbing my literary dispositions, which were characterized by more natural bad taste than the visible configuration of my brain had led her to expect. Besides, of course, a more philosophical training in the works of George Coombe and of that remarkable young philosopher called Buckle, she taught me how to write out of two excellent books, Blair's *Rhetoric* and Cobbett's *Grammar*, supplementing them with elaborate and admirably written commentaries of her own, and with horribly painful object-lessons in *corpore vili* of my adolescent works. These she criticized entirely from the point of view of good sense and good manners, although "ideality" and "poetic feeling" were what she praised most in literature. She was, in truth, at once intensely poetical and excessively prosaic; permeated with cynicism yet beyond description sentimental and idealizing; philosophically abstract and passionately personal in all her judgments; more logical than all the *Encyclopédistes* rolled into one, and childishly unreasonable and credulous whenever herself and her belongings were concerned. She regarded all religions as the invention of ambitious priests; but she was convinced she had had a magical vision of her future husband (only he bore more resemblance to her future brother-in-law) on All-Hallows' Eve in consequence of dipping her shift with due incantations in the pond at the end of the policies. Similarly, while denouncing all Biblical genealogies as ridiculous imposture, she never had a doubt about herself being descended from "Robert the Bruce, the Counts of Vermandois, many kings of France, and the kings of England up to Edward III." She was, briefly, a mass of contradictions; but these were all grown into each other, made organic and inevitable by her passionate and unmistakable individuality, which recognized no law but its own, and, while unceasingly influenced by others, was never once checked or interfered with. She was tyrannical and self-immolating more than any of us are or can imagine in these days; overflowing with sympathy and ruthlessly unforgiving; dreadfully easily wounded and quite callous of wounding others; she was deliciously tender, exquisitely humorous, extraordinarily grim and at moments terrifying; always difficult to live with and absolutely adorable. She had a high notion of the dignity of literature, and of the divine quality of genius, which she took for granted in all her belongings. While my father thought poorly of writing, describing it (I now think not quite unjustly) as a " gift of the gab," my mother had made up her mind that I had to become, at the very least, another De Staël. I disagreed with all her criticisms, trembled before them; smarted and secretly rebelled under her teaching; and in my heart adored it, like her. And when I now look into my literary preferences I find that I care for a good deal of what I have read, and even for some of what I myself have written, because in some indirect manner it is associated with her indescribable, incomparable person. And the above is all that I feel sure of on the question *whether Writing can be taught.*

IX

WHAT WRITERS MIGHT LEARN . . .

AS already remarked, the intention of this postscript is to make good some of the omissions of which I have become aware while correcting and putting together the older portions of this volume. With one such omission I have just dealt, discussing *whether*, and *how*, writing can be taught. There remains another, a far graver one, at least to my present thinking. It concerns the relation, not of words to one another nor of Writers and Readers to words, but, owing to the nature of that, the relation, both as it is and as it should be, of writing to life. Whence arises the further question: To what use should those who read put those who write? *Use* suggests *misuse*. But I am not alluding to what is often spoken of by moralists as the *misuse of literary gifts*. This is always put to the account of the Writer, and turns upon his applying his special talent either to the diffusion of such doctrines as we happen to be afraid of, or to the unguarded treatment of subjects such as we English call "unpleasant," meaning more pleasing than is good for us. The drawbacks of literature, those at least which I am most struck with, are of an opposite kind. They depend far less on the misapplication of literary gifts by the Writer as on abuse, like that of narcotics and stimulants, by the Reader, that is to say, by the world at large, not educated as yet to discriminate such beneficent yet dangerous cordials and sedatives from the food of facts and reasons.

For the preceding studies have convinced me (and I trust suggested to a few others) that the handling of words is nothing but the handling of the associations and habits, especially the emotional ones, existing potentially in the mind of the Reader. Such " handling of words " is a rearrangement of values for the sake of an alteration of mood, just like the *modus operandi* of other kinds of art. But whereas neither painting nor sculpture, still less architecture and music, can practise such unperceived and unintended deception, the artistic processes of literature pretend to transfer facts and opinions from one man to the other, while most of the time they are merely transmitting orders how to act or at least how to feel. Have we not seen how, without letting slip a single tell-tale " good " or " bad," the combination of seemingly neutral adjectives. the bare concordances of tenses and placing of prepositions and adverbs, may carry the implication of the highest praise or most violent blame ? Does not the bringing in of certain abstractions like *Duty, Justice, Honour,* the employment of *my* and *our* instead of *yours* and *theirs*, often prejudge, decide a question, say, of peace and war ? May not the word *Truth*, of all others the most difficult of definition, set up incipient willingness to go to the stake or send others to it; when the word *opinion*, of which we know the precise meaning, would merely make us shrug our shoulders or stifle a yawn ?

Thus, when not an evident superfluity like other art, literature is mainly persuasion and exhortation in the guise of statement. And we are all so accustomed to such use (which I call *misuse*) of literary power, as to overlook that persuasion means *making others feel as you wish them to feel* upon a given matter, instead of letting that matter, whatever it is, make them feel by its own relation to them and to their circumstances. *Persuasion* signifies a vote in your favour, a decision to your liking. While as to *Exhortation*, *that* is oftenest compassed by invoking the Past, and the hoarier or more infantile the better, to come and queer judgments concerning only the Present and Future.

And here I must interrupt myself to say that we are all of us so hagridden by . . . [there! *Hagridden* is an act of just such literary prejudging; strike it out and read instead: we are all *so given over to*] a habit of praise and blame instead of mere *remarking and stating*, that what I have just said will almost inevitably be read as an attack upon, a condemnation of, all literature except that of scientific primers. Have patience! and

I may show you that it is only a statement of how things seem to me, with an implicit suggestion of how, were this duly recognized, they might become different; an implicit explanation also of why they could not have been otherwise than they are. I mean in this matter of literature as an instrument of Persuasion and Exhortation. Can we conceive literature having become anything else, indeed coming to exist at all, when we bear in mind that classical Antiquity made a man's civic importance and sometimes his legal status depend on his capacity for public speaking, that is, on *persuasion*; while, on the other hand, theocratic civilization has always required impressive formulæ regulating Man's attitude to the Divinity and attuning his mind to piety with an appeal unanswerable as that of church organs and more primitive bull roarers? Nor is it credible that the mere wish to record facts and impart one's *whys* and *wherefores*, would have sufficed to evolve a literary art until the mediæval recognition that quite a trifling theological fallacy may damn you everlastingly (as *vide* Dante), and the even more recent application of "natural" science to everyday convenience, which between them gradually turned the stream of literature from persuasion and exhortation to the (at least) ostensible statement of how things are and the discussion of the causes thereof. Meanwhile, perhaps in proportion as mankind has got engrossed in material improvement, its intellectual training has been left to the doctors of *divinity* and graduates in *humanities, Humaniores Literæ* as opposed, no doubt, to *Diviniores* ; but *Literæ* in any case : written or preached *words*, books, sermons, newspaper articles and political holdings-forth. All these forms of literature have maintained their classico-theological status of legitimate instruments for making people feel and act differently from how those people might be prompted by their own circumstances and inclinations, but in accordance with the convictions and aims of somebody else.

That is a state of affairs as old as literature itself ; but just by reason of its being so very ancient and unaltered, by no means one to be invariably desired. How undesirable nowadays was brought home to me by noticing the universal, unflagging persuasion and exhortation wherewith the writers of all the belligerent nations made the war welcome and kept it going : indeed, as much execution was done by the horrible power of words as by the more new-fangled engines which did the mere brute destruction of bodies and material goods. That was indeed an object lesson (in *corpore vili* and, alas! also *anima nobili*) of the power of Literature, far surpassing that fabled of music (vide *Alexander's Feast*), to sway the Soul of Man.

I am not proposing, in Mr. Gradgrind fashion, that Man should let himself be swayed only by Facts. Nor solely by what is rather different from Facts, namely, Realities. As much as by these, and in proportion, the Soul of Man needs swaying by the unrealities, deliberate and unmistakable, of Art. *Swayed* in the sense of being made to live, for however brief an interlude, according to the heart's desire, in the more vivid, steadier, essential and harmonious modes of its own invention, which means, of Art. That kind of swaying and the instinct for it have, indeed, no value for such survival as the human race shares with other vertebrates and invertebrates, shares with such lowly somethings, neither plant nor animal, which just survive and nothing besides. But are we sure that odd, unaccountable superfluity called a soul would have survived without some such superfluous responses to some such superfluous activity? At all events such activity and such responses, such *swaying*, are felt as a human need, and should therefore, like the needs for bodily survival, be accounted honourable. Only, there might be advantage in pointing out and bearing in mind that "*being swayed*," as we are swayed by music, architecture, the other visual arts, by lyric and dramatic poetry, and even the fine spectacles of Nature, is not the same kind of swaying as that by eminent statesmen, preachers, journalists, and even by plain men of letters, as exhibited, for instance, during the war years and all the other years since Man's Creation. There is the difference that, as men of action and moralists are for ever complaining (*vide* Tolstoi), art and poetry lead to nothing, whereas other human activities do frequently lead to something often far better not led to. Art—or call it "poetry" if you choose—does not *Sway*, manipulate our mind and will with the object of getting us to *do this* or *refrain from that*; it has no "constructive plans"—such as every latter-day man of letters among us is hawking about, or whimpering for, only to pull down and "reconstruct" to-morrow. But in some yet unascertainable manner such handling by art, and by the art of words, is, I believe, building and rebuilding the shape and substance of ourselves. And even if it does not, it makes us happy without putting us up to mischief, and that is surely to be thanked and prayed for!

Neither are incitement to mutual slaughter—war and civil war—and justification thereof, the only drawbacks of our over literary habits of mind. The excessive importance thus given to the manner of stating (usually faking the values!) as compared with the things stated, has done more than to place in irresponsible literary hands the incalculable destructive apparatus which we degrade our science into inventing. That science should be set to purveying, not habits of thought and rules of judgment, but telephones, electric light, aeroplanes, poison gas and antiseptic treatment, seems quite as it should be to us who are trained by and to literature, and are so far incapable of recognizing in Science the sovereign teacher not only of the ways of things—*Rerum natura*—but more essential even, of the ways wherein to conduct the mind.

Consonantly with my sorrow at the neglect of the philosophical training which science could give us, what I would deprecate even more than the sensational damage with which literary persuasion and exhortation helps, every now and then, to overwhelm the community, what strikes me as grievous is the daily unheeded wasting and spoiling of the man of letters himself and his influence.

For, just as words are employed both to tell how things are and, on the other hand, used like all art to make people feel differently from how they would otherwise be feeling; so,of course, we Writers stand half-way between thinkers and artists, akin now more to the philosopher and again to the musician. This much is evident, that with our verbal gift there goes more general lucidity of thought (since lucid thought *is* verbal) than is indispensable in other walks of life; and there goes also a greater sensibility and less inhibition of impulse than other walks of life would always tolerate. To possess, as the French vulgarly put it, *la langue bien pendue,* conduces to that glib tongue becoming an unruly member, set wagging for the pleasure of impressing others, or pleasure of feeling and hearing ourselves. Especially as the faculty for putting forth metaphorical wings leads to giddy flights and poising not without *bombinating,* like Rabelais's chimæras, *in Vacuo;*

whence instability, self-indulged and at times irresponsible. *Volubility*, remember, which in English is synonymous with *talking fast and easily*, in the original Latin and some Latin languages, signifies *undue facility for changing feelings and views*. Now, obviously the oftener you change your feelings and views the more you will have to say, and with grateful variety; which, to us Writers, is surely of consequence. No doubt there is some peevish exaggeration in the old saw that speech is of silver and silence of gold. But golden or not, we Writers cannot afford to pay in that kind of cash; and worse luck to us!

Now, recognition of these our natural drawbacks, and occasional acts of confession and contrition like my present one, might grow into a habit of keeping alive to the transgressions our literary nature is prone to. More easy to compass and even more efficacious could be such recognition on the part of our Readers, teaching them to take us with rather more grains of doubt, and enjoy our performance like a play or concert, without necessary influence on the rest of their conduct, which might be safely left to the less fascinating admonitions of Reality. This would seem natural enough; but here we come up against another bad business about all Literature, namely, its origin in political and forensic persuasion, and in the exhortations and sacramental exorcisms of religion. Are not we Writers the (however usurping!) successors of priests and wizards

What Writers Might Learn

and medicine men, of prophets and sibyls? Like theirs (*teste David cum Sibylla*, as remarked in the *Dies Iræ*), our words are often taken seriously, and we nearly always, at the moment at least, take them seriously ourselves. We pontificate, consecrate, anathematize, we elaborately purify (as witness the late war!), and prophesy without a blush. We have been brought up to this solemn insistence on our particular ritual and liturgy, never venturing to wink, like the honest haruspex, nor put our tongue, for relief, in our cheek; indeed, never guessing we may be absurd and even odious. Meanwhile, being Writers, we are to that extent artists (and quick-change artists!); and art legitimately requires self-expression and self-exhibition. So the world, in the intervals of other business, takes us for its Sunday mornings and Saturday evenings; bowing before our gestures of consecration to God or the Infernal deities, while the next moment it claps and cries *encore* to our vocalizations and chest notes.

All this is, of course, natural and could not have been avoided in the past. But if acknowledged it may perhaps become less excessive and less of a subject of self-congratulation. There might arise some division of spiritual labour; or rather, a differentiation between the various wants of man's soul and the trades which cater for them. Thus priests and prophets are needed by a (smaller and smaller?) set of people who cannot feel comfortable except when ordered about and swallowing the nostrum labelled "certainty." Experimenters and analysts must, on the other hand, increase in numbers as Mankind grows more and more complicated and recognizes more complexity in its surroundings. While, just in proportion to such dealings with Reality, artists and poets, musicians, actors, singers, all such as express themselves and exhibit counterfeit presentments, will be necessary to make up for reality's shortcomings. Thus, paying more tribute to truth and doing more honour to fiction, the world might be none the worse for a few thinkers taken among those who are gifted for literature, and an increasing number of philosophers who were admittedly poets, and *vice versa*; though one hopes their philosophy would be learnt rather in the practice of science than in the sibylline books of purely literary ages.

Be all this as it may, my second postscript, rectifying previous omissions on the subject of Literature, comes to this: that besides the nature and use of words for and by the Writer, some study should be devoted to the nature and the use, also the misuse, of the Writer.

Moreover, as regards a Writer's position in his own eyes: that surely would grow more satisfactory if we retired awhile from persuading and exhorting other people, and grew more careful of our own consistency and genuineness; recognizing and admitting that what we express and exhibit is not Eternal Law nor Transcendental Truth, but just our preferences and opinions, a part, and if possible the least faulty, of our individual selves.

There is, however, another trade which, when a Writer happens thus to express himself, is frequently attributed to him: namely, that of standing on his head to amuse the Reader or to attract attention. To those who enjoy such alleged antics, and feel that topsy-turviness is the best means to their notice, it is difficult to know what to answer. But among the literary weaknesses we Writers are often conscious of, there is also the kind of self-expression and self-exhibition which the French call *Boutade*, expression and exhibition not of that self which has matured through recurrent acts of agreement and disagreement, but rather of momentary impatience and unmannerliness. Confessing my own failings of this sort, I want to say that I am not guilty of them in the immediately foregoing pages. Crude as may be the mode of statement, all I have just written is the matured (even if nowise rare or precious) fruit of a lifetime of being not a Writer only, but likewise a Reader. A Reader weary, indeed, of a good deal of . . . I scarcely know what to call it!—to be found in literature: But a Reader, no less, quite unspeakably grateful for what other Writers have given me of their substance and revealed to me of my own.

X

CONCLUSION

"WHAT we find words for is that for which we have no longer any use in our heart." Thus wrote one among the half-dozen greatest verbal artists of modern times. And added: "There is always a grain of contempt in every deed of speech."

Nietzsche was telling us, according to his wont, rather what he experienced with mingled complacency and disgust in his own self, than what he valued in others. To him the word—and he was apt to feel it rather as the spoken than the written word—was essentially the response, almost the reflex, the impatient, violent, contemptuous and often self-contemptuous venting and easing of his inner distress, of his instability, soreness and frenzy. To such, as he called himself, a Dionysiac man, and to all mankind in its Dionysiac moods, the word is a cry, sometimes a curse, at best an invocation of the unattainable. And being such, the Dionysiac word, like all Dionysiac art, may, for a moment, relieve by bringing to a head the misery of life, or stir life's lethal sluggishness to change and hope.

Conclusion

But there is another use for the word, that to which it —and by the word I mean, of course, literature—has been put by men, say, like Goethe or Browning, enabling both them and us to take up position to what is not ourself and to whatever in ourself had better not be. It is thus the vehicle through which some of the small clarified portions and moments of the Writer's soul can be transmitted to that of the Reader, helping him to see and feel if not the same thing, at least his own share of things in the same serene and lucid manner, remodelling himself and the world, however little, according to his choice. The word is then no longer what Nietzsche called Dionysiac and described with mixed self-satisfaction and disgust. It does not deal with self at all except as part of the great otherness of contemplation and understanding. We may call it *Apollinian* : an instrument of lucid truthful vision, of healing joy, and perchance even of such prophecy as makes itself come true.

ADEL NEAR LEEDS,
August 1922.